TEACHERS, GENDER AND CAREERS

EDITED BY

SANDRA ACKER

The Falmer Press
(A member of the Taylor & Francis Group)
New York • Philadelphia • London

UK The Falmer Press, Falmer House, Barcombe, Lewes, East Sussex, BN8 5DL

USA The Falmer Press, Taylor & Francis Inc., 242 Cherry Street, Philadelphia, PA 19106-1906

First published 1989

British Library Cataloguing in Publication Data

Teachers, gender and careers
1. Women teachers. Equality of opportunity.
I. Acker, Sandra
331.4′813711
ISBN 1-85000-426-9
ISBN 1-85000-427-7 (pbk.)

Typeset in 11/13 Bembo by
Mathematical Composition Setters Ltd, Ivy Street, Salisbury

Printed in Great Britain by Taylor & Francis (Printers) Ltd, Basingstoke

Contents

Acknowledgments

My appreciation goes to all the contributors to this volume for their dedication to its aims. Of these, Edith Black must get a special thank you for reading through all the chapters to give me a 'consumer's view'. Len Barton, Sara Delamont and Anthony Hartnett all gave valuable advice on the editor's role. My greatest debt is to Geoff and Dorothy Millerson for domestic and intellectual support.

Sandra Acker
University of Bristol
June 1988

Introduction

Sandra Acker

Why a book on teachers, gender and careers? Like Tyack and Strober (1981) I believe that 'gender is one of the fundamental organizing principles in society, as important a category for analysis as class or race or age' (p. 131). For many years I have been puzzled not only by the reasons behind gender divisions within teaching but also because their existence is so taken for granted. Teaching is interesting because it is not a single-sex monopoly like engineering or secretarial work; on the contrary both sexes are well represented, albeit differently distributed by phase and subject. Teaching is thought of as an appropriate — perhaps even 'the best' — career for women, the best paid and highest status of the traditionally female professions, with holidays and hours that allow combined responsibilities in work and family contexts. Yet a closer look shows that 'career chances' of women and men teachers sharply diverge. Women constitute most of the nursery and infant teachers and hold most of the headships at that level, but as we go up the age range, both their representation in the teaching force and their access to management positions diminish. Evidence is accumulating, in the chapters of this book and elsewhere, that there are further differences between the sexes in subjects taught, administrative responsibilities held, and simply in the daily experience of being a teacher. Mapping these variations, and indeed explaining them, is a task of this volume.

The book is divided into four sections. In Part 1, 'Starting Points', my chapter discusses the concepts and themes which underpin the contributions to follow. Alison Oram shows that gender divisions and conflicts have characterized the occupation of teaching over many years. Rosemary Grant summarizes and criticizes work to date on gender and teaching, and points to the need for a new framework.

Part 2 begins to unpack any notions one might have that all women teachers are alike, or even that all feminist teachers are alike. Calling upon in-depth interviews and personal reflection, three chapters give us a vivid picture of how teaching is experienced from different perspectives. Using four case studies from New Zealand, Sue Middleton considers how teachers become feminists. Barbara McKellar analyzes the impact of race, class and gender on black women teachers. Gillian Squirrell investigates the experiences of gay and lesbian teachers and suggests reasons why this topic is rarely researched and imperfectly understood.

Part 3 picks up the concept of 'reproduction', much used in sociology of education in recent years. Here we ask how it is that the sexual division of labour in teaching persists and what consequences it has for gender divisions generally. Christine Skelton and Joan Hanson consider a neglected topic, the role of teacher training in the process of perpetuating sexism in the classroom. Sheila Riddell takes us into a rural comprehensive school, where pupils make subject option choices in their third year largely along sex and social class-based lines, and explores the sustaining role of teacher ideologies in this process. Edith Black reports on secretarial studies teachers in a further education college, a group whose route into teaching differs from that of schoolteachers and has consequences for their outlook and the messages they convey to students. Sheila Cunnison's ethnographic study of a secondary school shows how 'gender joking' in the staffroom acts as a form of control over women teachers.

The final section of the book contains three papers which broaden the focus still further. Kathleen Casey and Michael Apple describe changing discourses in the literature on teachers in the United States, moving towards scholarship which highlights women's own views of their experience, in their own words. Julia Evetts makes a conceptual advance in her analysis of the internal labour market for primary teachers, drawing on evidence from her career-history study of women headteachers. Finally, Miriam David pulls together many themes in the book in her contribution, which is both a personal view of her experiences moving into academic management and an assessment of the potential for feminist educational reform.

The chapters in this book present an unusual range of topics. They draw on currently popular methods of investigation — ethnographies, depth interviews, life-history analyses, personal reflection — which also in large measure match those featured in discussions of feminist research. Apart from the contrasts of New Zealand and the United

States, all the other chapters are based on studies undertaken in England, with locations scattered around the country.

Teaching has been called a divided profession. This book aims to highlight the gender divide without suggesting either that this is the only one that matters, or that each gender group is internally homogeneous. It gives an account of what research is now available and of what new ideas are emerging. We hope others will follow in the same direction and fill in the gaps remaining.

Reference

TYACK, D. and STROBER, M. (1981) 'Jobs and gender: A history of the structuring of educational employment by sex', in SCHMUCK, P. *et al.* (Eds) *Educational Policy and Management: Sex Differentials*, New York, Academic Press, pp. 131–52.

Part 1
Starting Points

1
Rethinking Teachers' Careers

Sandra Acker

This chapter is a starting point for the others which follow, presenting as it does the conceptual foundation for a book that links teachers, gender and careers. Bringing these three terms together serves multiple purposes. The concept of teacher career can be extended and revamped by taking into account its gender ramifications, which have been ignored or approached stereotypically in the past. We have a chance to explore teachers' roles in the reproduction of gender divisions in society, and to ask how and why their own experiences seem inexorably to follow sexually divided paths. We can also question whether the cards will always be stacked against women teachers by a patriarchal society, or whether social change, feminist activity and informed sociological scholarship can reshuffle the pack.

Teachers' Careers

The concept of career is one which evokes a deep fascination among certain sociologists. Whilst the public, one imagines, thinks of a career as simply a series of upward or sideways moves within or between occupations, sociologists have invented alternative meanings, for example, using 'career' as a synonym for a set of changing experiences within a given role, as in 'the career of the hospital patient'. The major application, however, has been to occupational roles.

If we think of a career as an individual experience, we may chart work histories, enquire about aims and ambitions, elicit someone's feelings about and perceptions of what happened and why. 'Career' has a structural side too. First, political and economic features of a given historical era provide the context within which careers occur.

Additionally each occupation offers a typical sequence of positions, together with rules or conventions for their allocation. These rules or conventions appear to facilitate career progression for some and impede it for others. From this standpoint 'career chances' appear structurally imposed rather than individually chosen. Research on teachers' careers has rarely found a way to integrate these alternative conceptualizations. From one extreme teachers are rational individuals, plotting 'career maps' (Lyons, 1981), while at the structural end of the continuum they are simply 'victims' of the system, unable to exercise any freedom of choice.

Recent British work in the sociology of education strives to avoid this polarization. Two main approaches can be discerned. One, exemplified by Lawn and Ozga (1981), views teachers as workers. As educational workers, they argue, teachers are subject to long-term changes in the nature of white collar work, generally in the direction of taking away skill and autonomy. Recent moves towards a government prescribed national curriculum, regular external pupil assessment, hiring unqualified teachers to meet shortages and teacher appraisal can all be seen as part of the process which Lawn and Ozga term the proletarianization of teaching. Whilst some workers are 'deskilled', a smaller number are reskilled to specialize in management and related functions, especially within complex secondary and tertiary institutions. There is a career structure created for a few — mostly men — based on the lack of one for the masses of teachers.

The other, more dominant, trend in British work rests on a revival of interactionist approaches such as those of Hughes (1971) and Becker (1970), and focuses on ways in which teachers develop and change their perspectives, interpretations and strategies in response to circumstances. Becker (1970) depicts adult life as a process of 'situational adjustment':

> The person, as he moves in and out of a variety of social situations, learns the requirements of continuing in each situation and of success in it. If he has a strong desire to continue, the ability to assess accurately what is required, and can deliver the required performance, the individual turns himself into the kind of person the situation demands (p. 279).

A 'variety of social situations' may shape and structure teachers' careers. So researchers study sponsorship, colleague relationships, school micropolitics (Ball, 1987), critical incidents in the classroom (Measor, 1985), the nature of teaching itself and teachers' lives outside school.

Alongside a changing theoretical framework methods of investigation have altered. Large-scale surveys of teachers seem increasingly rare, and sample size no longer seems to matter in view of the depth of insight generated by intensive interviewing and observation, even with a few individuals. Ethnographic investigations, life-history or career-history data, and to a lesser extent personal reflection have been the methods of choice in recent work.

The articles in the collection edited by Ball and Goodson (1985) provide good examples of such theoretical and methodological approaches. They tend to shift the concept of career away from its vertical imagery towards 'teaching as a path in life' (Connell, 1985, p. 157), a series of experiences in coming to terms with situations and making choices subject to constraints. There are two criticisms which may be levelled at such work. One is Julia Evetts' point, expanded in her chapter in this volume, that there is a largely absent level of conceptualization: the internal labour market for teachers. The other is the sometimes inadequate level of understanding displayed of the impact of divisions within the teaching profession, especially those based on gender.

Social Divisions in Teaching

Numerous writers have commented on the 'divided profession' (e.g. Lacey, 1977), and it is sometimes difficult to see how we can manage to give the same occupational title to people who teach an enormous range of skills and ideas to big and little children and adults, inside and outside educational institutions. As suggested above, individuals called teachers face a structure of opportunities outside their own control. Their chances of achieving the rewards offered by these structures, should they want them, are significantly altered at different times in history. Demographic changes resulting in falling or rising school rolls; social changes in the acceptability of married women and mothers working outside the home; the age structure of teachers or academics now in post (a consequence of earlier social events); political decisions about expansion or contraction of certain curriculum subjects or extensions of education to younger or older children or adults — all these produce what feel like historical accidents to individuals who are relatively advantaged or disadvantaged by their operation.

Opportunity structures not only exist, they vary for those differently situated in what Connell (1985, p. 164) calls 'a kind of institutional grid within which teachers locate themselves'. That is, teachers' career chances differ according to factors like the age level and subject they teach and the size and type of school in which they work. Most important is 'phase' (age level of pupil or students). Compared to secondary school teachers, those employed in the primary phase have a relatively 'flat' career structure (Pollard, 1985). This means that beyond deputy headships and headships, there is little differentiation among the rest of the teachers, especially in smaller schools. Secondary teachers have greater chances to increase their salaries with allowances for middle management responsibilities. As Sheila Cunnison shows in her chapter, secondary teacher career routes are tacitly divided into 'pastoral' and 'academic' pathways. British universities are rather oddly like primary schools in career structure: they hold the majority of their academics in a bottom 'lecturer' career grade. Apart from a small number of high flyers, those who progress up through the system may have to wait for twenty years or more before they can do so. Further education recruits many of its teachers from earlier careers in commerce or industry, as Edith Black's chapter shows. There is a relatively clearly defined sequence of positions in further education colleges, with a specified blend of teaching and administrative activities expected at each level. What the chapters in this collection call to our attention is an important point about the operation of structures: all the patterns in the 'institutional grid' are bifurcated by gender.

The majority of nursery and primary teachers, 78.1 per cent, are women (DES, 1987). Representation varies by school type. Nearly all teachers and headteachers in nursery and separate infant schools (containing children of ages 5 to 7) are women. Combined infant/junior schools (ages 5 to 11) and separate junior schools (ages 7 to 11) have higher percentages of men teachers (25 per cent and 34 per cent respectively) and are likely to be managed by men, who hold 69.4 per cent of the infant/junior headships and 79.6 per cent of the junior headships. In secondary schools 54 per cent of teachers, and 83.8 per cent of headteachers, are men.

Such figures tell us what proportions of which headships are likely to be held by men or women, a kind of message about gender divisions in teaching broadcast to the outside world (and to pupils). We can also approach the figures differently, looking at how a given category of teacher (such as women in primary schools) is distributed across the ranks. This approach gives us some idea of 'career chances' for each sex. Table 1.1 shows that career chances for men teachers in primary education are exceedingly good: around half hold headships or deputy

Table 1.1 Percentage Distribution of Each Sex across the Grades for Full-Time Primary and Secondary Teachers, England and Wales, 1985

	Nursery and Primary		Secondary	
	Men	Women	Men	Women
Heads	31.5	7.4	3.2	0.7
Deputy Heads	19.6	8.3	4.3	2.1
Second master/ mistress/ senior teacher	0.4	0.2	5.4	2.6
Scale 4	0.3	0.1	17.5	6.1
Scale 3	12.1	7.6	26.9	19.3
Scale 2	26.9	41.5	23.3	29.4
Scale 1	9.2	34.9	19.4	39.8
Total %	100.0	100.0	100.0	100.0
N	(37,587)	(133,691)	(127,790)	(108,915)

Source: Calculated from DES (1987), pp. 24–7.

headships, compared to 16 per cent of the women. In secondary schools neither sex is especially likely to achieve a headship, as there are few such posts available, but men are better distributed across middle management posts than are women, who remain disproportionately on the lower scales (Table 1.1). Since October 1987, the Burnham salary scale system for primary and secondary schools, the basis for Table 1.1, has been replaced by a main professional grade scale plus incentive allowances. As national figures typically run two or three years behind (Interim Advisory Committee, 1988), it is not possible to provide tables to show the new system in operation. But given that incentive allowances initially went to those on the higher Burnham scales, and fewer incentive levels are available for primary schools, gender disparities are likely to remain.

Tables 1.2 and 1.3 show 'career chances' for women and men in further and higher education in England and Wales. Like secondary school teachers, relatively few academics reach the higher grades, but men's chances are considerably greater than women's. Women are a minority among full-time academic staff in further education colleges (25.6 per cent), polytechnics (15.0 per cent) and universities (17.2 per cent) (DES, 1987; UGC, 1987). Their minority representation overall, together with their poorer promotion chances, results in heavy male dominance of the higher grades in tertiary education. Above senior lecturer level in further education colleges only 9.3 per cent of staff are women; for polytechnics the figure is 7 per cent (DES, 1987).

Table 1.2 Percentage Distribution of Each Sex across the Grades for Full-Time Teachers in Polytechnics and Other Further Education Establishments, England and Wales, 1985

	Polytechnics		Other Establishments of Further Education[1]	
	Men	Women	Men	Women
Principals	0.2	—	1.0	0.1
Vice Principals and Heads of Departments	6.0	2.5	5.9	1.8
Readers and Principal Lecturers	22.3	9.7	5.7	1.8
Senior Lecturers	63.4	65.8	28.1	15.2
Lecturer Grade 2	7.7	20.7	25.9	26.3
Lecturer Grade 1	0.4	1.3	33.3	54.9
Total %	100.0	100.0	99.9	100.0
N	(13,003)	(2,299)	(47,560)	(16,557)

Note: 1 'Other establishments' refer mostly to further education colleges. Although polytechnics are usually classed as higher rather than further education, the DES figures give polytechnic staff numbers in tables on further education. A smaller group of 'miscellaneous establishments' such as adult education and youth welfare centres is not shown here.
Source: Calculated from DES (1987), pp. 35–6.

In universities 7.8 per cent of readers and senior lecturers and only 2.8 per cent of professors are women. What these figures mean in practice is that at many universities there is only a handful of women in senior posts. When figures are shown separately by subject area, they can be startling: for example, in university Departments of Education (including Adult and Continuing Education) in 1986–87, there were only nine women professors and thirty-five readers or senior lecturers in all of England and Wales (UGC, 1987). As Table 1.3 shows, women academics are disproportionately likely to be off the main grades and in a category called 'others' which includes miscellaneous personnel such as language assistants but is mostly made up of researchers. Most 'others' (89 per cent) are *not* 'wholly university financed' (compared with about a quarter of the other three groups) (UGC, 1987, p. 67). This means that the jobs of 'others' are likely to be less secure and their salaries lower.

I have argued elsewhere (Acker, 1983) that until recently sociological work on teachers' careers approached gender simplistically and stereotypically. Women teachers were seen as choosing to prioritize family over career, thus lacking commitment and impeding teaching's claim to full professionalization. In some versions women teachers were naturally subordinate and amenable to bureaucratic controls as well as being intuitive and unintellectual. The 'facts', as Rosemary Grant points

Table 1.3 Percentage Distribution of Each Sex across the Grades for Full-Time Academic Staff[1] *in Universities, England and Wales, 1986–1987*

	Men	Women
Professor	11.1	1.6
Reader/Senior Lecturer	21.3	8.7
Lecturer	59.4	67.1
Other	8.2	22.7
Total %	100.0	100.0
N	(31,925)	(6,649)

Note: 1 Academic staff are defined as those whose function is teaching and research, or teaching only. Researchers, although not given the same titles as teaching staff, are included in the equivalent grade in this table (UGC, 1987, p. 71).
Source: Calculated from UGC (1987), p. 63.

out in her chapter, to some extent were, and are, there: women do apply for headships less often than do men; many women want and have children; women usually shoulder the bulk of domestic responsibilities. The mistake is in closing the analysis with such observations. Even in the early 1980s, when gender divisions among pupils were beginning to be regularly noted, analysts stopped short of investigating those among teachers much beyond the description above (e.g. Woods, 1983). In Ball and Goodson (1985), gender figures in the editors' introduction and the first two selections and is absent (other than implicitly) thereafter. Sikes *et al.* (1985) note differences in the perceptions and experiences of the male and female teachers they interviewed about careers, but do not make gender a major dimension in their book. In contrast, gender is central for Apple (1986) writing from the United States, and Connell (1985) from Australia. Two British books of the mid-1980s also manage to take a non-stereotypical view of gender and give it a high profile in the analysis of teacher careers and experiences: Ball (1987) and Lawn and Grace (1987). The present volume continues in that direction by making gender *the* central theme.

Reproducing Gender Divisions

Why are these gender divisions in teaching so persistent that we can find them with ease both in historical accounts (see Alison Oram's chapter) and in accounts of our own time? Perhaps the concept of 'reproduction' will help us answer this question. Sociology of education has carried on a love/hate affair with this concept in recent years.

Clearly social divisions and the cultural understandings which sustain them persist over time, though not unproblematically. Schooling is widely believed to play a major part in such a process. The persistence of the sexual division of labour is less well theorized but schooling figures here too. For women teachers there is an ironic touch, insofar as their own subordination appears to limit the chances for change in the next generation.

There are various theories as to why, ultimately, gender reproductive forces operate (Acker, 1987). In this volume Alison Oram and Sheila Cunnison both suggest that the status quo suits the interests of men, who have little to gain by changing or challenging it. Thus the history of teacher union efforts to equalize women teachers' status with men's is marked by inertia and sometimes open opposition. Cunnison's study in one secondary school reveals a great deal of latent hostility among men towards women. Chapters by Sheila Riddell and Edith Black point to local labour market forces which limit job choices students can make and reinforce conventional sex-typed provision in schools and colleges. In Riddell's case the teachers' convictions that the school should not interfere in 'free' choices made the outcomes all the more predictable. Kathleen Casey and Michael Apple also invoke labour market forces when they argue that criticisms of education and subsequent tightening of controls over (women) teachers' working conditions and practices in the United States are ways for the capitalist economy to 'export the crisis' — to blame the schools for current ills such as unemployment and poverty rather than review the dominant economic arrangements.

The very existence of hierarchies, some believe, favours men (Illich, 1983), and there have been biological arguments advanced for this thesis (Golberg, 1977). Feminist arguments about hierarchies tend to suggest women do not simply lose a competition, but consciously choose to reject such hierarchies as politically oppressive (see Casey and Apple's chapter). Research documents the preference of many women to define career commitment as good classroom teaching rather than upward mobility through the system (Grant's chapter). It is unlikely that rejection of hierarchies is biologically built into women; women's socialization and satisfying experiences of alternative values and forms of organization, together with a kind of 'situational adjustment' — coming to terms with a situation unlikely to be changed by wishing it so — provide a more credible explanation.

It may be futile to speculate on *why* gender divisions exist, but chapters in this volume give us insights into the ways they operate within teaching. As Miriam David's chapter suggests, little overt action is necessary. 'Business as usual' is sufficient. Christine Skelton and Joan Hanson show this vividly in their account of a primary teacher training Postgraduate Certificate in Education course, where 'gender' had not surfaced as a recognized curriculum issue. Paradoxically, the same students who were sensitive to sexism in their own relationships were unthinkingly perpetuating sexism in the classroom by their taken-for-granted practices. Similarly, 'business as usual' selection procedures for headships result in male preferment. As Grant points out in her chapter, when most secondary and junior school heads are men, the image of how a headteacher looks and behaves is powerfully 'male' in the minds of the selectors, and this becomes the norm to which they compare candidates.

A discriminatory system continues when it is underpinned by powerful ideologies. Most prominent are the beliefs that tightly tie together women with marriage and children, and the complementary beliefs about men's role as breadwinners. Over time the image of a woman teacher has changed from that of a dedicated spinster to a married woman. The images hold contradictions, as Oram shows: the spinster, of uncertain sexuality and not quite a 'real woman', is a second-best model, yet 'normal' married women teachers, by working outside the home, are also compromised. That women are believed to 'belong' with *young* children has given them a route to headships of infant schools largely denied to men (see Julia Evett's chapter) but continues to disqualify them from management positions where *older* children are concerned (Grant, this volume). Other chapters in this collection give support to the influence of ideology on women's experiences: promotion is thought to be based on merit and individual striving (Evetts); women's choice to have children is free, yet equivalent to renouncing interest in a career (Riddell); career breaks mean self-evident lesser commitment (Cunnison); men, the breadwinners, have a *right* to promotion (Cunnison, Oram).

Oram's chapter shows how hierarchical structures of the Burnham pay scales worked indirectly to disadvantage women. Instead of rewarding classroom teachers across the board, the trend in pay settlements has often been to increase differentials (recently termed 'incentives') so that a smaller number (the 'reskilled' few) get greater rewards. In situations where there are rigidities such as age norms and penalized career breaks (most returners to teaching after career breaks revert to the lowest scale) it almost goes without saying that one consequence is the disadvantage of women who do any dividing of energies between family and work. Oram argues that while direct discrimination through government policy on pay, promotion and marriage bars (in the not very distant past) has ended, a strong residue of indirect discrimination remains, less checked because less overt, and sometimes disguised as 'market forces'. Examples might be the recent availability of bursaries for teacher training in subjects of physics and mathematics, teaching in such shortage subjects being listed among possible grounds for receiving incentive allowances, 'new blood' lectureships in universities given almost exclusively to scientists while cuts fell disproportionately on arts and social sciences. The indirect disadvantage of such practices to women — who are less often mathematicians and physicists and more often in arts subjects — is almost never noted in public discussions.

Hierarchies mean competition. Hilsum and Start (1974) show that many fewer male secondary teachers will be promoted to headships than express an interest, commenting dryly, 'Reality is going to come as a surprise to many teachers' (p. 267). It may be that a competitive, hierarchical system, plus men's belief in their right to promotion, encourages extra efforts and sacrifices for male teachers, creating a kind of motor for the whole system to carry on despite the undoubted stresses and paltry rewards on offer. Many teachers must come to terms with disappointment as they age (Sikes *et al.*, 1985). Nor is the system necessarily fair in its rewards and promotion procedures, even to men, for example favouring people in certain subject areas or with certain qualifications over others, being amenable in internal promotions to a certain amount of negotiation between teacher and head and in external ones relying heavily on first impressions at interview. Cunnison's chapter shows how some of the anger and resentment of the disappointed men may be deflected onto women, especially those apparently on their way 'up'. Women may not be consciously deterred from seeking promotion by the prospect of being a target for hostility (see David's chapter) but there are likely to be subtly discouraging effects of an institutional ethos that defines reality for its members in this way.

There are also a variety of constraints which work against innovation in schools in general and against feminist reform in particular. For example, the teacher's role in Britain has been constantly expanding and continues to do so with plans for a National Curriculum. Morale is thought to be low (Interim Advisory Committee, 1988, p. 21). Teachers have so many 'innovations' to which they have to accommodate, often under conditions of resource deprivation and high levels of stress, that there is little surplus energy available for optional extras such as implementing anti-sexist initiatives or working to equalize opportunities for the sexes in teaching (Acker, 1988).

Moreover, as chapters in this volume show, women are rarely in high-level positions and thus not well placed for instigating reform. There is also a tension between individual career progress and bringing about feminist social change. The former may be necessary to accomplish the latter, but being publicly associated with the latter may stop one achieving the former. David's chapter illustrates the painful dilemmas of balancing the two objectives. Perhaps this is why, Riddell suggests, women teachers who have achieved success in conventional terms may be those least inclined to challenge the status quo. Both Riddell and Cunnison see women teachers as divided by ideologies and social control processes and hampered in bringing about reform by the divisions among them.

Working to advance in a career takes considerable energy, especially when one's attributes are not those of the dominant group. As Barbara McKellar's chapter indicates for black women teachers, such individuals may have had to work twice as hard already. Sue Middleton shows that certain varieties of feminism may bring a negative response from colleagues. Lesbian teachers, Gillian Squirrell finds, may temper feminist inclinations either because others are likely to believe that their sexual orientation discredits their politics or because they keep a low profile generally to avoid homophobic reactions from colleagues and the community.

In my analysis so far, individual teachers appear as players in a complex, and frequently unjust game. Part of the game is deciphering the rules, written in a language better understood by some than others. Widespread ideologies and vested interests make inequality of outcomes difficult to alter over the generations. It is time to bring the people back in to this scenario and assess the prospects for change.

New Directions

Earlier in this chapter I commented critically on approaches which see teachers as calculating individuals making decisions in a socio-political vacuum. But I certainly do not mean to dismiss individuals from this volume's compass. On the contrary, they pop up bravely in many of the chapters, a testimony to unquenchable human spirit. First, individuals devise strategies. Evett's headteachers, for example, benefited from sponsorship and community networks — but to do so, they had to 'trigger' such networks by making themselves visible, taking on responsibilities, being aware of innovative schemes, etc. McKellar reports exactly the same sort of activity in her own past. Early awareness of discrimination against black people was painful, but paradoxically gave her a head start, as she learned even as a child the need to plan ahead, gather information, set clear goals. Black's secretarial studies teachers, reactionary and socially reproductive to some, also planned and worked and advanced within the limits set by 'women's work'. They took pride in their work — 'you've got to have it all the way round'.

Second, people on the margins may develop greater insight. The teachers Squirrell interviewed, suffering as they did from victimization real or anticipated, still felt they had gained a kind of extra sensitivity to others' tribulations. Middleton's feminist teachers' own painful personal experiences of discrimination or marginality based on sex, race and class left them poised to develop a feminist understanding once they came across theories that helped them to articulate and understand their own biographies.

Third, people help each other. Middleton's teachers were able to turn their understandings into practical support for other women teachers. Similarly the women headteachers in Evetts' study were part of occupational networks wherein women were encouraged and sponsored. David's experiences show that a position in educational management and a feminist vision are not, after all, incompatible.

Casey and Apple document for us the dramatic changes in American scholarship on teachers, under the impetus of feminism. Taking gender seriously need not de-emphasize the social divisions which cut across it, nor suggest a hierarchy of oppression. What it does make clear is that many possible questions about teachers' careers and experiences have not yet been answered, or even asked, because the dominant model has limited the scope of our collective imagination. For example, what is the impact on teachers of working in a school catering for a particular social class, religious or ethnic mix, or a single-sex pupil body? Are these effects different for teachers who themselves possess different characteristics? Are the experiences of teachers from Asian backgrounds different from those of the Afro-Caribbean teachers McKellar writes about? What about rural/urban differences, or regional effects? Would Riddell's findings be replicated in an urban area where opportunities for girls might be less restricted? Why is it that when nationally women were 16 per cent of secondary school headteachers, in the LEA studied by Davidson (1985) there were *none*? Only through an accumulation of studies like those reported here will we begin to answer such questions and do justice to the full variety of teacher careers.

Individuals clearly do make choices and develop strategies. But the model of individuals negotiating their way through the complexities of occupational, social and historical structures must be modified again to recognize these individuals as heterogeneous. For those belonging to particular groups there are blockages and barriers making their passage more difficult. Individuals possess different currencies (qualifications, length and type of experience, subject specialties) but their probabilities of holding these also depend on their class, sex, race, age and other identifications and memberships. Even qualities like motivation and personality may be differently received and interpreted by others according to who displays them.

Some time ago Peter Berger (1963) observed that a humanistic sociology might still depict individuals as puppets controlled by social forces, but that they would retain the capacity to look up and see who pulls the strings. With some modification this image suits this book. Through scholarship and reflection we come to understand the levers of our lives. But we cannot but try to challenge and control them too.

References

ACKER, S. (1983) 'Women and teaching: A semi-detached sociology of a semi-profession', in WALKER, S. and BARTON, L. (Eds) *Gender, Class and Education*, Lewes, Falmer, pp. 123–39.

ACKER, S. (1987) 'Feminist theory and the study of gender and education', *International Review of Education*, 33, pp. 419–35.

ACKER, S. (1988) 'Teachers, gender and resistance', *British Journal of Sociology of Education*, 9, 3, pp. 307–22.

APPLE, M. (1986) *Teachers and Texts*, London, Routledge and Kegan Paul.

BALL, S. J. (1987) *The Micro-Politics of the School*, London, Methuen.

BALL, S. J. and GOODSON, I. F. (Eds) (1985) *Teachers' Lives and Careers*, Lewes, Falmer Press.

BECKER, H. S. (1970) *Sociological Work*, New Brunswick, N.J., Transaction Books.

BERGER, P. L. (1963) *Invitation to Sociology*, Garden City, N.Y., Anchor Books.

CONNELL, R. W. (1985) *Teachers' Work*, Sydney, Allen and Unwin.

DAVIDSON, H. (1985) 'Unfriendly myths about women teachers', in WHYTE, J. *et al.* (Eds) *Girl Friendly Schooling*, London, Methuen, pp. 191–208.

DEPARTMENT OF EDUCATION AND SCIENCE (1987) *Statistics of Education: Teachers in Service England and Wales 1985*, London, HMSO.

GOLDBERG, S. (1977) *The Inevitability of Patriarchy*, London, Temple Smith.

HILSUM, K. and START, K. B. (1974) *Promotion and Careers in Teaching*, Slough, National Foundation for Education Research.

HUGHES, E. (1971) *The Sociological Eye*, Chicago, Ill., Aldine-Atherton.

ILLICH, I. (1983) *Gender*, London, Marion Boyars.

INTERIM ADVISORY COMMITTEE ON SCHOOL TEACHERS' PAY AND CONDITIONS (1988) *Report* (Chairman: Lord Chilver), London, HMSO.

LACEY, C. (1977) *The Socialization of Teachers*, London, Methuen.

LAWN, M. and GRACE, G. (Eds) (1987) *Teachers: The Culture and Politics of Work*, Lewes, Falmer Press.

LAWN, M. and OZGA, J. (1981) 'The educational worker? A reassessment of teachers', in BARTON, L. and WALKER, S. (Eds) *Schools, Teachers and Teaching*, Lewes, Falmer Press.

LYONS, G. (1981) *Teacher Careers and Career Perceptions*, Slough, National Foundation for Educational Research.

MEASOR, L. (1985) 'Critical incidents in the classroom: Identities, choices and careers', in BALL, S. J. and GOODSON, I. F. (Eds) *Teachers' Lives and Careers*, Lewes, Falmer Press, pp. 61–77.

POLLARD, A. (1985) *The Social World of the Primary School*, London, Holt, Rinehart and Winston.

SIKES, P., MEASOR, L. and WOODS, P. (1985) *Teacher Careers: Crises and Continuities*, Lewes, Falmer Press.

UNIVERSITY GRANTS COMMITTEE (1987) *University Statistics 1986–87, Vol. 1: Students and Staff*, Cheltenham, Universities' Statistical Record.

WOODS, P. (1983) *Sociology and the School*, London, Routledge and Kegan Paul.

2
A Master Should Not Serve under a Mistress: Women and Men Teachers 1900–1970

Alison Oram

In theory there are now no formal barriers to women's equality in the teaching profession. Marriage bars were abolished by the 1944 Education Act, equal pay established in 1961, and discrimination in promotion outlawed by the 1975 Sex Discrimination Act. In practice, however, women's position in teaching remains in many respects much the same as it was at the turn of the century; average salaries are lower than men's, and women are found in the lower status posts. Indeed women teachers' promotion prospects have notably worsened. In 1927 women teachers held 57 per cent of headships of primary and secondary schools, yet in 1984 they held only 39 per cent. This puts paid to any simple notion that career opportunities have improved for women teachers in the post-war period, the era of equal pay and opportunities.

In fact major differences of status and position have divided men and women teachers throughout the twentieth century. In this chapter I will first describe the major inequalities between women and men teachers from 1900 to the 1970s, taking as parameters those issues identified by women teachers themselves: pay, union involvement, promotion and the marriage bar. I will then examine the overt and covert supports for this situation, and argue that legislatively imposed inequalities have been supported by far less formal mechanisms. Although the formal constraints imposed by central and local government were lifted after World War II, the informal controls have remained, and indeed strengthened. A third section of the chapter will briefly discuss the conflicting images of women teachers, arguing that marital status and the assumptions which accompany it have been a crucial division for twentieth century women teachers.

Change and Continuity in the Position of Women and Men Teachers

Recruitment and Training

As a career, teaching was supposed to hold different attractions for girls and boys. It was frequently assumed to appeal to girls because of their 'natural' maternal instincts and other feminine qualities. The 1925 *Report on the Training of Teachers* described elementary school teaching as 'a field of effort for the girl of average intellectual capacity and normal maternal instincts', but this image helped to contribute to its lower status as an occupation for men. The *Report* identified 'a feeling that for a man to spend his life teaching children of school age is to waste it in doing easy and not very valuable work, he would not do it if fit to do anything else ...' (Board of Education, 1925, pp. 34, 41). Recent feminist studies of the class background of women teachers in the late nineteenth and early twentieth centuries discuss the attractions of teacher training for the predominantly lower middle-class female entrants. They show that, rather than the motherly girl, the potential teacher was the bright, more academic type of girl, with expectations of teaching as a career which were probably not very different from the expectations of boys; she looked for security, status and a reasonable salary (Widdowson, 1980, 1986; Copelman, 1986).

Real differences did exist, however, in the class background and training experience of women and men entering the profession. A higher proportion of girls than of boys came from lower middle-class backgrounds throughout the century. Boys were rather more likely to come from skilled working-class families. This indicates the relatively circumscribed employment opportunities for girls; the civil service, office work or nursing were the most likely alternatives to teaching (Floud and Scott, 1961; Widdowson, 1980, 1986).

Discrimination against women teachers began at the very point of their entry into training. Although access to training college was much easier after World War I than previously, and most teachers did pass through a training college, for most of the inter-war period women found it harder to get a training college place than men. Once at college, women received substantially smaller grants than men, and their college places were not subsidized to the same extent. Most teachers were trained in single-sex colleges, but even ostensibly mixed colleges were segregated until after World War II. However, men and women took the same Certificate Examination which gave them the same professional status and entitled them to compete in the same field of work.

The Emergency Training Scheme after World War II was first aimed mainly at men, and the proportion of men teachers in the schools, which had been 32 per cent in 1938, had risen to 37 per cent by 1955. But at the same time mature married women began to be required as teachers, partly to ease the teacher shortage, and by the late 1960s married women were for the first time encouraged to enter teacher training.

Salaries

Before World War I, women teachers' salaries were on average 75 per cent of those of men with the same qualifications and status. Teachers' salaries were bargained for locally by the local education authorities (LEAs) and the National Union of Teachers (NUT), and so varied among areas. In a very few areas such as parts of outer London, where women teachers were strongly organized, they achieved a near approximation to equal pay. From 1904 women teachers campaigned within the NUT for equal pay, resulting in acrimonious debate at successive NUT conferences. Resolutions calling for equal pay were always heavily defeated until 1919, when a referendum of the membership strongly endorsed equal pay and it was accepted as NUT policy. However, the union failed to press this demand on the newly formed Burnham Committee, and women teachers' salary scales were set at 80 per cent of men's. While this represented an improvement in most women teachers' salaries relative to men's, it was a proportion which was to remain unchanged for forty years.

During the inter-war years education cuts led to across-the-board reductions in teachers' salaries in 1922 and 1923, and again in 1931. In 1925, however, women teachers' annual increments were cut considerably more than men's. In these economic circumstances equal pay did not resurface as a serious issue until the late 1930s and during World War II (Oram, 1985, 1987b). An attempt to include equal pay in the 1944 Education Bill was defeated by the government. Although the Royal Commission on Equal Pay which reported in 1946 did not support equal pay, and post-war governments were reluctant to implement it, pressure from women's organizations and white collar unions (including the NUT) intensified in the early 1950s. In 1955 the introduction of equal pay by stages to 1961 was agreed for the civil service and subsequently for teachers (Gosden, 1972; Partington, 1976).

Marriage

Before World War I only about one-third of LEAs operated a marriage bar. Indeed in certain parts of the country, including rural areas and London (where 25 per cent of women teachers were married), it was accepted practice for women to continue their teaching careers after marriage (Copelman, 1986). During the war, when there was a need to replace men who had enlisted, most LEAs suspended any such restrictions.

By 1921 almost 19 per cent of women teachers in elementary schools were married. But between 1921 and 1923 the vast majority of LEAs introduced a marriage bar in a panic response to teacher unemployment and education cuts. Thousands of serving married women teachers were sacked in some areas, while others required single women teachers to resign upon marriage. By the 1930s the proportion of women teachers who were married had dropped to about 10 per cent nationally, but many authorities continued to employ married women as supply teachers. In one or two areas the bar was raised in the 1930s if there were recruitment difficulties or local pressure (Oram, 1983).

During World War II married women were encouraged back into the schools in all areas, and due to concern over teacher supply, marriage bars were outlawed under the 1944 Education Act. After the war a deliberate policy of retaining the 'wise married woman' was further encouraged by the increased wastage rate of women teachers, in a reversal of the policy in the 1920s (Littlewood, 1988). In 1952 one-third of all women teachers in service were married, and by 1960 this proportion had reached 42 per cent (David, 1980, pp. 168–9). In the 1960s married women were urgently sought as part-timers or returners, or new trainees, but were not regarded as 'career teachers' in the way that men were.

Promotion Prospects

Throughout the early decades of the century to World War II there was intense public debate and antagonism between women and men teachers over the issue of relative promotion prospects. Each side accused the other of stealing headships rightfully belonging to their own sex, in a debate that was fuelled by anxiety over the amalgamation of schools and the significance of gender in teaching. For example, some women teachers complained that headships were going unfairly to men:

> Men were an almost insignificant section of the whole, yet gradually the chances of promotion for women were becoming less and less. The practice was growing of combining infant departments with mixed schools and putting men in charge. That was how economy worked when coupled with sex prejudice. (*Manchester Guardian*, 7 January 1933)

In fact women's promotion prospects did not worsen to any greater extent than men's in the years to 1939, although both sexes suffered from the reorganization of the elementary school system from the mid-1920s. This, coupled with falling school rolls, meant that schools were increasingly separated into junior and senior departments, and a growing proportion was mixed, raising the question of whether women should be heads of schools with a mixed staff.

The sexual division of labour in the schools became more rigid, however. Women teachers were increasingly likely to work and find promotion only within infant and junior departments, while men teachers were found at higher stages of the education hierarchy, in charge of older children and boys (Oram, 1987a).

But women teachers' promotion prospects did worsen after World War II in comparison to men's. By 1959 women held less than half the headships in state schools for the first time this century, and the proportion continued to decline. One contributing factor was the increase in co-education, especially in secondary schools, which has reduced the number of headships that are traditionally reserved for women in girls' schools. Another was that since the war a gender differentiated career pattern emerged alongside the increased employment of married women. Women teachers were expected to take a break for child-rearing and often returned to part-time employment. In addition there is evidence that in direct competition with men, married women teachers in particular are discriminated against (Partington, 1976; NUT/EOC, 1980; Littlewood, 1988).

Union Involvement

The rate of unionization among women teachers has been far higher than among other groups of women workers, and there was never any formal barrier to women's participation in NUT business or to holding honorary office in the union. However, although women teachers always made up the majority of the NUT's membership from 1905, this was never reflected within the union hierarchy. Only about one-third of the delegates to annual conference, the union's policy-making body, were women in the years to 1939, and fewer than 25 per cent of national executive members were women in the same period, sometimes as few as 12 per cent (NUT *Annual Reports*). The NUT elected its first woman president in 1911, and subsequently the position was held by a woman in 1918, 1920, 1930 and 1938, five in forty years.

Women teachers were particularly influenced by and linked to the wider feminist campaigns of the early twentieth century. Pressure groups of women, such as the National Federation of Women Teachers (NFWT), were formed within the NUT before World War I to demand equal pay, union support for women's suffrage, and to encourage more women to join the union and hold office within it. But the resolutions on equal pay and the suffrage were blocked, shouted down and defeated at annual conferences between 1911 and 1918. The NUT's refusal to push for equal pay in the Burnham negotiations (after accepting the principle as union policy) capped the disillusionment felt by the feminist teachers in the NFWT. They decided to secede from the main union and set up their own National Union of Women Teachers in 1920, taking many of the most active and able women with them (Pierotti, 1963). Women's involvement in the offices and executive of the NUT dropped off sharply in the 1920s.

The issue of women's equality also split the NUT in the other direction. Anti-feminist men teachers who were resolutely opposed to the NUT's adoption of the principle of equal pay in 1919 left to set up the National Association of Schoolmasters (NAS), who thereafter campaigned for a family wage for men and men teachers for boys (Littlewood, 1985; Oram, 1987a). The NUT denounced both secessionist groups, criticizing the 'sex conscious efforts' of the foolish 'pre-suffrage feminists and misogynists' (*Schoolmaster*, 26 January 1923, p. 127), but put far more effort into wooing the men back to the fold. During the inter-war period equality issues were suppressed under an ethos of unity; the NUT's equal pay policy was never mentioned and promotion issues rarely discussed. Women's issues and women members were more dispensable than men (Oram, 1984).

In the 1950s and 1960s women teachers' involvement in the NUT was no better than before the war. Women's representation on the executive continued to be only around 15 per cent, and women presidents were infrequently elected. The NUT rather belatedly joined the equal pay campaign when it became 'practical politics' after the war, but continued to cross swords with the NUWT, who wanted equal pay introduced all at once, rather than by stages. The NUWT wound itself up in 1961, after equal pay had been achieved.

Constraints on Sex Equality

The factors contributing to the unequal position of women in the teaching profession can be classified into several areas. One is direct discrimination through government policy; a second area covers the pressures on state policy, that is, the rationale for discrimination. These in turn are strongly influenced by the ideological assumptions about women's rightful place. Finally, men teachers' antagonism and the ways in which they protected their privileges must also be considered.

Direct Constraints

Many of the inequalities facing women teachers for most of the century were overtly and unabashedly written into the system. State policy at both local and national levels intentionally discriminated against women teachers and favoured men's position in the profession.

A general feature of the whole period was the gradual transference of power from local authorities to central government in the area of education. Even when control of policy was nominally in the hands of LEAs (and the Board was always anxious to disclaim responsibility for contentious policies whenever possible), there is frequently evidence to show that the Minister for Education encouraged or endorsed discriminatory policies (Oram, 1984).

Salary policy after 1918 was determined by the Burnham Committee, made up of two panels, one from the LEAs, the other from the NUT. In practice the attitude of the Board of Education also had some influence on proceedings. In any case the Burnham Committee never seriously considered the question of equal pay during the inter-war years; the principle was not supported by either panel, and in the post-war years the Committee maintained that it was up to the government to approve the policy. Even when governments in the

1940s and 1950s reluctantly agreed to the principle, they were unwilling to fund it.

The implementation of a marriage bar was a local decision, but there is evidence that the Board colluded in it, at least in the early 1920s (Oram, 1983). But because it was a local bar, pressure to lift it could be brought to bear locally as it was in London. The appointment of headteachers was also a matter for local decision-making, or more commonly an unwritten rule. Women were employed as heads of most junior mixed schools, but rarely to senior mixed schools with a mixed staff; as one handbook for educational administrators said: 'it is not customary for a master to serve under a mistress' (Ikin, 1926, p. 64). Many LEAs advertized for men as heads of mixed or combined junior and infant schools throughout the period.

Where government had exercised influence over policy, so it had the prerogative to change it. Both the raising of the marriage bar in the 1940s and the implementation of equal pay in the 1950s were effectively central government decisions. However, although the Burnham settlement of 1956 ended direct sex discrimination, it replaced it with a new pay and promotions structure which indirectly penalized women. Rather than distributing rewards equally to all classroom teachers, higher salaries were available for a smaller number who could display a (typically male) career pattern of continuous service, managerial and other extra responsibilities and work in larger (secondary) rather than smaller (primary) schools (Littlewood, 1988; Grant, this volume).

Indirect Pressures: The Rationale for Policy

The main factors which affected state policy towards women teachers were finance, the supply of teachers, and structural changes such as amalgamation and co-education in schools.

Lack of money was always a handy excuse for governments faced with demands for equal pay. It was particularly relevant during the financial crises of the early 1920s and 1930s, but served them right up to the 1950s. This was also a rationale for the marriage bar. It was argued that married women were more expensive to employ, due to higher absenteeism, and it was also hoped that the policy might save money in the short term, as married women were senior teachers, and so higher up the scale.

An oversupply of women teachers for much of the inter-war period also made it easier for governments to argue that they were already paying reasonable and attractive salaries to women teachers based on market values. It provided further justification for the marriage bar; exclusion of married women would make way for unemployed college leavers. Wartime needs and periods of expansion of the education system, as in the 1940s and 1950s, clearly illustrate how married women teachers were used as a 'reserve army of labour'. The World War II and post-war shortage of teachers, particularly of women teachers, contributed to the raising of the marriage bar in 1944, and added to the pressure for equal pay in the 1950s (Partington, 1976).

The reorganization of the primary school system has also affected women's position in teaching, although more indirectly. In the inter-war years falling rolls and the decision to implement a break at 11 led to the amalgamation of departments and separation into junior and senior schools, along with increasing co-education. Women teachers had a decreasing preserve of girls' schools available to them and were more likely to compete directly with men for jobs. This led to a hardening of the sexual division of labour in teaching for both classroom teachers and heads. The extension of co-education to the secondary school became increasingly important in the post-war era. However, these structural changes only affected women teachers' position because of the deeply embedded familial ideology of the school: the man as head of the family, supported by women teachers, who were supposed to be particularly suited to the education of the younger children.

A Woman's Real Place...

Discriminatory policies were implemented and upheld in the last resort because they were supported by contemporary notions of women's role. The most common argument against equal pay was that men needed more money because they had wives and children to support. The ideal of the nuclear family complete with male breadwinner, dependent wife and two or three school age children and its opposite, the self-supporting spinster, was central to sex inequality in the profession, and it was constantly invoked to justify discrimination against women teachers. In accordance with this scenario, it could be alleged that giving men and women equal salaries would result in unequal standards of living: '... teachers were divided into two main classes, married men with children and unmarried women. The first mentioned in receipt of £250 a year were poor men not able to dress properly, educate their children as they wished, or take part in social amenities which single women comparatively well off with £250 could enjoy' (report of speech in *The Times Educational Supplement*, 5 June 1919). Likewise the employment of married women was depicted as unfair and unnatural since: 'If marriage does not appeal to a women she should remain single', and 'the husbands should be compelled to keep these women, not the public' (letters to the London County Council, 1922). It was considered to be self-evident that women should not be placed in positions of authority over men in mixed schools. 'Only a nation heading for the madhouse would force on men, many married with families, such a position as service under spinster headmistresses' (*TES*, 15 April 1939, report of speech). Obviously this vision of the family bore little relation to reality. Many men teachers were unmarried but still earning more than their women colleagues, while a high proportion of single women teachers had to support dependent aging parents or other relatives (Oram, 1987b).

In the 1950s a new archetype emerged of the mature married woman teacher, and increasing numbers of married women were encouraged to come back into the teaching profession (as in other occupations). Yet this change was framed against a background ideal for women of singleminded motherhood and domesticity (Birmingham Feminist History Group, 1979). The divided responsibilities of married women teachers were expounded and emphasized by both legislators and male colleagues, a process which had negative effects on the status and prospects of all women teachers. Thus ideology served to sustain state policy and guarantee to men the advantages of higher pay and status, a greater chance of a headship and housekeeping services in the home.

Union Attitudes: Men's Antagonism

Generally speaking men teachers' interests and the state's converged. The conflict between men's interests and equality within the profession emerged most nakedly in the inter-union battles over feminist issues. As the body representing the profession as a whole, the NUT had an obligation to support its women members on the equality issues. Equal pay, women's suffrage, promotion prospects and the marriage bar were all matters of *professional* concern to a union which was trying to raise the status of all teachers. Lower salaries, insecurity of tenure, lack of political representation and other inequalities which applied just to one section of the profession were a threat to the status of the whole. But this fact was generally obscured by the male-dominated hierarchy of the NUT behind the smokescreen of gender.

The NAS attitude, by comparison, was more that of a 'macho' industrial trade union. It was happy to use the family wage as a bargaining lever and argue for a reasonable level of subsistence, rather than demand the professional rate for the job. It is clear that many NUT men shared the misogynist attitudes of the NAS, but did not want to give up the benefits of belonging to the larger union.

The NUT was willing to fudge the issues, try to ignore them, or say these were not union issues. In theory women were equal members of the NUT. In practice their efforts to organize on issues of concern to them as women teachers were blocked by the men. In the 1920s and 1930s this was because the union was afraid of male members' reactions, and did not want to lose any more men to the NAS. It was only in the 1940s and 1950s that equal pay began to be voiced as a union issue again, once public opinion had swung its way. Men continued to control the powerful positions in the union through to the 1970s. Men's advantages which enabled them to exercise power in the union were the same as those they were trying to protect and enforce as teachers: support services at home, higher pay and status and a male-orientated ethos. There was no getting away from the fact that if women teachers were to have equality, then men would have to give up some of their power in the union and in schools. Only the NUWT was clear about the distribution of power both in the NUT and in conventional households: 'A man who marries obtains an unsalaried housekeeper for life' (Board of Education, 1918, Vol. 2, p. 69).

A Real Woman's Place? Femininity and Teachers' Marital Status

The image of the woman teacher has always held contradictions. On the one hand teaching has been sold as an undeniably feminine occupation, linked to women's role as mothers and nurturers of children. The younger the children the more apt is women's place as their teacher. The sexual division of labour in the profession has emphasized this familial structure. On the other hand teaching has offered twentieth century women economic independence with relatively high (though unequal) salaries, responsibility and status both within the profession (for instance as heads) and in the local community. These images have been linked to a great extent (although not inevitably) with women teachers' marital status. The former role reflects the woman teacher's position as wife and mother, while the latter more powerful and therefore threatening image came to be associated with spinster teachers.

There can be no doubt of the dramatic changes in marital status of women teachers during this century. Until World War II only 10–15 per cent of women teachers were married, but with the raising of the marriage bar this figure reached 42 per cent by 1960. Accompanying this change — indeed preceding it — has been an insidious and damaging shift in the public perception of women teachers.

There was always some ambiguity about spinster teachers. Teaching was seen as an appropriate role for unmarried women, but an implication of personal failure was always there. The possibility that women might choose to be single, although teaching was one of the few occupations that allowed them the economic freedom to make such a choice, was never entertained. During the inter-war period spinster teachers were increasingly portrayed in a negative way, as neurotic, lonely and frustrated (Oram, 1988). On the other hand married women teachers were dismissed as greedy, unfeminine and neglectful of home, husband and family. To some extent married women teachers began to be rehabilitated in the 1930s, with the emphasis on domestic subjects in school and domestic virtues outside, although they were still excluded from the profession by the marriage bar (David, 1980).

By the 1950s this had been translated into policy. Women teachers were seen as having acquired desirable skills and qualities via marriage and motherhood. But despite the employment of many 'returners' full-time as well as part-time, women teachers began to be perceived as temporary teachers, divided between home and school. 'Since the war women [teachers] have become casual workers' (quoted in Partington, 1976, p. 85). This also left unmarried women teachers in an uncertain and often invisible place. Although women teachers had gained the right to work after marriage, they had lost some of their former power and professionalism along with the disparagement of the spinster teacher.

Conclusion

The sexual imbalances in the teaching profession in the twentieth century were inevitably accompanied by conflict between women and men teachers, since real economic advantages for men teachers and for employers were at stake. Men teachers' dominant position was maintained in the first part of the period by a combination of legislative methods and ideological pressures. Central and local government directives on pay, appointments and employment after marriage were justified by reference to woman's true place as dependent wife and mother, and often tacitly supported by the male dominated teachers' unions.

While these official inequalities were removed in the 1940s and 1950s, the informal constraints on women teachers' position remained, and indeed were strengthened by the 1956 Burnham pay settlement. This process was enhanced by major changes in women teachers' marital status. Although the change from spinster schoolmistress to mature married woman was only partial, the transformation of image was complete. The greater emphasis on the importance of marriage, proven heterosexuality and actual rather than proxy motherhood reached its apotheosis in the 1950s and 1960s, while at the same time men teachers tightened their grip on headships and union hierarchies.

References

BIRMINGHAM FEMINIST HISTORY GROUP (1979) 'Feminism as femininity in the nineteen-fifties?', *Feminist Review*, 3, pp. 48–65.

BOARD OF EDUCATION (1918) *Report of the Departmental Committee for Enquiring into the Principles which Should Determine the Construction of Scales of Salary for Teachers in Elementary Schools*, London, HMSO.

BOARD OF EDUCATION (1925) *Report of the Departmental Committee on the Training of Teachers for Public Elementary Schools*, London, HMSO.

COPELMAN, D. (1986) '"A new comradeship between men and women": Family, marriage and London's women teachers, 1870–1914', in LEWIS, J. (Ed) *Labour and Love: Women's Experience of Home and Family 1850–1940*, Oxford, Basil Blackwell.

DAVID, M. (1980) *The State, the Family and Education*, London, Routledge and Kegan Paul.

FLOUD, J. and SCOTT, W. (1961) 'Recruitment to teaching in England and Wales', in HALSEY, A. H., FLOUD, J. and ANDERSON, C. A. (Eds) *Education, Economy and Society*, New York, Free Press.

GOSDEN, P. H. J. H. (1972) *The Evolution of a Profession*, Oxford, Basil Blackwell.

IKIN, A. E. (1926) *Organisation and Administration of the Education Department*, London, Pitman.

LITTLEWOOD, M. (1985) 'Makers of men: The anti-feminist backlash of the National Association of Schoolmasters in the 1920s and 30s', *Trouble and Strife*, 5, pp. 23–9.

LITTLEWOOD, M. (1989) 'The "wise married woman" and the teaching unions', in DE LYON, H. and MIGNIUOLO, F. (Eds) *Women Teachers: Issues and Experiences*, Milton Keynes, Open University Press.

NUT (1980) *Promotion and the Woman Teacher*, Manchester, Equal Opportunities Commission/NUT.

ORAM, A. (1983) 'Serving two masters? The introduction of a marriage bar in teaching in the 1920s', in LONDON FEMINIST HISTORY GROUP (Eds) *The Sexual Dynamics of History*, London, Pluto Press.

ORAM, A. (1984) *'Sex Antagonism' in the Teaching Profession: Employment Issues and the Woman Teacher in Elementary Education, 1910–1939,* Unpublished MSc thesis, University of Bristol.

ORAM, A. (1985) '"Sex antagonism" in the teaching profession: The equal pay issue 1914–1929', *History of Education Review* (Australia) 14, pp. 36–48.

ORAM, A. (1987a) 'Inequalities in the teaching profession: The effect on teachers and pupils, 1910–1939', in HUNT, F. (Ed) *Lessons for Life: The Schooling of Girls and Women 1850–1950*, Oxford, Basil Blackwell.

ORAM, A. (1987b) '"Sex antagonism" in the teaching profession: Equal pay and the marriage bar, 1910–39', in ARNOT, M. and WEINER, G. (Eds) *Gender and the Politics of Schooling*, London, Hutchinson.

ORAM, A. (1988) '"Embittered, sexless or homosexual": Attacks on spinster teachers 1918–1939', in INTERNATIONAL CONFERENCE ON WOMEN'S HISTORY (Eds) *Current Issues in Women's History*, London, Routledge.

PARTINGTON, G. (1976) *Women Teachers in the 20th Century*, Windsor, National Foundation for Educational Research.

PIEROTTI, A. M. (1963) *The Story of the National Union of Women Teachers*, London, NUWT.

TROPP, A. (1957) *The Schoolteachers*, London, Heinemann.

WIDDOWSON, F. (1980) *Going Up into the Next Class: Women and Elementary Teacher Training 1840–1914*, London, WRRC Publications.

WIDDOWSON, F. (1986) '"Educating teacher": Women and elementary teacher training in London, 1900–1914', in DAVIDOFF, L. and WESTOVER, B. (Eds) *Our Work, Our Lives, Our Words*, London, Macmillan.

3
Women Teachers' Career Pathways: Towards an Alternative Model of 'Career'

Rosemary Grant

Fifteen years ago, when I was a beginning teacher in a middle school, I knew that I wanted to pursue a career, though I had no set goals, no real idea of what might constitute a source of professional satisfaction, no 'ambition' in the sense of knowing where I was going or how I might get there. During the first few years promotional scale points were plentiful and I received two fairly rapid promotions. Although my progress was never formally reviewed, I began to acquire a positive 'teacher' self-image and felt that my professional expertise was on a par with that of my peers. Gradually, through their activities, my awareness of the promotional system in a wider context grew. I saw that teachers of my age and experience were moving into deputy headships and headships. Some of these appointments I found frankly surprising. Could it be that someone who expended much energy bawling out kids and was reputed to hate teaching had undergone a dramatic transformation? I found the promotional system strange and baffling. I began to think that I too should be entering the arena. After all, I convinced myself, if they could do it, so could I. I duly applied.

Nothing happened and meanwhile I began to think quite hard about the system itself. I had a need to make sense of it. How did teachers receive promotion? What qualities were in the minds of the promoters? Did their mental map of a 'good' teacher match mine? Then a short news item appeared in the local newspaper. It was a list of newly appointed primary headteachers and deputies. Nine out of ten were men. Was there some career advantage in being a man in teaching? Conversely, were women disadvantaged and, if so, how did that disadvantage operate? This question became the focus of my subsequent research into teachers' careers.

Gender Divisions in Teaching

Further investigation showed that differences I had noticed in the percentage of women and men attaining senior posts in schools in my home town reflected the picture nationally. It also emphasized other gender-related divisions, for although teaching is a career highly associated with women (DES, 1987) and one in which levels of feminization are likely to increase over the next few years (McNamara, 1986), it is a career in which women tend to be found in some roles and not others and in receipt of certain responsibilities rather than being represented across the range. For example, women are more likely than men to be the teachers of young children or the pastoral carers/special needs teachers in secondary schools and, significantly, their roles more frequently focus on class teaching than the management of schools (Byrne, 1978; Deem, 1978; Acker, 1983; Marland, 1983). The marked differences in scale post allocations in schools of different types (England and Wales) are shown in Table 3.1. This compares the percentage of women and men in headships with those in scale one posts.

The data also show that the percentage of women attaining headships is inversely (though not proportionately) related to the percentage of men in the staffing cohort of each school sector. Thus as the proportion of men increases, women's representation at headship level decreases. Whereas 12 per cent of women in infant schools currently hold headships, this is the case for only 0.7 per cent of their counterparts in the secondary sector, a difference not wholly dependent on other factors, such as the relative availability of headship posts. Rather it would seem that as competition from men for scarce promotional awards strengthens, women fare increasingly badly.

Research on Women Teachers' Careers

The early work on teachers' careers either ignored gender differences or 'explained' them in terms of women's deficiencies. In a critique of a number of studies Acker (1983, p. 124) concluded that most researchers portrayed women teachers as 'damaging, deficient, distracted, and sometimes even dim.' More recently, however, researchers have started to take gender differences into account.

A number of reported studies rely on surveys, often using a questionnaire format close to that designed by Hilsum and Start (1974).

Table 3.1 Percentage of Women and Men in Headships and in Scale One Posts in Primary and Secondary Schools, England and Wales, 1985

	Primary		Secondary	
	Headships	Scale One	Headships	Scale One
Women	7	35	0.7	40
Men	31	9	3	19

Source: Calculated from DES (1987), pp. 24–7. Figures are for full-time teachers in maintained schools.

Surveys have been initiated by the NUT both locally (for example, NUT Coventry, 1984; NUT Kent, 1986; NUT Suffolk, 1985) and nationally (NUT, 1980). Most of the local studies fail to meet rigorously applied research standards, but they have been effective in raising contentious issues, such as the practice of asking discriminatory questions at interviews. Partington (1986) has criticized the national study for not collecting data on men so the sexes could be compared. Two other larger-scale studies (ILEA, 1984; INTO, 1985) and two of smaller populations (Evetts, 1986; Grant, 1983, 1987) included both women and men. Of these, ILEA (1984) and Grant (1983, 1987) surveyed teachers in large cities noted for their radical local socialist policies, whilst Evetts (1986) drew on data on teachers in a midlands town less well known for its political stance. The INTO (1985) study reported on practices in Eire with its very different religious, cultural and political traditions. The studies also varied according to type of teachers surveyed. The ILEA (1984) focused on secondary teachers with ten to fifteen years' service, the studies by INTO (1985) and Grant (1983, 1987) were of primary teachers, whilst the NUT (1980) and Evetts (1986) did not differentiate between primary and secondary teachers. Finally, Evetts' (1986) study did not use a questionnaire but analyzed data recorded for statistical purposes by the LEA on Teachers' Service Cards.

Despite these important variations which make cross-comparison somewhat problematical, several consistent findings have emerged. First, women are disproportionately under-represented at management levels in all schools in which men form a significant group. Although some of the difference can be explained by factors known to correlate with career achievement, principally length of service, this does not tell the whole story (ILEA, 1982; NUT Coventry, 1984; Evetts, 1986; Grant, 1987). Other factors must be at work to explain the career patterns of women. There is also some suggestion (Partington, 1986) that career disadvantage is particularly marked for women teachers in primary schools. Second, a number of studies have reported that men are more active in seeking promotion than women (Hilsum and Start, 1974; ILEA, 1984; Grant, 1987). They apply for more jobs and are more persistent in their applications. In my survey, for instance, men were twice as likely to apply for five or more promoted posts over a two-year period than women. Third, women have been found frequently to perceive themselves as being disadvantaged on account of their sex (NUT, 1980; ILEA, 1984; Grant, 1987).

Though such studies are important in establishing that women's career experiences are different from men's, they do little to extend our understanding of the issues. They are largely atheoretical and likely to mislead if the researcher does not define key concepts such as 'career ambition' adequately (Acker, 1983). In comparing the career patterns of women with those of men there is a danger of presenting men's experiences as the norm against which, correspondingly, women's experiences are defined as deviant. Stanley and Wise (1983) have equated this kind of approach with 'malestream' rather than feminist research methodology, and other researchers have questioned its usefulness in helping to redress the power balance which it so powerfully exposes (Davies, 1986). I wanted the extension of my own research to fit more readily into the feminist tradition. I decided, therefore, to change its focus. Rather than charting women's career failure, I wanted to celebrate the 'success' of a group of women who had achieved deputy headships in secondary schools and, in particular, to work towards an understanding of the way that they viewed their careers. The methodology, too, was more compatible with feminist ideology. I selected loosely structured interviews, described by Burgess (1982, p. 107) as 'conversations with a purpose'. The research fulfilled other criteria of feminist research. It made women visible and gave them a voice. It was an exploration of power relationships between women and men (Purvis, 1985) which had the potential to be emancipatory (Acker *et al.*, 1983). In addition it had meaning for me personally (Scott, 1986), for in seeking to understand the career experiences of other women I was searching to know more about my own.

To date I have interviewed thirty-eight women deputies, the full complement in post in comprehensive schools in one northern city. My findings, albeit from a limited sample and thus reported tentatively, support the view that the career perceptions and concomitant experiences of women are different from men's in important ways, and suggest the need to develop an alternative model of 'career' which fits more readily with the realities of women's lives.

Towards an Alternative Model of 'Career'

Lyons (1981, p. 64) describes the career-orientated teacher as one who is single-mindedly purposeful in the pursuit of career goals.

> The task for those who want to achieve promotion was thus to recognise their location in career stages and timetable terms, to diagnose the necessary conditions for movement to the next (and ensuing) stages, to take stock of their assets measured against the attributes they need in order to move to the next or subsequent career stage, and then to begin the task of preparing and presenting themselves as suitable candidates.

This set of promotional behaviours does not seem to have been matched in the practices of the women in my survey who had achieved deputy headships. This may be in part because it is such a rigorous model that it is only likely to be met in full by a few teachers, but the interviews suggest other explanations. In particular, it does not take into account the powerful effects of home and family circumstances on career, which made it impossible for most of these women to adopt such a calculated and self-conscious approach to their career progress.

Few of the deputies had received effective career advice prior to teaching. A number spoke of drifting into teaching because it was the sort of job that women were expected to enter. At first some were not aware of a clearly defined promotional structure, and some of the older deputies remarked on how things had changed in this respect. One said: 'I wanted to do my job well, to enjoy it. I never wanted to do anything else. We didn't ... we didn't think of a career structure. You waited to be asked. We belong to a group of people who did our best and hoped it would be recognised and an offer would be made'.

In contrast to the career achievers in Lyon's study (1981), few of the women deputies had started teaching with a definite career plan in mind. Furthermore, a number claimed never to have acquired one. Some explained this as in part a consequence of their role expectations. They had anticipated taking time out of teaching to start a family, and this affected their ability to plan ahead. One deputy explained: 'I think like many women, I had hoped to have children. I didn't. I think therefore that I felt the need to be flexible.' For others role obligations in the form of motherhood temporarily took precedence over career plans. In a study of married women primary headteachers Evetts (1987) found that the women with children had frequently begun to consider developments in their own careers *after* they had returned to teaching and their children were settled in school. This was also the case for the few women in my study whose careers had followed this pattern. Other women continued in service on becoming mothers, and for some this meant a relative period of career inactivity. For example, one woman deputy who had the additional responsibility of single parenthood said:

> At that stage, I was not making any conscious decisions about my career. Because I'd got a young baby, I was always doing something convenient that fitted in. I was just coping with a young baby and I knew I was doing something I enjoyed and I was good at. I certainly wasn't, at that stage, making any career decisions.

As the children grew older, family needs often constrained career mobility. A widowed deputy in the sample explained why she had decided against applying for a particular post:

> The old head there, he's dead now, he rang me up and said, 'I'm advertising my deputy headship, will you apply for it?' I thought about it and rang back and said, 'No.' Because my kids were still young, then. I live at Greenside. This school is ten minutes the bottom way. It's a hell of a long way to Browndale. You consider the family. You've got to consider the family in my position. ... I didn't think about it at the time, but I obviously put family before money then. This place is centre of town. It's not far from home. If the kids were poorly, it wasn't far away.

This example may go some way to explaining why women tend to apply more readily for promotion in the schools in which they are already in post than others in the wider community (Grant, 1987; ILEA, 1984).

Other evidence supports the suggestion that combining teaching with the care of children has a negative effect on women's intentions to seek promotion. The ILEA (1984) found differences in application rates for women in different marital and family circumstances. Single women made the most applications, women with children fewest. This is understandable in the light of additional findings which indicate that women in partnerships assume major responsibility for child-care. Few women who intended to return to teaching after a period of maternity leave expected substantial help from their partners with either domestic or child-care chores (ILEA, 1985). Similarly, a study of teachers in service found that whereas nearly three-quarters of the men surveyed relied on their partners to provide at least partial care for their young children (under 5), this was true of only 11 per cent of the women teachers (ILEA, 1984). Shortage of adequate child-care provision may also deter some women from pursuing a career more vigorously; 22 per cent of non-promoted women with children of pre- or primary-school age in the Irish survey (INTO, 1985) said that they would be more likely to seek promotion if child-care facilities were improved.

I am suggesting that given traditional role expectations and responsibilities it is inappropriate to expect the majority of women to adopt the consistently single-minded approach to career advancement attributed by Lyons (1981) to so-called 'career ambitious' teachers. Nor do they necessarily wish to do so if this means forfeiting other equally fulfilling aspects of their lives. The impression gained in my survey was that motherhood was a highly valued role, so much so that one or two childless women regarded the development of a career as a second-best alternative. The probability is that many women will attempt to juggle family and career roles and that there will be times — possibly in mid-career — when their career advancement may be constrained by family demands. It is important, therefore, to regard women's avowed intentions to pursue career goals as being subject to fluctuation and change (Long Laws, 1976). There are times in the course of their careers when they might be more — or less — 'career ambitious'. The concept of aspiration levels as a static and objective measure of career intentions which differentiates ambitious teachers from the rest is built on male norms and experiences and serves further to dislocate women from the promotional processes.

Long Laws (1976, p. 33) also contends that aspiration levels are defined and adjusted according to received feedback. This implies that experiences in school might also be important in prompting teachers to become 'career ambitious'. Evetts (1987) reports that the advice and encouragement of 'gatekeepers', a phrase coined by Lyons (1981) to describe people with the power to control the promotional system, was a significant factor in the career achievements of the women primary headteachers in her survey. Similarly, career encouragement at critical times was a recurring theme of my interviews. Sometimes this amounted to sponsorship allied to opportunities for career development over a number of years. One woman deputy, for example, said that she began to acquire a career map about six years into teaching as a result of the relationship she established with a new headteacher. She supported his ideas and became involved in developing innovative courses in school. As a result of his advice and encouragement, she subsequently applied for a deputy headship. In other cases the encouragement was a matter of a word from an influential person at the right time.

> After about seven years, I started to feel fed up with the school. ... I decided that I wanted to move. I was looking round for other head of history jobs. At that time, Tom King was history adviser ... he rated what we were doing in the department. I can remember now exactly where we were sitting in the staffroom one lunchtime and he said to me, 'What are you going to do next? You know, you shouldn't be applying for any more head of history jobs, you can do that standing on your head. Get applying for deputy headships.' I said, 'You're joking. I can't possibly do that.' He said, 'Yes, you can, take my word for it.' So I did.

We do not really know whether women are as likely as men to receive this kind of encouragement. My 1983 survey suggested that this was so in the case of headteachers, but that women were slightly less likely to receive encouragement from advisers.

In a promotional system which does not make use of a formal method of career appraisal or generally make explicit the criteria by which appointees are selected, the way in which male preferment operates can only be guessed at. Teachers perceive that advisers' judgments, in particular, are more likely to be based on activities outside school than classroom competency (Grant, 1983), which Freedman (1987, p. 152) suggests often goes unrecognized.

> Who are the busy little bees that do all the dirty work ...? Women. Who's on the negotiating committee? Men. And I think if you don't do those things, there is no other way they get to know you because they certainly don't go in classrooms. No one would ever recognise you for that. And that's what I've done all my life, and I don't think they know me from a hole in the wall. Or if they did, it doesn't really count.

There were echoes of Freedman's sentiments amongst the group of 'successful' women in my sample. They explained their teaching commitment in terms of doing the job well (Nias, 1981), and some attributed their relatively slow climb up the promotional ladder to their involvement in routine, class-based activities during their early years in teaching. One, for example, referred to the hours she had spent at nights and weekends planning and marking work, which whilst providing a source of intrinsic professional satisfaction had not been rewarded through promotion. A number of studies have reported that women teachers attach great importance to working with children (Smith *et al.*, 1977; Grant, 1983; ILEA, 1984); there is less evidence to show that it is also valued by the promoters.

In sum, it seems clear that 'gatekeepers' have the power to support or impede teachers' bids for career advancement, though it is not known how teachers are selected for this form of sponsorship. Nor did my 1983 study provide any evidence that either headteachers or advisers were using their potential powers to redress the imbalance of women in management posts. To do so it may be necessary to rethink the organization of the current promotional system. Clear identification of the criteria to be met for particular posts would be one way forward. Given that women teachers' career routes are less predictable than men's, the opportunity for regular career review could help women to develop their careers more effectively.

There is another form of feedback which may operate differently for women and men with important consequences. Lyons (1981, p. 134) suggests that teachers assess their own performances by comparing them to those of their 'significant peers'. Through this referencing process teachers acquire a shared understanding of the appropriate time-scale between promoted posts, and develop the necessary tactics and strategies to stay on target. Unlike men, most women do not have a same-sex peer reference group moving alongside them through each stage of the promotional system to whom they can refer, and for those in the lower rungs there are very few female role models ahead of them. There is some indication in the literature that this might be important. In Hilsum and Start's (1974) study, for instance, women infant teachers who were more likely to have experience of working for women heads and deputies reported higher levels of 'career ambition' than women in junior or mixed primary departments. One interesting finding of my present study is of a group of six women now holding deputy headships around the country who previously taught at the same school. These women provided a reference group for each other and also had the strong support of their woman deputy head. She said:

> One of the things I considered to be one of my real successes at

> Carr Lane was that I provided a role model for other women that increased their aspirations. Now this is purely in my head, I've never discussed it with anyone. I think, I hope, I suspect that I had quite a strong influence on those women. I went into the school and was seen to be successful fairly early on. I certainly pushed Dawn to apply for Elmtree. ... There was certainly a feeling when Dawn got Elmtree that was really good. Carole, Anne, Margaret, Dawn and I worked very closely together as a year tutor team and I think that was an important reference point for those women as well.

Teaching has been described as having a bureaucratic promotional structure (Lyons, 1981) in that each step provides the necessary qualification for entry to the next and subsequent steps. Though there is no guarantee of a smooth passage for any teacher, the NUT (1980) contended that it is most likely to be effective for those who play by the rules, that is, those who remain in continuous service. The vast majority of teachers who break service — and by that I mean teachers who resign from teaching for a significant period rather than take periods out for secondment or maternity leave — are women. The NUT (1980) estimated that about 65 per cent of all women teachers broke service in this way during their teaching career. Subsequent research has indicated that such a break has a negative effect on career achievement (NUT Coventry, 1984; INTO, 1985; Evetts, 1986; Grant, 1987). In the sample of women deputies, for example, only five of the thirty-eight had taken substantial time out of teaching (between eighteen months and seven years) in order to care for young children.

These findings suggest that the disadvantage experienced by women who follow traditional career patterns is too great for most to overcome. In part this may be because promotion is tied to age-related norms. Evidence is accruing which supports this assertion. A study of teachers' careers by Sikes (1985, p. 43), for instance, reported that male teachers grew increasingly anxious to be at 'appropriate age-associated career stages' as they became more experienced. To be on a scale one at age 28, for example, was not thought to be appropriate. The data relating to the women deputies suggest that this 'male' timetable of events had also operated for them. With the exception of one teacher, a mature entrant to teaching, the mean age of the other deputies appointed over the last five years was 35. Women returners, who forfeit all previous promotional gains on their re-entry, cannot be expected to meet these age targets. This effectively limits management posts to women without children or those who are prepared to combine the early years of motherhood with a full-time teaching role. No account is taken of the alternative pattern of career followed by the majority of women. Thus the status quo of male managers and female teachers is insidiously perpetuated. One deputy summed up the confounding effect of this situation.

> Women who're diffident because they've come back into teaching should see that other women, preferably women who themselves have had time out, are in fact still moving up through the grades. Here Beverly (the other senior woman teacher) doesn't have a family and I don't have a family. I fear that the message that we give to our young colleagues is that you can do this, you can move up through the profession, but only if you sacrifice the chance of having a family.

As well as failing to follow the normative ('male') career pattern women may be further disadvantaged by the stereotypical attitudes held by many promoters towards women's careers (NUT, 1980). Despite having ultimately achieved career 'success', a number of the women deputies referred to instances which illustrated such discriminatory attitudes. Some of the married women without children had, at some time in their careers, been asked at interview about their future family plans. This is a finding reported elsewhere (NUT, 1980; ILEA, 1984; NUT West Kent, 1985), and one which suggests that many promoters are operating from constructions of gender roles defined in narrow, traditional terms which accentuate women's roles as wives and mothers and diminish their roles as teachers. This can have profound consequences for the women concerned. One of the deputies in my sample recounted how the governors of a former school refused to ratify the headteacher's recommendation that a post of acting deputy headship should be made permanent. They thought that she was too young and as the mother of two young children had too many family commitments. Such overt discrimination may well have been outlawed by the Sex Discrimination Act (1975), but other deputies perceived that underlying attitudes had not changed significantly. Women appeared to be in a 'no win' situation. One woman without children said that she had been regarded as an 'oddity' by a previous headteacher, who was openly baffled by the fact that any woman could want to concentrate on a career and 'not be at home having babies', whilst another felt that her role as a mother had militated against her. She felt that single women or women without children were more likely to be encouraged to apply for promotions, whether or not they displayed the appropriate professional abilities, simply because they were perceived as having fewer commitments out of school.

Given the wide differences in age and experience reported by the women and the loosely framed nature of the interviews, a relatively high proportion (eleven of the thirty-eight) referred to the way in which they felt they were compared unfavourably — and against their wishes — to a promotional yardstick built on 'male' norms. One said:

> The tenor of the interview seemed to suggest that the ideal person for this job would be a man of a certain age, certain male attributes. Do you think you could live up to this? Would you find it difficult to take assemblies? How would you deal with a fight? I suspect they would have assumed that any man can deal with a fight in the playground. ... I have male colleagues who can't do it at all. I don't find it difficult. But all the time, you are being compared with some standard you're not actually prepared to admit is morally superior.

Speaking from a recent interview experience, a second deputy endorsed this view:

> I have a very strong feeling about what happened. The day in the school went very well. I interviewed well. I know all that went well. ... John who got the headship, he is 6 ft 2, 15 stone, has a loud voice. He plays — he is a bully — and he plays a very hard line in that school. Now within Carlton Green there is a perception that it's a tough school and it needs a big strong man. I think they have made a big mistake. Not in appointing me, but in appointing John. What they're going to do is perpetuate a style that hasn't worked in that school. When it comes to the rock solid crunch, there's always an issue for women about control and discipline, and that's the crunch I'm at now. ... This thing about control, discipline and people's perceptions, parents' perceptions and governors' perceptions about the school being in control. ... I do think that was the crunch issue in the end. They took the safe bet and went for the man saying the right things. I feel that I'm disadvantaged because I can't become a 6 ft 2 rugby player with a loud voice and I ain't gonna do. But there are a lot of perceptions around about responsibility. It's to do with needing to be tough to do this job. And it's all couched

> in male language. I'm quite convinced that women are at a disadvantage in that sense.

In the light of present promotional practices most people with the power to promote are men. In the Irish study (INTO, 1985) over 90 per cent of candidates for principalships had been interviewed by all-male, or predominantly male boards. It may be, as these women suggest, that the promoters' perceptions of qualities which mark out potential candidates for management posts are affected by this gender imbalance. Thurow's 'queuing' model of occupational selection (reported in Joseph, 1983, p. 211) explains how this might happen. Thurow suggests that as posts become scarce, a 'queue' forms. The individual's place in the 'queue' is partly determined by what the promoters define as desirable endowments or attributes. If one attribute is related to stereotypical expectations of 'maleness', then, as these deputies perceive, women will have difficulty in reaching its head. Morgan, Hall and Mackay (1983) suggest that one consequence of consistently appointing male candidates to management posts has been the development of a model based on traits stereotypically attributed to men against which women are assessed unfavourably. In this way 'male preferment' may continue to operate in spite of legislation which seeks to outlaw it.

Summary

My interest in researching women teachers' careers arose out of my own teaching experiences. I found that my perceptions of gender-related disadvantage were shared overwhelmingly by other women primary teachers, but less so by men (Grant, 1987). Further study of women teachers, this time in the secondary sector, suggested the need to develop a model of 'career' which applied more readily to the circumstances of women's lives than the one outlined in the traditional research literature. The data on women deputies suggest that this should take account of the following factors. First, women are unlikely to begin teaching with a definite career plan in mind. Their career pathways are locked into, and shaped by, developments in their personal lives. As such, the notion of once and for all career decisions is irrelevant to most women. Their 'career ambition' is likely to fluctuate as is their determination to seek promotion. Second, sponsorship is likely to be an important aid in gaining promotion for women and men.

LEAs which profess a commitment to redressing the promotional imbalance in teaching should look to ways of forwarding women's careers through sponsorship. A more formal process of career review and development could benefit women, especially if this takes greater account of classroom expertise as an important criterion for promotion. Third, traditional child-care arrangements mean that many women experience a different service pattern from men. A woman-friendly promotion structure would reward women for gaining expertise in this field, rather than exacerbating the effect of a career break by stripping them of any previous promotional gains and establishing an age-related career structure which is disadvantageous to many women. Fourth, attention should be paid to the composition of interview panels. Women should have equal representation with men, and all participants need to be made aware of the insidious ways in which male preferment might operate.

We also need to know more about characteristics which may combine with gender to increase or depress women's chances of promotion. So far existing surveys have paid little attention to charting either differential career routes or opportunity structures available to women teachers from different class, ethnic or other groups; this is clearly a direction for future research.

The alternative pattern of 'career' followed by women needs to be acknowledged and legitimized by those with the power to promote. This would have far-reaching consequences, requiring a revision of present employment practices as well as questioning the roles currently played by advisers, headteachers and governors. But it might also result in an equal representation of women in management posts in schools and all the ensuing benefits that would bring.

References

ACKER. J., BARRY, K. and ESSEVELD, J. (1983) 'Objectivity and truth: Some problems in doing feminist research', *Women's Studies International Forum*, 6, 4, pp. 423–35.

ACKER, S. (1983) 'Women and teaching: A semi-detached sociology of a semi-profession', in WALKER, S. and BARTON, L. (Eds) *Gender, Class and Education*, Lewes, Falmer Press, pp. 123–39.

BURGESS, R. (1982) 'The unstructured interview as a conversation', in BURGESS, R. (Ed.) *Field Research: A Source Book and Field Manual*, London, George Allen and Unwin, pp. 107–11.

BYRNE, E. (1978) *Women and Education*, London, Tavistock.

DAVIES, L. (1986) 'Researching gender, educational administration and the third world', Paper presented at the British Educational Research Association Annual Conference, Bristol, 4–7 September.

DEEM, R. (1978) *Women and Schooling*, London, Routledge and Kegan Paul.

DEPARTMENT OF EDUCATION AND SCIENCE (1987) *Statistics of Education: Teachers in Service England and Wales 1985*, London, HMSO.

EVETTS, J. (1986) 'Teachers' careers: The objective dimension', *Educational Studies*, 12, 3, pp. 225–44.

EVETTS, J. (1987) 'Becoming career ambitious: The career strategies of married women who became primary headteachers in the 1960s and 1970s', *Educational Review*, 39, 1, pp. 15–29.

FREEDMAN, S. (1987) 'Burnout or beached: Weeding women out of woman's true profession', in WALKER, S. and BARTON, L. (Eds) *Changing Policies, Changing Teachers*, Milton Keynes, Open University Press, pp. 41–58.

GRANT, R. (1983) *Promotion in Teaching with Particular Reference to Gender Differences*, Unpublished MEd dissertation, University of Sheffield.

GRANT, R. (1987) 'A career in teaching: A survey of middle school teachers' perceptions with particular reference to the careers of women teachers', *British Educational Research Journal*, 13, 3, pp. 227–39.

HILSUM, S. and START, K. B. (1974) *Promotion and Careers in Teaching*, Slough, National Foundation for Educational Research.

INNER LONDON EDUCATION AUTHORITY (1982) *Female and Male Teaching Staff in the ILEA*, RS 833/82, London, ILEA Research and Statistics Branch.

INNER LONDON EDUCATION AUTHORITY (1984) *Women's Careers in Teaching: Survey of Teachers' Views*, RS 921/84, London, ILEA Research and Statistics Branch.

INNER LONDON EDUCATION AUTHORITY (1985) *Teachers on Maternity Leave*, RS 971/85, London, ILEA Research and Statistics Branch.

IRISH NATIONAL TEACHERS' ORGANISATION/EMPLOYMENT EQUALITY AGENCY/EDUCATIONAL RESEARCH CENTRE (1985) *Gender Inequalities in Primary-School Teaching*, Dublin, Educational Company of Ireland.

JOSEPH, G. (1983) *Women at Work*, Oxford, Philip Allan.

LONG LAWS, J. (1976) 'Work aspiration of women: False leads and new starts', in BLAXALL, M. and REAGAN, B. (Eds) *Women and the Workplace*, London, University of Chicago Press, pp. 33–49.

LYONS, G. (1981) *Teacher Careers and Career Perceptions*, Slough, National Foundation for Educational Research.

MCNAMARA, D. (1986) 'The female profession', *The Times Educational Supplement*, 14 February, p. 21.

MARLAND, M. (1983) *Sex Differentiation in Schooling*, London, Heinemann.

MORGAN, C., HALL, V. and MACKAY, H. (1983) *The Selection of Secondary School Heads*, Milton Keynes, Open University Press.

NATIONAL UNION OF TEACHERS (1980) *Promotion and the Woman Teacher*, Manchester, Equal Opportunities Commission/NUT.

NATIONAL UNION OF TEACHERS, COVENTRY (1984) *Primary Teachers in Coventry*, Equal Opportunities Sub-committee of the Coventry Association of the NUT.

NATIONAL UNION OF TEACHERS, KENT (1986) *Top Jobs in Kent Schools*, Pamphlet published by the Kent Division of the NUT.

NATIONAL UNION OF TEACHERS, SUFFOLK (1985) *Equal Opportunities in Suffolk*, Pamphlet published by the Equal Opportunities Sub-committee of the Suffolk Division of the NUT.

NATIONAL UNION OF TEACHERS, WEST KENT (1985) *Unequal Opportunities and West Kent Teachers*, Pamphlet published by the Equal Opportunities Group of the West Kent Association of the NUT.

NIAS, J. (1981) '"Commitment" and motivation in primary school teachers', *Educational Review*, 33, 3, pp. 181–91.

PARTINGTON, G. (1986) 'It depends what you mean by equal', *The Times Educational Supplement*, 22 August, p. 17.

PURVIS, J. (1985) 'Reflections upon doing historical documentary research from a feminist perspective', in BURGESS, R. (Ed.) *Strategies of Educational Research: Qualitative Methods*, Lewes, Falmer Press, pp. 179–205.

SCOTT, S. (1986) 'Feminist research and qualitative methods: A discussion of some of the issues', in BURGESS, R. (Ed.) *Issues in Educational Research: Qualitative Methods*, Lewes, Falmer Press, pp. 67–83.

SIKES, P. (1985) 'The life cycle of the teacher', in BALL, S. J. and GOODSON, I. F. (Eds) *Teachers' Lives and Careers*, Lewes, Falmer, pp. 27–59.

SMITH, B. *et al.* (1977) *The Woman Teacher*, Pamphlet published by a group of Northamptonshire Deputy Heads and Senior Mistresses.

STANLEY, L. and WISE, S. (1983) *Breaking Out: Feminist Consciousness and Feminist Research*, London, Routledge and Kegan Paul.

Part 2
Institutions and Individuals

4
Educating Feminists: A Life-History Study

Sue Middleton

Teachers draw their ideas from many different sources. As Esland (1971, p. 82) expressed it, 'within the teacher's stock of knowledge are fragments of multiple paradigms — arising particularly through the interplay of subject and pedagogical knowledge.' For example, teachers' theories about the nature of curriculum knowledge and teaching methods will be influenced by their pre-service training, what they read, courses they attend, interactions with colleagues, involvements with political groups and networks. The question of why certain teachers are attracted to certain methods and theories and repelled by others can usefully be addressed through a life-history approach. By means of four case studies drawn from a larger investigation of feminist teachers in New Zealand (Middleton, 1985), I shall argue that teachers who come to adopt a feminist analysis of education have, themselves, experienced discrimination, victimization or marginality within the education process — in their own schooling, teacher training, and/or as teachers in the schools. To explain these personal experiences as social issues rather than signs of personal inadequacy, such teachers must have access to feminist theories at a time and in a form which makes the connection between the personal and the political or social. Each of the case studies focuses on the woman's feminist position which has substantially (but not solely) shaped her orientation toward teaching. The chapter begins with a brief outline of the dominant theoretical tendencies within contemporary feminist educational theory, then through the case studies shows how people become attracted to, practise and develop such theories in their everyday working lives.

Feminist Educational Theories: An Overview

Contemporary Western feminists have generated a variety of approaches to teaching. In the main these have been shaped by four discourses: liberal feminism, radical feminism, socialist feminism, and Black women's critiques of these positions (see Acker, 1987; Middleton, 1987c). Liberal feminist educational strategies aim to bring about equal representation of the sexes throughout current educational hierarchies. Liberal feminists support strategies of affirmative action to encourage more women to apply for senior positions in teaching and educational administration. A second aim is to remove 'sex-role stereotyping' from schools, for example from textbooks and from pupils' subject choice. Liberals argue that boys and girls should be exposed to all subjects, and girls compensated for any 'deficiencies' in their socialization which may influence them not to attempt traditionally 'male' subjects or jobs. Liberal feminists have observed that girls' subjects, such as domestic science, often have the lowest status in the hierarchy of school knowledge, and argue that encouraging boys to take such subjects is a means of raising the status of 'women's work'. Drawing explanations from psychological models of learning, liberal feminists view social equity as achievable through changes in individuals' attitudes. Another curricular strategy consistent with this approach is to 'add women in' to existing curriculum subjects, for example including women in history courses and making women artists' work visible in art lessons. While the aims of liberal feminists are to seek an equal balance of the sexes within current hierarchies, feminists of more radical persuasions, such as socialists who choose to work 'within the system', may also support these measures as reforms which are a necessary first step towards wider, more revolutionary, social change (Eisenstein, 1981).

The strategies advocated by radical (and some socialist) feminist educators have a different emphasis. Rejecting liberal ideals of sexual equality within the inequitable hierarchies of contemporary capitalist societies, radical feminists focus on male dominance, or patriarchy, as the cause of female subordination: while liberals regard women as individual victims of discrimination, radical feminists view women as an oppressed class. Schooling is believed to reproduce patriarchal social relations. Single-sex schools are favoured because they free girls from day-to-day experiences of male dominance within the peer group and from teachers. They also provide opportunities for the development of feminist knowledge. Influenced by the relativist, phenomenological approaches to knowledge characteristic of the 'progressive' educational theories of the 1970s, radical feminists view knowledge as socially constructed, and argue that men have constructed an education system which oppresses women largely through the way 'academic knowledge' is generated and taught. Within the 'patriarchal paradigm' in education (Spender, 1981) women's experiences are denied visibility in both course content and teaching methods, or are interpreted through male eyes. Educational institutions, especially those at secondary or tertiary levels, are structured on the basis of academic 'disciplines' with hierarchical patterns of organization (e.g., 'departments'). This pattern of organizing knowledge fragments and compartmentalizes it so that students find it difficult to gain a sense of integration in their studies. Feminists have viewed this fragmentation as largely a 'historical accident', the categorizing and social organization of knowledge reflecting the power struggles between male academics rather than any conceptual unity within 'subjects'. Radical feminist educators have sought to break down disciplinary walls — the struggle to establish new transdisciplinary subjects such as women's studies is an example.

Socialist feminists agree with radical feminists that the liberal goals of equal distribution of the sexes within the hierarchies of capitalism will not liberate women; for this to occur a social revolution is necessary. Socialist feminist educationists criticize radical feminists for their analyses of 'girls' and 'boys' as unitary groups, for seeing schools as reproducing patriarchal relations in which males universally oppress females. Drawing on Marxist analyses of class, socialist feminists argue that

> The same sort of power dynamic which Spender and others indicate disadvantages girls in the classroom also happens *among* groups of girls, and with the same effect: knowledge is 'differentially distributed' *on the basis of race and class* to different groups of girls in the classroom. Girls as members of race and class groups receive quite different knowledge about learning and teaching and about their own ability. (Jones, 1988, p. 144)

For socialist feminists, radical feminism cannot explain the oppression of racial minorities or of working-class men.

Both radical and socialist feminist educators have criticized the dominant models of education for impersonal, bureaucratic, authoritarian patterns of social relations, which deny the validity and relevance of students' personal experiences in the classroom context. Such women have advocated teaching styles premised on the belief that 'the personal is political', that learning starts with the sharing and analysis of personal experiences. Many radical and socialist feminists working within formal institutions have advocated 'consciousness-raising' as a teaching style which allows students to explore themes which they perceive as directly relevant to their own lives. As Bernstein (1975) has pointed out, the pedagogy associated with infant and pre-school levels of schooling allows for greater flexibility in time-tabling, in integration of curriculum subjects, and a less rigid mode of assessment of pupils than the pedagogy of secondary schools and tertiary institutions. He notes that the levels of formal education with the more 'child-centred' pedagogies are also those where women teachers predominate and which have the lowest status in the teaching profession. The levels of schooling in which men predominate as teachers, the secondary school and tertiary levels, are more bureaucratically organized and have higher status. Teachers have less flexibility in what they teach, when and how to teach it; methods of assessment tend to be more formal and quasi-scientific in accordance with the increasingly dominant ideology of 'technocratic rationality' analyzed by American curriculum theorists such as Apple (1979, 1983) and Giroux (1982). Feminist teachers' preference for 'child-centred' or humanistic approaches to teaching has brought many into conflict with educational administrators in institutions run on technocratic lines (Bowles and Klein, 1983).

Life-history interviews allow us to gain an understanding of how feminist teachers' own consciousness has been raised, and how it is applied in their practice in schools. The four case studies which follow illustrate how feminist ideologies can display both similarity and diversity.

Four Case Studies

Jane: A Liberal Feminist

Jane attributed her feminism to her experiences of discrimination, victimization and marginality as a student and teacher of home economics. As a student teacher, she had become aware that the pupils and teachers of home economics were regarded by their peers as 'dumb' or 'thick'. During one of her teaching practice placements at an all-girls' school, Jane first encountered feminist thinking through feminist colleagues, and she began to make connections between feminism, the status of home economics and the professional status of women teachers. These women taught history and social studies classes, including in their courses lessons on nineteenth century feminist struggles, such as the suffrage movement. They encouraged Jane in her reading and analyzed with her the close affinity between the first-wave feminists they were studying and the contemporary struggles of women for promotion within teaching. For Jane the personal was becoming political, or, as Mills (1975) expressed it, personal troubles were being translated into social issues. She was beginning to theorize her 'sense of something wrong' (Mitchell, 1973, p. 38) as something structural, not merely a sign of personal inadequacy.

On completing her training Jane began teaching home economics and other subjects in a brand new co-educational secondary school in a provincial city. From the very beginning she worked hard at upgrading the image of home economics. Her strategies included actively encouraging academic stream pupils and boys to take the subject, becoming active in her local home economics teachers' group and attending in-service courses. Jane helped plan the curriculum so that all pupils experienced all the technical subjects in the first two years of their secondary schooling. Many of Jane's students opted to continue home economics for School Certificate. Her success in attracting 'brighter' students challenged the image of home economics as a 'dumb kids' subject: 'We managed to dispel quite a few myths. At the end of my first fifth form year, I was suddenly being asked by the Department of Education Advisors to give workshops at home science meetings, which I did.'

At the end of her fourth year of teaching Jane applied for and won a first-level position of responsibility (PR 1) at her school. Apart from the 'Senior Woman', no other woman on the staff had a PR. She then gained a PR 2 at the same school. This elicited sexist responses from some of her male colleagues, which expressed their disdain not only of women, but of what was seen as 'women's knowledge', associated with 'women's work': 'When I got the PR 2, there was a lot of "anti" feeling among the males on the staff. Although many of them said, "You deserve it, Jane, because you work harder than most people around here", [they also said], "but really, should a home economics person have a PR 2?"' However, her achievement impressed her women colleagues in home economics and began to have a 'consciousness-raising' effect on some of them: 'I was the only home economics teacher with a PR 2 in town at that time and in the next few years more people got PR 2s. But I remember that at workshops people would say, "Jane got a PR 2 in home economics" and everyone would say, "Wow! How did you get that?"'

Jane was using feminist ideas to articulate her experiences of discrimination as social/political questions rather than personal problems. In the evenings Jane took university courses in the social sciences. She began to read feminist theory, and mentioned Friedan's *Feminine Mystique* (1963) — a key text in the resurgence of contemporary liberal feminism — as having particularly influenced her thinking. These ideas helped her to analyze the position of women in teaching: 'Then I would have been a liberal feminist — "equality of opportunity" — those sorts of things. I thought, "That's where it's at, that's what we've got to do, we've got to change things from within the system. We've got to talk to the Department of Education."' Recognizing that her own teaching situation was unusually non-sexist, Jane worked to help others in worse situations by starting a feminist teachers' group to tackle issues such as 'women not applying for senior positions, why they didn't apply; and if they did apply, why they didn't get the jobs, the PRs; also why the subjects of home economics and clothing were "put down."'

At the time she was interviewed Jane had taken a break from teaching to care for her pre-school child and to complete her social science degree part-time. She also became very involved in pre-school groups and parent education courses. A university course in women's studies led her to connect new feminist theories to her own changing experiences:

> I've had all these loose ideas floating around from the last four or five years — from teaching, from Playcentre, from being a Mum, from being a Mum back in education after all that time. And suddenly there are people talking about *things that have happened to me*. I spent a lot of time last year changing my position. When I wrote an essay for a women's studies course, I kept changing, thinking, 'I think I'm a Marxist — no, I'm definitely a radical feminist.' I'd have doubts, the more reading I did. And people would say to me, 'It's good that you're changing.' I think that feminism is something that isn't constant.

Aroha: A Bi-cultural Perspective

Aroha saw her feminism as based on an awareness of the strength and history of Maori women and on her exposure to Western feminist theory in a university context. She described her educational strategies as 'liberal feminist' in the sense that she encouraged other Maori women teachers to attain senior positions in order to combat racism amongst teachers and pupils and to promote the teaching of Maori culture and language. Aroha, a primary school teacher, attributed her own success in attaining a position of responsibility to the support and encouragement of other Maori women in education.

Aroha's sense of pride and confidence in being a Maori woman had come partly through her awareness of their importance in history. She had read the writing of Rangimarie Rose Pere (1983) on the status of Maori women in her tribal traditional modes of learning, and described this book as having been highly significant in her appreciation of the 'different but equal', or 'complementary' status of the sexes within these traditions:

> Tuhoe Potiki and Ngati Kahungunu women, prior to the introduction of Christianity and the 'original sin of Eve', were extremely liberated as compared with [my] English tupuna [ancestors]. With the exception of slaves (male and female), the women were never regarded as chattels or possessions; they retained their own names upon marriage. Retaining their own identity and whakapapa [genealogy] was of the utmost importance and children could identify with the kinship group of either or both parents. (Pere, 1983, pp. 51–2)

Aroha had also learned of the power of Maori women through conversations. She described an encounter with a leading male Maori scholar, versed in both Maori and Western scholarly traditions, about the symbolic role of women on the marae (tribal meeting place). No formal occasion could begin unless both sexes were present; both were of equal status and importance:

> We discussed the importance of Maori women in traditional Maori society and it made me think that we were really important, in fact we had an elevated status in some instances above men and according to Maori myth woman was the first being ahead of man; but you look at the Christian things — it's Adam isn't it before woman? Adam created woman. He said that the tangi [funeral] situation and the Pakeha [European] interpretation of that is that the man, the male, has the most important part of that situation because they're doing all the

> speeches. But he said the most important part is the woman when she gives that initial call to welcome everybody back to the marae and to bring the dead back into the marae. He was saying it was because of Hine-nui-te-po. Hine-nui-te-po was the off-spring of Tane who was one of the gods, and Tane mated with his own daughter. She got whakama [embarrassed] and so she went into hiding and he went to try to get her to come back and she said, 'No, you go and I'll stay here. You go and you have our children now and I will receive them on death.' And he was saying that when these sorts of things were written up she was the personification of death. The Pakeha or Christian interpretation, I suppose, was that woman represented evil, the unknown. Whereas for the Maori it was just the other place, the place to go back to mother. I felt good listening to that. So the woman that does the initial call on the marae, there's a dedication to Hine-nui-te-po to say 'there we are bringing back your off-spring.' So the woman is the giver of life and taker back of life.

Western liberal feminist demands for the abolition of differentiated sex roles were antithetical to this tradition, which Aroha regarded as enhancing, rather than demeaning, women's status. However, within the context of her teaching career Aroha believed that the liberal feminist goal of encouraging women into senior positions was an essential first step to wider social change. She was concerned that so few women aspired to these positions and noted, as have many researchers (Department of Education, 1982), that many women express a preference for classroom teaching rather than administration: 'I do encourage other women around me to get into these positions, but a lot of them have the attitude that I used to have; they're quite happy to stay in the classroom. It's sad.'

Her work after promotion took Aroha into many schools, and her observations there had led her to believe that women's own child-rearing experiences made them better teachers than men and more concerned with 'social issues'. She observed that when women did come forward to serve on professional bodies, such as teachers' union committees, these qualities of deep social concern made them more dedicated to the job. Also she believed that women, who tended to disapprove of corporal punishment, rather than men, who had been socialized to accept violence, should assume greater responsibility in administration. Her beliefs here sound like those of radical feminists, although she did not say that this position had influenced her thinking. Her strategies were liberal feminist and above all were aimed at contributing to the achievements of Maori women:

> I feel proud when I hear mention of Maoris in general and Maori women in particular. I've come to hear more and more about Maori women. Previously, it was only Maori men we ever heard about. Lately I seem to hear that there are so many Maori women coming to the fore. I think that is fantastic — I think they can do a hell of a lot.

Marie: Radical Feminism and the Experience of Marginality

Marie had been a 'high school dropout', who had lived a 'hippy' lifestyle in the late 1960s and early 1970s. She re-entered formal education after marriage, when her children were young. Her husband had encouraged her to take adult education classes, and her teachers there encouraged her to go to university. At the time she was interviewed Marie had graduated from university and was at teachers' college studying to become a primary school teacher. She had encountered feminist ideas at university and had synthesized these with her anarchistic 'hippy' view of the world. She did not believe that emulating male career patterns would liberate women, and felt that women's mothering role gave them a certain moral superiority over men, whose career patterns and socialization for masculinity deprived them of the opportunity for reflection on moral issues and interpersonal relationships. Marie believed that child-centred methods of teaching were superior to the pseudo-scientific technocratic behaviourism she was being taught at teachers' college. Her strong radical feminist views drew antagonistic responses from her fellow students, from lecturers and from teachers she met on 'section' (her teaching practice placement).

At teachers' college, Marie's attempts to be critical of sexism in courses were met with derision: for example, 'If I'm doing an English course and I make any comments about how sexist the book is, I get, "Oh, no — not *you* again." There's just this general attitude that feminism's not something nice.' As a feminist, Marie found relationships with her fellow students difficult. She believed them to be 'good conformists', and questioned their acceptance of the 'technocratic rationality' of the college, for example, the emphasis on statistical measuring of 'intelligence' in children and the regimented, hierarchical and bureaucratic style of the college itself: 'It epitomised the high school environment and I hated high school. The teachers and students have got a sort of wall between them.'

In particular Marie came into conflict with students whose views were explicitly anti-feminist, including the large number of fundamentalist Christian students at the college (Openshaw, 1984; Ryan, 1988), whom she saw as actively reinforcing sexism:

> They see me as something rather vile and low. They have tunnel vision. They see the natural role of women as in the home. When they go out to teach they will encourage little girls to 'be little girls'. They are actually putting the boundaries up. They're good conformists — they don't question anything.

Marie also encountered overt sexism and anti-feminism on teaching practice when she was teaching an infant class:

> When I was out on section, my associate said to me, 'Of course — you're a *feminist.*' She picked it up in the classroom by the way I taught the children. One boy had made a comment that girls couldn't do a certain task, so I asked the rest of the children whether they thought that was correct. And we talked about it, and we looked at instances where girls were doing the same jobs as boys.

As at teachers' college, Marie found her feminism within the school 'was mentioned as if it was a negative against me, rather than something in my favour.' In a school structured according to 'technocratic' principles Marie found her child-centred philosophy of teaching held in similar disregard:

> I'd like to teach the children so that they can be thinkers. So that, when they are grown up they'll be able to make choices for themselves. So they can think of all the alternatives. But if you have that sort of attitude or that sort of philosophy, you want to open them up to all sorts of experiences. Now, see, when I was on section, I did a unit on classical music, and we talked about composers and things like that. Then I did one on ballet, and I took along tutus and pointed shoes. ... I let them put on the costumes, and I said to them, 'You can put on a ballet.' Well, that went on all day. ... They were so engrossed. ... That's very threatening to a teacher who sticks to a rigid programme, because she can't see where it applies to everyday life. I felt I was

providing those children with a living experience that they would remember for the rest of their lives. You know, 'the day I wore the tutu, danced.' So I tend to, sort of, excite the children to a high degree and the poor teacher can't cope.

Marie felt marginal in teaching in two respects. First, her feminist consciousness made her sensitive to sexism amongst her colleagues and pupils. In conservative contexts, such as schools premised on technocratic assumptions, or amongst fundamentalist Christian colleagues, this was regarded negatively, putting her in a defensive and marginal position. Second, her 'child-centred' approach to teaching (characteristic of, but not unique to, radical feminist approaches to education) was at odds with the dominant educational ideology. Her position of continuing marginality acted as a further stimulus to radicalization.

Terry: A Socialist Feminist

At the time of her interviews Terry was teaching adults in a tertiary institution. Her sophisticated knowledge of Marxist and feminist theory had been put into practice in her teaching, and she had become well known in feminist circles for her innovative, non-hierarchical approach. Terry said that she had developed these skills during her early teaching days in primary schools. From a working-class background, she had struggled during her own schooling to articulate the sense of inferiority she felt in the academic stream of a girls' school dominated by the daughters of the town's professional and business élite: 'my schooling was just so influential in what I've ended up espousing as a philosophy, my experience as an individual.' At primary teachers' college in a large city in the 1960s she encountered 'people who were incredibly involved in race issues and Vietnam, black consciousness — we were always having people in to talk to us in assembly about those issues — it was the 'red' teachers' college.' While school had failed to make connections between her personal experience of oppression as female and working-class, the 'red' teachers' college helped to make them through exposing her to radical theories of the time. While at teachers' college, Terry became active as a folk singer in local coffee bars and regarded this experience as an important part of her political awakening: 'I seemed to identify instantly with class-based songs of my ancestors, my Scottish and Irish ancestors. ... That whole working-class experience was opened up to me there and I loved it from the start. It was really important, and I still identify with a lot of that.'

Terry's musical talents also proved a valuable asset in her primary school teaching. Her 'child-centred' teaching style was inspired not by educational theories from college or university texts, but was grounded in her own experience:

> Some of it was instinctive, out of the things like not feeling recognized as a child in myself, or as an adolescent, and feeling that needs of mine had not been fulfilled. So I tried to do them for the children. Dad was very anti-'play-way', and I felt I'd never ever had any 'play-way' and I wondered what the hell it was — and it felt all right to me. My natural way was the way I felt I learned. The way I felt I learned was what I tried to do with children. So, if I found rote-learning rather boring, then I never tried to do that with the kids. I also tried to find out about the child individually and therefore tailored the course around the child and tried not to impose structures.

Moreover, Terry drew on her own experiences of victimization, discrimination and marginality in educational settings to devise teaching strategies which would help students to come to terms with these experiences in their own lives. Like many Marxist feminists of her generation, Terry's Marxism had preceded her feminism (Mitchell, 1973). Her feminist consciousness-raising came about when she enrolled in university social science courses as a mature student. Her feminism, however, remained strongly Marxist in orientation:

> My feminism also influences me at the personal methodological level, like trying to break down the structures that are there. I feel alienated from them naturally ... the system is not just patriarchal, but it's also a class system and, of course, it's also a race system. What's created is a whole hierarchy of winners and losers. ... It's only starting to break down very slowly and it won't really break down until you've got people of different races and classes and sexes in positions of power to bloody select people.

Conclusion

Although the women's theories and biographies differed, several common themes emerge. The first is the importance of personal experiences of discrimination or marginality as grounding, or generating the preconditions for, an adoption of feminist educational theories in later life. For some these experiences had occurred during their own schooling (Middleton, 1987a, 1987b) and they regarded these as important in shaping their teaching practice as adults: '... my schooling was just so important in what I've ended up espousing as a philosophy' ... 'needs of mine had been unfulfilled, so I tried to do them for the children' ... 'I hated high school. The teachers and students have got a sort of wall between them.' As student teachers, and later as trained teachers, the women continued to experience sexism in the workplace: '... really, should a home economics person have a PR 2?' Not only was this evident amongst their colleagues, but also amongst the children: 'one boy had made a comment that girls couldn't do a certain task.'

A second important theme of the case studies is that the women had access to radical social theories with which to articulate these personal experiences of oppression and their deep feelings of alienation from sexist, racist and/or class-based ideologies in their own education and their teaching contexts. These theories came from a variety of sources; what was important was that they were accessible at a time and in a form which enabled each woman to conceptualize her personal sense of oppression as a wider social issue. Aroha, for example, learned from Maori elders that her understanding of gender relations in traditional tribal cultures had been mediated, and distorted, by Pakeha Christian interpretations, and she learned to value her heritage of power as a Maori woman. Jane encountered feminism from feminist teachers in schools and at university: for the first time history and social theories included her experiences as a woman — 'suddenly, there were people talking about *things that had happened to me*.' Terry learned to theorize her deep feelings of oppression as working-class, her sense of marginality in academic settings, through folk singing: 'I seemed to identify instantly with the class-based songs of my ancestors, my Scottish and Irish ancestors.'

A third theme in these women's experiences is their continuing marginalization within schools because of their teaching styles and their explicit feminism. Their preference for child-centred, individualized teaching styles put them in conflict with senior teachers who operate in a more technocratic mode: 'sometimes the lesson would go on for a long time, so it meant that other routines had to be put aside. [My associate teacher] felt very threatened because of that'; ... 'what is created is a whole hierarchy of winners and losers ... [educational structures] were devised primarily by men of a certain class and race ... I feel alienated from them naturally.' In addition to their rebellion against bureaucratic modes of organization and teaching, their explicit feminism earned disapproval: 'they see me as something rather vile and low' ... 'feminism is not regarded as something nice.'

While their degrees of radicalism differed, all of the women used the liberal feminist strategy of seeking senior positions in teaching as at least a first step towards wider social change: 'I do encourage other women to get into these positions ... there are so many Maori women coming to the fore ... I think they can do a hell of a lot'; ... [sexism, racism and class inequality] 'won't really break down until you've got people of different races and classes and sexes in positions of power to bloody select people.'

For feminist teachers, then, schooling and teaching need not merely reproduce patriarchal capitalist social relations, but can provide students and teachers with theories to help them connect personal experiences of oppression and marginality to structural inequalities in the wider society. Education provided these women with a vision of both the desirability and the possibility of change.

References

ACKER, S. (1987) 'Feminist theory and the study of gender and education', *International Review of Education*, 32, pp. 419–35.

APPLE, M. (1979) *Ideology and the Curriculum*, London, Routledge and Kegan Paul.

APPLE, M. (1983) 'Gender and teaching', *Teachers College Record*, 84, 3, pp. 611–28.

BERNSTEIN, B. (1975) 'Class and pedagogies: Visible and invisible', in BERNSTEIN, B. *Class, Codes, Control*, Vol. 3, London, Routledge and Kegan Paul.

BOWLES, G. and KLEIN, R. DUELLI (Eds) (1983) *Theories of Women's Studies*, London, Routledge and Kegan Paul.

DEPARTMENT OF EDUCATION (1982) *Teacher Career and Promotion Study*, Wellington, Government Printer.

EISENSTEIN, Z. (1981) *The Radical Future of Liberal Feminism*, New York, Longman.

ESLAND, G. (1971) 'Teaching and learning as the organisation of knowledge', in YOUNG, M. F. D. (Ed.) *Knowledge and Control*, London, Collier Macmillan.

FRIEDAN, B. (1963) *The Feminine Mystique*, Harmondsworth, Penguin.

GIROUX, H. (1982) *Ideology, Culture and the Process of Schooling*, Philadelphia, Pa., Temple.

JONES, A. (1988) 'Which girls are "learning to lose"? Gender, class, race and talking in the classroom', in MIDDLETON, S. (Ed.) *Women and Education in Aotearoa*, Wellington, Allen and Unwin/Port Nicholson Press.

MIDDLETON, S. (1985) *Feminism and Education in Post-War New Zealand: A Sociological Analysis*, DPhil thesis, University of Waikato, Hamilton, New Zealand.

MIDDLETON, S. (1987a) 'Schooling and radicalisation: Life histories of New Zealand feminist teachers', *British Journal of Sociology of Education*, 8, 2, pp. 169–89.

MIDDLETON, S. (1987b) 'Streaming and the politics of female sexuality: Case studies in the schooling of girls', in WEINER, G. and ARNOT, M. (Eds) *Gender Under Scrutiny*, London, Hutchinson.

MIDDLETON, S. (1987c) 'The sociology of women's education as a field of study', in ARNOT, M. and WEINER, G. (Eds) *Gender and the Politics of Schooling*, London, Hutchinson.

MILLS, C. WRIGHT (1975 edition) *The Sociological Imagination*, Harmondsworth, Penguin.

MITCHELL, J. (1973) *Women's Estate*, Harmondsworth, Penguin.

OPENSHAW, R. (1983) 'Saving femininity from the feminists: Some underlying values of a New Zealand "Back to Basics" group', *Discourse*, 4, 1, pp. 32–48.

PERE, R. (1983) *Ako: Concepts and Learning in the Maori Tradition*, Hamilton, Department of Sociology Monograph, University of Waikato.

RYAN, A. (1988) 'The "moral right", sex education and populist moralism', in MIDDLETON, S. (Ed.) *Women and Education in Aotearoa*, Wellington, Allen and Unwin/Port Nicholson Press.

SPENDER, D. (1981) 'Education: The patriarchal paradigm', in SPENDER, D. (Ed.) *Men's Studies Modified*, London, Pergamon.

5
Only the Fittest of the Fittest Will Survive: Black Women and Education

Barbara McKellar

People often ask me how I have managed to progress from the primary classroom to a post in the teacher education department at a London polytechnic. This question is pertinent when there is evidence of black under-representation in higher education. I would not find unreliable the informal survey of teacher education institutions carried out by the Anti-Racist Teacher Education Network (Table 5.1). This showed that I would be one of twenty-seven black teacher educators in England, Scotland and Wales (0.6 per cent).

Further information would be needed to establish how many of these black teacher educators are women. The small percentage the survey revealed is indicative of the way in which both race and gender operate to prohibit the recruitment and career advancement of black women in the teaching profession. Since the teacher education sector has to recruit from the pool of qualified and experienced teachers, what is needed is an analysis of the career progress of black teachers, in order to explain the percentage of 0.6 in post. What follows is an account of this progress with special reference to the ways in which race, class and gender relations have shaped the development of my career.

Table 5.1 Number of Full-Time Staff in Teacher Education, with Number of Black Staff Shown in Brackets

	Public Sector (including voluntary colleges)	University
England and Wales	2,150 (18)	1350 (8)
Scotland	709 (1)	17 (0)

Source: Anti-Racist Teacher Education Network (ARTEN) unpublished survey, 25 January 1988.

First I shall discuss the structural position of black women in society with a view to interpreting how this position influences the development of identity and images. Second, I shall discuss the processes of schooling which have assisted in shaping my potential to benefit from higher education. Finally, I shall look at the issues which black women face in sustaining a career in the teaching profession.

Black Women in Society

Historical Background

The position of black women in society is structured by political and economic developments, both nationally and internationally. The past holds as much explanation for the experiences of black women today as the present social and political climate. The development of racial and gender superiority coincides with the rise of capitalism as a major means of production in Europe. Such developments have also defined the roles played by all women in society and dictated the nature of the relations which could exist both between gender groups and across racial groups. It would be unrealistic to discuss the processes by which roles are structured without reference to the historical factors, not least because the same terms of reference operate to structure the progress of black women in education in Britain today. The experiences which are enjoyed in education are a reflection of the relations which exist in society at large. I would go as far as to say that when I walk down any street the reader would not necessarily know that I am a teacher educator but you *would* know that I am black and female. Therefore, the cultures to which one belongs are only important insofar as society attaches significance to them.

Throughout the last 200 years or more there has been a predominantly accepted image of black women, whereby they are portrayed as serving and/or servicing others. The subservient role played by black women was related primarily to the development of indentured societies in the Caribbean, Central and North America. The role of black women in such societies is not dissimilar to one played by working-class women in Britain during a parallel historical period. But in the black diaspora the women were invariably performing this role in all spheres of life without any of the social differentiation which would have been normal to the African societies from which they came. Such societies had the potential to allow a diversity of social and economic activity, but slavery introduced the limitations of domesticity wholesale to successive generations of black women.

Quite apart from the restrictive range of social and 'economic' activity, the period of slavery marked the point at which gender segregation occurred amongst black people in slave societies. Thus the gender role reconstruction, as well as cutting men and women off from each other, removed from black women the privilege of being able to exercise the trading skills which had been part of their heritage. Whilst this is the case, entrepreneurial traits are still to be found in the cultural practices of modern Caribbean societies where women are market holders and participate in international trade, mostly dealing with the American mainland: 'Buying and selling, or higglering as it is called, is a common form of livelihood for women throughout Jamaica. ... Higglers buy from the primary producers in the market at wholesale prices and retail them in villages nearby' (Clarke, 1979). This practice has expanded beyond the scale of fruit and vegetables to include all forms of commodity items. The shopfront or pavement site has been replaced by business enterprises which trade with the Americas, organized predominantly by females. So although slavery and capitalism have united to thwart the development of traditional economic patterns, despite the odds some things have managed to survive. The revival of African culture in the post-independence period has probably accelerated the trend of women adopting a higher profile within their communities.

Contemporary Forms of Oppression

The survival of traits related to the gender division of labour has occurred against a background of political struggle and extreme hardship, and as such the forms of oppression have assisted the construction of the particular kinds of gender relations which are to be found in black British communities. The norm of economic and political leadership being distinct from each other and attributable to separate gender groups has rendered both black women and black men unable to assert themselves in the British context. This is because within British society women are not seen as the prime leaders in the field of business, and black men do not have access to the means of enfranchisement to the mainstream political spheres. The expectations of black people are that they would fit into the existing patterns of gender differentiation which are not in fact familiar to them. Moreover, when black women become part of British society, they were expected to assume the patterns of dependency experienced by white women, as well as to maintain continuity in the role assumed during the period of colonial rule. Colonialism had the effect of guaranteeing compatibility with the needs of industrial capitalism. Thus the possibility of fulfilling the cultural and social needs of black women is limited by the structural position of women in Britain per se. The degree to which British (white) women are second-class in status has been the source of discrimination for black women in particular and for minorities in general. One only has to refer to countries in Eastern Europe or to other moments in Britain's historical past to see how artificial is the allocation of gender roles. The existence of a correlation between power and economic activity, in addition to the conscription of women to the secondary labour market, has rendered women incapable of having access to equal status in society. The failure to meet the needs of black women is further worsened by the considerable gap in social and educational experience between the ethnic culture and the British one. When one then considers that for reproduction to occur women must perform a dual role, it can be seen that black women have more with which to contend. That there has been social fragmentation in most parts of the black diaspora during the past cannot be disputed, and this has also meant that there was and is a greater need of urgency to stabilize the family base. The activities of many black women have this stabilization process as a prime concern.

Racism within Gender Groups

White male supremacy in international relations has been promoted via the development of patriarchal structures in European societies and via the extension of European power and influence in all parts of the world. This, in itself, has presented black men with an insuperable task in trying to regain a position of equality. In turn the inferior position which black men hold makes more problematic the gender relations within black groups. In fact, the frame within which black women operate has to include favourable interactions with both of these groups, that is, a double source of dominant oppression. The resolution of conflicts which stem from male dominance has resulted in black women relying on their own resources. This is due in part to the fact that the dominant perspectives which influence the organizations and lobbying machinery within the women's liberation movement have not always recognized the racial dimensions of black women's experience.

The birth of a movement called 'Women against Racism and Facism' sought to redress the balance. However, it has been suggested that: 'the different strands of feminist and left politics were real impediments to thrashing out a common anti-racist position' (Bourne, 1984, p. 9).

The inability to fuse the two perspectives which would address the issues related to black women's experience has been one of the major criticisms made by black women of the women's movement as a whole. Reasons suggested for this failure relate to the assumed differences which exist due to differences of race. When one considers that 'race' is an artificial term, then many of the distinctions with regard to physical qualities, intellectual capacity and the taboo subject of sexuality can be regarded as myth. Of the qualities referred to, it is often the physical and visual differences which are given prominence and then integrated via cultural and media representations to reproduce the ideologies that maintain the idea of significant difference. An example is the assumption that European standards in beauty are the ones by which to judge all others. Indeed the idea of racial superiority feeds assumptions about the qualitative distinctions which are mentioned above. For a long time there was assumed to be a scientific basis for the distinctions in academic achievement. The research of Mackintosh and Mascie-Taylor (Committee of Inquiry, 1985) suggests that IQ is not a reliable indicator of potential for academic achievement: 'These findings tend to argue against those who would seek to provide a predominantly genetic explanation of ethnic differences in IQ' (p. 147). It is further explained that West Indian children do better in public examinations than IQ scores would indicate.

The other of the assumed differences, namely sexuality, is problematic because little has been written about sexuality and sexual relations, and what has, has tended to remain in departments of higher education institutions and has not percolated to the world outside. It is unfortunate that this is the case, as stereotypes with regard to sexual prowess prevail to influence inter-racial interactions. Once again the period of slavery in the Caribbean has encouraged an image of black women as sex objects for the use of black and white men alike. It is unfortunate the current media portrayal adopts these stereotypes to keep alive the idea that black women are strippers and prostitutes (e.g., *Eastenders*, 27 March 1988).

Campaigning and political black women leading ordinary lives are rarely seen, so the predominant stereotype is perpetuated and used for referral by all. Consequently the inter-gender relations of the black community have tended to over-emphasize the reproductive role which women perform. It shocks many people to find out, for instance, that I have no children. It is important, therefore, that the experiences of all women are related to the political processes which express resistance to oppression. Feminists of all varieties need to ask the question, 'what does it feel like to be a black woman in British society?' Until this is seen as crucial in policy development, the effect of feminist activity will always be only to liberate white females. There has been a change in consciousness with regard to women's issues and much of this has started to influence the processes of education. However, it is not apparent that black female identity and social development have so far been included as high priorities in either resourcing or developing educational policy. It may be a major concern of teachers in inner-city areas where there are significant numbers of black pupils, but there needs to be full permeation of anti-racist and anti-sexist perspectives in curriculum development, regardless of geographical location. Moreover, it would be common to find the cultural isolation I experienced in the 1950s and 1960s replicated today in the non-metropolitan areas of Britain. Pupils in the all-white school need to develop anti-racist and anti-sexist practices as much as, if not more than, pupils from multi-racial schools. It was my experience that girls within my peer group were able to develop hostile patterns of behaviour in a subtle way which often went undetected by the staff. The way in which pupils interact with each other has not always been a major concern of teachers, yet the implications for the development of racial attitudes in society are just as important as the transmission of values by the mass media.

Summary

Although this is a brief account of the factors which shape the structural position of black women in Britain, what is revealed is that multiple factors operate to ensure that gender-related experiences are racially differentiated. The relations between European people and those of 'African origin' have been moulded by the exploitative nature of colonialism. Society's institutions which are concerned with cultural reproduction — family, church, judiciary — have all played a part in sustaining these relations. Responses to the economic, political, social and cultural forms of oppression which have resulted from the complex interaction of factors mentioned earlier have in turn confirmed the shape and form of the political platforms of resistance.

Race, Class and Gender in Schooling

> Women, whether black or white, experience relations of sexual domination and exclusion and this, too, was central to their thinking about their lives inside and outside school. (Fuller, 1983, p. 170)

> Unless their efforts to circumvent racial and sexual exclusion in employment are successful they are likely to find themselves in unskilled and semi-skilled jobs and being paid at even lower rates of pay than their male counterparts. (Fuller, 1983, p. 179).

It is dangerous to analyze racism or sexism in terms of individual achievement because, where it may be possible for small numbers of racial minorities or women to achieve success, often the structural position in society of both black people and women is not altered by such progress. Women are predominantly found in the lower paid sectors of employment. Together with sexual differentiation in employment, racism in employment and education combine to produce a climate in which black girls perceive and experience the processes of schooling in an entirely different way. Evidence of racism in education can be seen in the fact that pupils from black and ethnic minority groups are rarely selected into higher education. Rather than examining all the issues simultaneously and thereby risking the creation of more generalizations, I shall look at the race and class dimensions briefly before considering the impact of gender on my school career.

Race and Class

My parents migrated to Britain from the Caribbean in the 1950s at a time when there was a positive recruitment policy for attracting workers from the Commonwealth. The flow of immigration in itself has 'class' implications which, although never explicitly stated, were soon realized on arrival:

> After the war, which had killed off so many people, Britain was so desperate for workers to operate the factories, run hospitals and maintain transport and other services. In 1948 the Government passed a Nationality Act making all colonial and Commonwealth citizens British and actively recruited Black people. ... (IRR, 1986)

The hidden consequences of such recruitment practices had the effect of designating the housing class to which black people were assigned, whilst having repercussions for the lifestyles of the first generation and the life chances of the second generation. Immediately prior to the arrival of significant numbers of racial minorities there had been an extensive period of imperialism during which the foundations of prejudice and the ideologies which underpin discrimination were laid. Despite the positive view that many of the new arrivals had of their white 'hosts', it rapidly became clear that at best they were ill-informed. A view of the world in which British is synonymous with best has permeated all aspects of culture and is transmitted via all institutions, for example, the family. On arrival at school children bring with them the tacit knowledge and values which are enshrined in their pre-school experiences. Similarly the other institutions in society like the school absorb the prevailing culture of society to produce low expectations of black pupils by staff and other pupils alike.

Such low expectations assisted in influencing the cultural climate of the schools that I attended and in structuring the patterns of socialization into school as well as subsequently British culture. Encoded in language and cultural practices are the predominant attitudes to 'race'. Teachers are educated and socialized to utilize this code as they are a group which is drawn from a cross section of society. The mere fact of being successful in school is indicative of being able to conform to the social control mechanisms. Those who are not able to comply would not normally have a smooth career through school, and achieving the necessary qualifications for entry to higher education would not be possible.

Pupil-pupil interaction is often dismissed as being secondary to teacher-pupil relationships in the discussion of race relations in schools. Interactions with pupils, both in the classroom and the playground, can have a long-lasting effect on one's personal, emotional and psychological development. The dynamics of social interactions in the case of minorities are numerically structured. Where the ratio of teachers to pupils is one : many, the reverse is true for a peer group to a given child. Educational research reveals that teachers can only offer a small amount of individual time with each pupil in a day. Time spent with one's peer group is considerably longer. In my case there came a point when the negative attitudes of the teacher actually served to increase my determination and motivation. I began to carve out clear goals and ambitions. Instead of accepting the academic downfall signalled by failing the 11 +, I sought avenues for achieving status, both in school and the world outside, as well as in the future which lay ahead of me. The swift results yielded by increased determination led to transfer to grammar school after only a year. The consequence of this kind of thinking is that at an early age an awareness of one's overall position in society develops. Ideas emerge as to how to overcome obstacles and how long it takes to achieve one's goals: 'Schooling and education provided an alternative and less undermining possibility in their search for greater freedom and control. Concentration on education as a way out was something which all the black girls whom I interviewed stressed ...' (Fuller, 1983, p. 172). Much of the research carried out by Fuller at a London comprehensive endorses my experience of receiving a British education.

Race and Gender

The brief account above of the 'class' specificities of 'race' reveals that oppression has a double edge for those of an immigrant background. Black women experience two sorts of oppression which combine to shape the development of self-concept, as a direct result of being brought up in a racist and sexist culture. Recent attention has focused on the relative educational success of Afro-Caribbean girls in comparison to boys: 'The average performance score obtained by girls was 17.7 compared to 13.7 for boys. In all ethnic groups, girls did better than boys' (ILEA, 1987, p. 7). It may be that this observation is accurate for areas outside the ILEA and relates to the differential treatment which each gender group receives, both in school and in society at large. At school the expectations of girls are that they will be quiet, docile and diligent and adopt the values that are presented by female role models in school. The fact that these values are 'middle-class' matches the aspirations held by black parents on behalf of their daughters.

During my education my father was an active source of encouragement, offering as much support as he was able to. More importantly, given that the links between the culture of the home and school may be weak, the link between the kinds of values which are fostered in black girls and those of the mainly male-orientated culture of the school are strong. It would seem that the female gender role constructed within black families displays features which are more often associated with the male gender role in British culture. Qualities such as independence, self-reliance, a sense of responsibility for others are very much a part of the essential attributes associated with black females. Research has shown that the school cultures actually favour those who possess such traits, and it is the view of the writer that it is this which operates to encourage the success of black girls in certain spheres of school life. It would need a deeper analysis than can be offered here as to why this does not assist the success of black boys in school. It has been suggested that negative stereotypes exist with regard to their behaviour (Tomlinson, 1983).

In theory I should have had a distinct advantage over my peers throughout my education, but the early periods of schooling were dogged by low expectations, and these were exacerbated by the absence of black female models. There was nobody within school or in an equivalent status position elsewhere in society with whom to identify. I would suggest that experiences such as these serve to ensure that a lack of awareness of self-worth develops. The position with regard to the social mobility of black and other ethnic minorities is changing but there is still a long way to go.

Due consideration of the fact that immigration did not distribute the black population vertically within the class structure nor geographically suggests that a culturally pluralist educational climate is still of importance today as it was when I started school in the mid-1950s. During my schooling I experienced racial harassment, mostly name calling. An experience of harassment which frequently occurred at grammar school related to name calling by a girl who was not even in my class but who was in my year group. Throughout most of the period of secondary school I combed my hair in about twenty plaits and consequently I had many partings. It became fashionable for the girl and her clique to call me 'streets'. I was thick skinned, but initially this remark hurt not least because others laughed and thereby condoned it. There were many other pranks that yielded nicknames, but these I would put down to high spirits and immaturity. The personal nature of being called 'streets' could not even be offset by having somebody with whom to share this. I find it sad that the incidence of racial harassment has increased not decreased:

> The Commission for Racial Equality's two latest reports — the one alleging widespread racial harassment in schools, the other detailing the shortage of ethnic minority teachers — came just as the all-party consensus which greeted the Swann report three years ago shows ominous signs of cracking (*Guardian*, 5 April 1988, p. 21).

The reports indicate that the ethos is not changing, nor are the black personnel with motivation to change the position being recruited. Currently the cultural climate is marked by a range of regressive political moves which have encouraged the collapse of consensus on issues of cultural pluralism. One such political development is the introduction of the Education Reform Act which does not appear to encourage the trends which had been initiated at grass roots level related to multicultural education. In fact, aspects of the reform have encouraged the expression of negative racial attitudes as illustrated by the case of the (white) Dewsbury parents' group who, in refusing places for their children at a nearby school with mostly Asian pupils, theoretically were taking up their rights under the new arrangements for open enrolment.

Personal Testimony

Rather than listing the catalogue of negative encounters which took place, I shall elicit what was done to combat the effects of stereotyping. The area of pupil-pupil interactions was made more favourable by developing competences displaying high prowess. I was able to accomplish peer group approval via athletics. It was possible in this area to have clear-cut results which were associated with my own innate skills, both physical and psychological. It is useful to point out, however, that towards the end of my school career there were clashes with the PE teacher who did not accept in my case that there would be times when academic work, such as summer public examinations, would take priority over practices and training. Nevertheless, athletics was an area where I could establish my worth. Doing this is important for all children as it is in this way that being the butt of scorn from one's peer group is avoided. However, it applies even more to a black child who may acquire unfortunate labels even more easily.

The reputation one develops throughout schooling has more to do with evidence of academic ability than the level of involvement in extra-mural activities, important though this may be. It is important to achieve academic consistency in order that achievements are not questioned. This may involve investing more time and effort across a range of subjects. It is worthy of note that the 'work twice as hard' theory applies to both black and female pupils. However, for those who make additional effort, such children are off-setting the disadvantage of an inadequate educational provision themselves. The educational system is actually making additional requirements of such pupils. The responsibility of schools should primarily be that of facilitating the educational attainment of all pupils, of whatever race, gender or class. As well as burning the midnight oil I developed other strategies, for example analyzing what my areas of strength were and applying them in other contexts. I found I was able to boost my confidence by previewing what I perceived as the next likely obstacle to achieving my aims. An example of this would be asking pupils in the year above me in school a range of questions about the procedures necessary to gain work experience, at the time when I was considering career choice. Eventually I was able to pass high status subjects and enter teacher training.

Black Women in the Teaching Profession

The experiences of being black and a woman overlap with being a black teacher and with being a woman teacher. What follows may not depart significantly from what is already known about either of these but may serve to highlight the concerns of both.

Teacher Education, Ideology and Gender

The effects of racism are that some doors open and others remain firmly closed, due to the lower position held by racial minority groups. One such door which has remained closed for many black school leavers is the one by which entry is gained to higher education institutions. The divisions which exist in society between different social strata are engineered via the way that higher education institutions devise the criteria which select and recruit. One effect of restricted entry procedures is that for those with overseas qualifications, or without the full complement of qualifications, access is barred.

'Access' courses have been developed for those who may have or may not have had a British education and not achieved success because of reasons outlined earlier or due to disruptions to their schooling. It is significant that Access courses which were set up specifically to attract mature students who have not been able to make use of the education system are now attracting younger applicants, the majority of whom have been educated here (mostly from primary school onwards). Research I conducted for an MA dissertation revealed that a third were fully educated here with many others arriving during the secondary period of schooling. Often the primary reason for taking an Access course is to satisfy vocational needs. It would appear that schools fall short of satisfying this need to the extent that Access is now a popular alternative. The expansion of the number and range of such provisions reflects the increase in demand.

For those with the correct qualifications the race to qualify only begins on deciding to opt for higher education. The first stage of choosing an appropriate institution is an important one. When I applied to college I read as much available literature as I could, and once again listened to the impressions which those who had already been interviewed had of those colleges and the courses for which they had applied. The main guiding principle which I adopted was that the college should above all be situated in or near a city with a cosmopolitan population. The idea of living in total cultural isolation for three years seemed unbearable. Eventually the decision to move from London to a city in the East Midlands was a correct one. No sooner had I been exposed to the 'middle-class' environment of the college campus then I found myself gravitating towards the schools in the city nearby. I did this in order that I could more easily identify with the pupils whom I taught. It became clear, too, that I could make specific contributions in such social and cultural areas because of the perspectives I could bring to the classroom and due to my ability to empathize with pupils. A black family who lived next door to my digs in my second year was a good cultural anchor.

The ethos of many teacher education institutions is so élitist with terms of reference that are middle-class that only the fittest of the fittest can survive. The advance preparation strategies which were utilized in order to jump all the 'hurdles' during school needed to be re-employed during training. I attended a campus style college in my late teens and so there was no escape at the end of the day by way of a home to go to. The predominantly middle-class students flew in from distant places laden with exotic souvenirs and revealed the social background from which they had come on the first day. Such experiences serve to highlight that teachers are on the 'official' side of the desk representing the establishment. The realization soon dawns that as a black teacher, by participating in the management of the education system, one is likely to be operating against the interests of the community from which one came. The responsibilities of being a teacher, coupled with the negative experiences black people have of school, tend to limit the appeal of teaching as a career. The same arguments can be applied to other professions: witness the low recruitment rates for black and ethnic minority groups to the police force.

However, teaching carries high status within Caribbean cultures and so there is a pull, particularly for women. Boys' negative experience of the school system may discourage entry to the teaching profession. Another feature of being a member of the teaching profession is that in many ways black teachers have, of necessity, to be bicultural at school and to prioritize developing a British cultural perspective during college and subsequently during their teaching career if advancement is the aim. The period of adolescence has often signalled a reassertion of ethnicity for many black male youths. Thus the secondary forces which operate to engender success are minimized. I would go as far as to say that at college the norms of ethnic cultures do not apply and could potentially be a source of clash. Black teachers need to develop a professional identity which whilst accommodating British values relates to the social status of black people in society after they qualify.

Role of the Black Teacher

The education system, having been founded by men for men, has tended not to reflect positively the contributions of women or black people. When any teacher presents or introduces a curriculum to the class which reflects this exclusionary perspective, it is clear that they are colluding with the system. The development of initiatives which respond to bias in the curriculum and to the management of pupils assists in establishing that black pupils can make a positive contribution in schools, and can also improve the educational climate of the school. It is clear that the current processes of education overburden those black pupils who are keen to succeed, and so it is essential that black teachers play their part in alleviating the burden. More significant than developing innovative practice in one's classroom is the permeation of such innovations throughout the school via curriculum leadership. In order to do this it is necessary to be a part of the process of forming structures or organizations which will articulate the necessary issues and lobby for change. To tackle the form and content of the education process in one's own classroom is adequate when one first starts teaching, but it is not enough in the long term for the black teacher. It is a part of the role of the black teacher to think of the wider concerns of education; the positions of groups in society; the differential rates of achievement of pupils; the way schools induct pupils into different roles in society. It could be argued that all teachers need to have an overview of the processes of education, but because black women teachers are most likely to be able to understand the issues involved in throwing off oppression then it becomes a part of their lot. One criticism which I would level at teachers is that the time has come for teachers to be involved in the development of non-educational issues in the wider community instead of confining themselves to what is traditionally seen as relevant to school. Initiatives like Industry-links are to be welcomed in encouraging a greater development of broader educational perspectives.

In my case I taught lower juniors but tried to develop links with the infant department and also worked in local youth clubs which assisted in the development of a longitudinal perspective of children with whom I worked. Where the organization of schooling fragments the experience of children, it is an important part of the politicization of the black teacher to develop a wide perspective on educational issues. One cannot form part of the discussion on the outcomes of schooling if one does not know what happens beyond the age of 10–11 in the education system.

Promotion and the Black Teacher

It is often reported that black teachers are on the lower grades, on temporary contracts, in posts designated as Teacher above Authorized Numbers, or Section 11 (Ranger, 1988). There is some evidence to suggest that black teachers may be employed as a last resort, when there is nobody else to fill a post and there is a danger that classes might be sent home. An experienced black London teacher has shared this problem since starting her career in 1970: 'she has done well at interview and then not got the job. One school told her that she was very good but we don't have many blacks here' (*Guardian*, 5 April 1988, p. 21). This teacher's experience can be seen to occur for reasons previously mentioned. She taught a subject which relates to a vocational field which is regarded as women's work. Ninety per cent of employees in secretarial work are women. The low status that such work confers on those women involved no doubt contributes to being perceived as inferior. Added to being black, opportunities for advancement are few.

My teaching career was marked by entering an expanding field in which opportunities were available vertically as well as horizontally. Primary education is also regarded as women's work, but the position I held as a language teacher involved having detailed discussions with all teachers about the curriculum they taught and the progress of their children in much the same way as the headteacher would do. The key to success is being farsighted, especially in analyzing the nature of the promotional levers. Career-minded teachers who do not ask questions about the educational developments on the horizon and how they can be a part of them are going to find the progress of their career stifled.

Career advancement is also based on the level of qualifications one has, both academic and professional. No doubt the lengthy process of qualifying may deter many from working to pursue other qualifications, but it is essential to see teaching and learning as inextricably linked, as well as essential to one's own professional development. There is a wealth of courses from which to choose: teachers' centre courses, DES short and long courses, higher degrees, etc. I started with the first of these in my probationary year and progressed from a diploma to Masters degree within ten years. In the intervening years (between taking the diploma and Masters degree) I tended to 'top-up' with short courses within the local authority for which I worked. Quite apart from the 'knowledge' gained, being involved in such courses allows contact with other teachers whose experience of teaching is as valuable as (if not more than) the course curriculum. In this way one can keep up with changing educational trends. Gaining extra qualifications alone is not sufficient from my observations. Having a good relationship with those in senior positions assists in ensuring that your professional needs are known. The possibility of communicating curriculum needs to those in a policy-making position, as well as the curriculum consequences of educational change for minority groups in schools, ought to be the aims of the black teacher.

Conclusion

The introduction of perspectives which put women, black people and other ethnic minorities on the agenda of the school's curriculum has increasingly become important. The success of black people in education is structured by external influences in society and extends the range of what counts as valued knowledge. The path of social mobility needs to be unblocked, and education is one way of achieving this. Black women have a central role in this process not least due to their role within the family and the wider community. Their role in education will continue to be an important one insofar as they can assist in ensuring that the extra effort which black people make is honoured by the school system. Racial and sexual differentiations have assisted in producing the position whereby black women are carrying the torch.

References

BOURNE, J. (1984) *Towards An Anti-Racist Feminism*, London, Institute of Race Relations.

CLARKE, E. (1979) *My Mother Who Fathered Me: A Study of the Family in Three Selected Communities in Jamaica*, London, Allen and Unwin.

COMMITTEE OF INQUIRY INTO THE EDUCATION OF CHILDREN FROM ETHNIC MINORITY GROUPS (1985) *Education for All* (The Swann Report), London, HMSO.

FULLER, M. (1983) 'Qualified criticism, critical qualifications', in BARTON, L. and WALKER, S. (Eds) *Race, Class and Education*, London, Croom Helm.

INNER LONDON EDUCATION AUTHORITY (1987) *Ethnic Background and Examination Results 1985 and 1986*, London, ILEA.

INSTITUTE OF RACE RELATIONS (1986) *The Fight against Racism*, London, IRR.

RANGER, C. (1988) *Ethnic Minority School Teachers: A Survey in Eight Local Education Authorities*, London, Commission for Racial Equality.

TOMLINSON, S. (1983) *Ethnic Minorities in British Schools*, London, Heinemann.

6
In Passing ... Teachers and Sexual Orientation

Gillian Squirrell

Plumbing the Gap

Conducting research on homosexuality twenty years ago, Magee discovered:

> ... almost all the literature fell into one of two categories. It was either technical ... or it was sensational. Most public discussion consisted in the expression of attitudes and was based on little knowledge, direct or indirect. In fact it was quite clear that the majority of those who had entered the public discussion had not even acquainted themselves with such serious literature as did exist. ... Consequently although public discussion was plentiful it tended only to spread or to reinforce existing attitudes. ... The paucity of worthwhile writing was probably one of the reasons why so many false beliefs were so widely held. (Magee, 1968, pp. 1–3)

Despite the insights from recent feminist and sociological writing, I have been struck by a lasting truth in Magee's comments, particularly when considering the issues of sexual orientation and their bearing on teachers and pupils. There is a dearth of sensible writing and discussion to counter-balance the sensationalism of press and parliament. The only works to hand are those of a few gay and lesbian teachers publishing to a limited audience (Leicester City NUT Association, 1987; London Gay Teachers' Group, 1987). Within mainstream academic research it would appear that sexuality and education are not thought a suitable coupling. There are a number of possible reasons for this, and a brief rehearsal will bring some major issues to the fore.

Firstly, educational researchers may suffer from a lack of awareness of the existence of gay and lesbian teachers and pupils. This is compounded because these teachers and pupils are not as easily identifiable as those within other areas of research interest, such as gender, race or special needs (Warren, 1984). The difficulties of detection are heightened when teachers and pupils choose not to be identified, but to 'pass' as heterosexual. There is a body of sociological literature on 'passing', fuller reference to which is made in the later section, 'Managing a Teaching Career'.

A second possible reason for the lack of research may be the prevalence of the corruption myths. These fall into two categories, those of physical and ideological corruption. Dobson (1983) explains that: 'The fear of physical assault arises from the belief that lesbians and gay men are predatory by nature, and the identification of homosexuality with paedophilia.' There is little done by the popular press to debunk these fears; most of the reporting on homosexuality deals with dismissals or court cases. Similarly the medical and legal professions sustain fears about homosexuality. A powerful example is that of the precedent-making ruling of the Employment Appeal Tribunal against John Saunders, which upheld the reasonableness of dismissing someone for being a homosexual if they had contact with children. The significance of this has not been lost on gays and lesbians. One respondent to the Lesbian Employment Rights Survey stated: 'Gay means that you're going to interfere with children, which makes me angry when it's heterosexual men who assault children' (Taylor, 1986). Work by the National Council of Civil Liberties (NCCL) has shown how strongly these prejudices and ignorance have gripped local authorities. One Yorkshire councillor wrote to a NCCL survey team: '... to suggest that homosexuals should be allowed to work with vulnerable children is appalling. I wonder would H. Samuels employ a kleptomaniac' (Ferris, 1977).

The second strain of 'corruption myths' is fears of ideological corruption. It is this which has lain behind a number of recent moves, the Halsbury Bill and the clause 28 amendment to the Local Government Bill, both designed to restrain local authorities from promoting homosexuality. Fears of ideological corruption have also been played upon by the media in their creation of controversy over *Jenny Lives with Eric and Martin* (Bosche, 1983). Billed as a 'REAL fairy story' by *The Sun*, it was portrayed as a tool to pervert 6–8 year olds' sexual development.

Nowhere within this sensationalism are there grounds for supporting the corruption myths. However, that does not preclude such crass assertions as the following: 'I have no doubt that a significant number of present AIDS carriers within our society were given positive education in homosexuality when they were at school' (Lord Fitt, recent House of Lords debate). This can be dismissed on grounds of chronological impossibility, if for nothing else. It is, however, not surprising that between the Scylla of press hyped abuse and the Charybdis of parliamentary discussions a researcher might feel sexual orientation too dangerous a topic to contemplate.

A third series of reasons for the absence of work in this area might lie with the powerful fear of being branded by association. Plummer writes of the stigmatized nature of research into homosexuality.

> ... it is still possible for research into homosexuality to invite condemnation from colleagues, community and family. Anybody embarking upon such research should thus give serious consideration to being discreditable or discredited. ... Anybody entering this field may become 'guilty through contamination'. (Plummer, 1981)

Socially conscious researchers may feel it safer to confine their interests and political perspective to areas such as gender or race, which perhaps do not have the same moral stigma and fear. This fear of guilt by association takes on a more profound significance at a time of insecure employment. In the light of current government moves and the rightist morality it would clearly be foolhardy for teachers, researchers or lecturers to write against the current and dominant homophobic ideologies.

A final reason for the absence of work in this area may be the difficulties of such research. Plummer writes of the moral gatekeeping of universities and funding bodies halting projects and failing to accredit work. Aside from this moral entrepreneurship there are 'technical' problems, primarily in gaining a sample group. Traditionally it has come from the analyst's couch or prison cells (Hooker, 1962, 1965). Although the situation for a researcher has improved, there is a reticence about identification which could endanger livelihood or result in vilification. My own process of gaining a group of teachers was tortuous and halting. Advertisements yielded few responses, not surprisingly so given the risks had my advertisements not been genuine. I came to rely on the method most commonly employed in this sort of research, that of word of mouth and personal contact, a process leaving power to vet and recommend the research in the respondents' hands.

A recent additional difficulty is that of the speed of national and local government actions piling restrictions on dealings with homosexuality. This makes it hard to keep abreast of what is happening. It also necessitates a delicacy from the researcher, for much of what is happening cannot be reported, lest those trying to innovate and resist heterosexism face reprisals.

The Existing Literature

What little writing there has been centres on three main areas. There have been several works on teenagers growing up gay, invariably with emphasis on the role of school (Trenchard and Warren, 1984). There has been work on revising the curriculum (Patrick, 1984), the bulk of which would appear to be in English teaching (Slayton and Vogel, 1986), and in personal and social education (PSE).

The other concern of the literature has been gay and lesbian teachers. Much of this has been written by the practitioners themselves. It is flawed, in that there is a tendency towards an insular view emphasizing individual 'coming out' stories with little political critique. 'Coming out' is in itself a problematic policy to recommend since:

> ... while it may secure some legal concessions under a liberal regime, it fails to challenge the domination of a heterosexist ideology and power structure which will only tolerate homosexuality on the grounds that it retain its deviant status. (Minson, 1981)

Rather than challenge this order of sexual definition, its tendency is positively to consolidate it:

> to make homosexuality the defining characteristic of the entire person is to make the very assumption made by those who are hostile to homosexuality, e.g. in an employer's justifications for giving someone the sack purely on grounds of their being a known homosexual. (Minson, 1981)

To these reservations can be added another. For lesbian teachers 'coming out' in the phallocentric environment of a school may not be practicable. Yet, in what has amounted to a campaigning literature, it is assumed that the lesbian experience is the counterpart of gay male experiences. This is a frequent flaw dogging much mainstream sociology in this area (Faraday, 1981).

The Interviews

In appreciating the problems of previous works on gay teachers and the need to produce 'campaign documents', I took as a brief the explication of a greater variety of experience through interviews with gay and lesbian teachers. The sample consisted of twenty-five, who taught in a number of counties, across the age range and with differing subject specialisms. The teachers represented a range of ages and lengths of teaching experience and were within various kinds of relationships. There is insufficient space here to allow for a full analysis of the data. I have selected interview material dealing with three areas: the management of the teaching role, teacher-pupil interactions, and differences between lesbian and gay male experiences.

Managing a Teaching Career: Issues of Passing

Reasons for Passing

In common with workers in many other occupations described in the sociological literature, the teachers I interviewed also felt some need to cover their sexual orientation. There were a number of ways that this may have been done, from a deliberate disguise to omitting to debunk colleagues' assumptions of the universality of heterosexuality. Some of the reasons for passing are given in the pamphlet, *Gays at Work*:

> By coming out we are aware that the attitudes of our friends and others and of superiors could be hostile and that we might harm our prospects and even lose our jobs. Therefore at work the majority of us pass as heterosexuals. Hiding our gay identity is necessary to avoid harassment and keep our jobs. (McFadyen *et al.*, 1980)

One can add to fears for job security and promotion, fears about victimization and of being discredited at work.

Job security and promotion

The interviewees spoke at some length about job security and promotion. Many teachers knew of a person who was sacked or squeezed out because they were gay. However apocryphal these stories, they are well augmented by the press: 'Gay staff face selective jobs ban' (*TES*, 23 November 1984); 'Lesbian love lesson miss quits' (*The Sun*, 3 July 1987); 'Gay job threat' (*TES*, 1 January 1987); and by a flourishing mythology in gay fiction, as these examples illustrate.

> They sacked me from teaching when they found out I was gay. They were scared that I might corrupt horrid little boys. (Ireland, 1984)

In the context of talking about job security and promotion, perceptions were given of the efficacy of Equal Opportunities Policies, many of which carried a clause about sexual orientation. A number were similar to this teacher's: 'they can still get you out if they want to ... it would be nearly impossible for a teacher not to do anything wrong and then they could be got out for that.' The lack of faith in the EOPs has an effect, especially when coupled with a lack of clear support from the teaching unions. Most gay rights pamphlets tell people to help themselves by joining a union. However, aside from NATFHE, the teaching unions do not have a policy on homosexuality, although they may support individual cases. It is not surprising that gay and lesbian teachers may be left with a sense of vulnerability and isolation:

> For the three years I was at H — I didn't tell anyone.

> Three people in the English department asked if I was gay — quite jocularly. I denied it. I was on probation and felt very much on probation. I knew that I didn't want to stay there so I was worried that I might not get a good reference.

Fears for promotion prospects may also lead teachers to keep silent about their sexuality. Such fears may be well grounded as there appears to be an emphasis on familial relationship before teachers gain entry to school hierarchies. One teacher, although quite successful, has been warned by his deputy head that he will be going no further unless he makes changes:

> He has coded conversations with me on the necessity for a conventional family life to achieve deputy headships and headships. He jokingly suggested that a single man shouldn't get a headship. ... They're coded ways of spelling out truths to me — there will be difficulties in getting those kind of jobs.

This equation of a 'normal family life' with promotion has led gays and lesbians to marry simply to advance their careers. A less dramatic solution is that of seeking promotion in the advisory service and local government where there seems less need to parade a family set up. There is an additional agenda for lesbian teachers trying for promotion, and this follows in a later section.

Victimization

It is a truism to say that people are victimized on grounds of their sexuality, and teaching is no exception. One teacher spoke of her head's behaviour towards two other lesbian members of staff. One, a deputy head, firm and competent, fell foul of the incoming head and her deputy. They made her life so unbearable that she eventually succumbed to early retirement. Another, living with a 'dear friend', was similarly victimized, and finally left through ill health. Not surprisingly the teacher I interviewed had no desire to let the head 'have anything on me. She tolerates me because I do a good job.'

The most recent manifestation of victimizing known, or suspected, gay members of staff has come about through the fear of AIDS. This led the London Gay Teachers' Group in 1985 to produce a pamphlet, *AIDS Hysteria*:

> This media coverage is helping to justify the discrimination and harassment of lesbians and gays. In the education system as in other areas people are refusing to work with or provide services for women or men who are openly lesbian or gay. For example in one London school two openly gay teachers have been ostracised with colleagues refusing to use the same toilets or even coffee mugs. Teachers who are, or are suspected of being, gay are suffering increased harassment from both pupils and colleagues.

One of my respondents, a deputy head, found that he became a victim of AIDS hysteria after an absence from school during which his homosexuality was revealed. On his return he found there was ill-feeling and fear surrounding him, his colleagues equating gay with diseased. This led to a distressing process of ostracism: some teachers would regularly leave the staffroom if he entered, and he was forced to take lunch on his own. This prejudice spilled into their working roles. His head refused to work with him, and tried to retain a supply teacher for his class once he had returned to school; while he was relegated to small-group support work in the cloakroom, the technician was told not to produce the resources he had ordered. Most irrationally of all, his pupils were ignored and not party to whole-school treats and events. The homophobic nature of the AIDS fears is well illustrated by the fact that lesbian teachers also fall victim to such ostracizing treatment.

The power of the knowledge

Three of the respondents said they feared that knowledge of their lesbianism or gayness might mean their professional judgment or competence would be discredited:

> If it got round the 6th form and to colleagues, it might not undermine my role as advisor to the 6ths, but there would certainly be a general prejudice against the value of the rest of my judgement.
>
> Once labelled you get put in a box and don't get taken seriously.

The same woman also said that she felt if she pushed against the WEA decision not to allow her to run a day course on sexuality, then her future employability might suffer: 'homosexuality puts into question all your other work. It makes it invalid and you don't get taken seriously. A deviant, a nut-case.' Fear of the effects of others finding out proved founded for one teacher: 'I've been in teaching for 17 years; 15 are logged up as very successful. Now the last two are known as a disaster. If people say it long enough then it'll stick.'

Strategies for Passing

There were a number of strategies which enabled teachers to pass for straight, ranging from silence to outright lying. However, as one teacher explained, silence was not a successful ploy as teaching and staffrooms are essentially interactive. 'It's a strain being anti-social when you're a social person. And they eek it out of you anyway, with questions: Where do you live? Do you live on your own?' Thus teachers tried to manipulate their social interactions:

> When they get too close I just steer the conversation away.
>
> I haven't told too many barefaced lies. I'm just economic with the truth.

> I concentrate on being neutral, on not letting certain conversations develop.
>
> I hold back, just keep acquaintances superficial.

In the staffroom there may be subterfuge, for example, the invented girlfriend miles away. 'I'd always say that I was going to Liverpool to see my girlfriend, I knew that a girl I had been friendly with at college had gone there.'

Colleagues' heterosexist blindness may be used against them; two teachers felt it kept them safe:

> But they'd say I couldn't be a lesbian because I've got two children.
>
> They think that I'm alright because I was married and I've got a child. I just share a house with a man.

Pupils, like colleagues, are curious about personal lives. 'Are you married?', 'Have you got a girlfriend, Sir?' are frequent questions, although they tend to be directed at the younger members of staff. With age comes an assumption that the teacher is married: 'Pupils feel that they can ask a lot more, can go further with a younger teacher than an older. It is more of a challenge to their discipline.' This can cause consternation to younger teachers who may not wish to lie but who know that not to might mean disaster. So there may be lies in response:

> Boyfriends? ... I've had hundreds.
>
> When they say things I just wink and they keep guessing.
>
> I ask them (irrespective of their sex) if they're going to make me an offer. That usually gets them so embarrassed that we just get back to the lesson.

As with colleagues, pupils' assumptions can also provide good cover: 'Because I'm young they assume that I'm having affairs with all the young female members of staff.' Teachers can also practise disguise in a number of ways, such as through clothing:

> I always wear a skirt — it makes me feel that I am normal.
>
> I was dressing straight and constantly conscious of suppressing a crucial part of my lifestyle of myself, me ... I tried to keep them separate — this sounds silly — by having a different costume for each.

or in the creation of another self for school. This could be achieved by a process of mental transposition, thus a partner would change sex or become 'friends': 'I can't say "we". It's hopeless, I always have to say "friends".'

Teachers may make themselves invisible in order to negotiate school functions:

> I became very adept at refusing invitations. That way I wouldn't have to have people back.

> There is a strong staff association. I never get involved with that. Those things are always geared around couples.

For those teachers who think that passing strategies may not help them, there are more extreme ways of coping. One male teacher described three that he had known fellow teachers employ:

> living a twilight existence. Just going out to clubs in the evening and keeping it at that, at a distance. Giving up an earlier gay existence and throwing everything into career and promotions. Or isolating oneself and living in a state of fear that something might eventually be said.

The Effects of Passing

Advantages may accrue from some strategies. A spin-off from wholesale engagement with work might be promotion: 'When I think of all the hours I used to spend on school work' was a comment from a man entering the advisory service. 'There are some advantages like working all night or going on field trips, not being tied down', commented a young scale 4. However, the effects are probably more likely to be negative:

> It takes something out of the working day not to be able to be yourself.

> I don't like feeling negated.

> With the 6th form that you get to know well, there is always an unnecessary sort of distance.

One woman found the usual feelings of leaving a job were exacerbated by her false position: 'I don't want them necessarily to know ... but I don't want them to think that I'm mad. They're incredulous that I'm leaving. People don't unless they go for a scale point or....'

At times when relationships go through periods of change it is often not possible to talk. One teacher had to sit and listen to her relationship with a colleague's wife discussed. '"She's left him for another woman". I could have died a thousand deaths. I felt sure that they knew it was me.' One teacher said that he wasn't sure if he would have spoken to anyone at work even if he had been heterosexual, but 'the possibility isn't even there if you are gay.'

The strain on relationships was frequently mentioned:

> I always answered the phone if it could be somebody from school. I didn't like being seen around with my boyfriend in case people 'sussed' it out. This led to arguments, 'Was I ashamed of him?'

> When I started teaching I was in the beginnings of a relationship with another man. The strain of starting teaching and keeping the teacher part of me and the gay man separate soon took its toll and I fell back on the tactic of throwing myself totally into my work. In fact after a year I went even further and tried to make a go of a relationship with a woman rather than come to terms with myself.

Other teachers noted that there was almost a pressure to have a heterosexual relationship and a curious release when the invisibility of being gay or lesbian was lifted:

> It was curiously liberating having a boyfriend for a bit, normal again, telling my dearest friend at school all about dear Graham.

> At school there was an extraordinary feeling of exhilaration and relief. I felt I could shout 'It's okay I'm like the rest of you.'

There is a strain in not being able to acknowledge anything of one's personal life in school. At one extreme a man who tried to keep things so separate went cottaging (impersonal sex in public toilets): 'then I used to try and pretend it was a binge, that it wasn't me. Then I'd throw myself back into work.' One woman commented on the feelings of professional and personal isolation: 'I found it difficult getting older and not having a relationship and not telling anyone anything.' Duplicity and lying also take their toll, as does not 'bearing witness'. This phrase was used by a number when describing the guilt they felt in not questioning homophobic comments or when they ignored jokes.

'Sometimes I just don't have the energy to take them on and I get up and walk out of the staffroom. Then I feel really bad about not having bothered.'

Self-consciousness, conflict and the need to keep things hidden may change with time and experience. Yet there were several experienced teachers who still denied things and felt uncomfortable. However, many had confided in a few colleagues at work, or at least felt comfortable that it was tacitly known: 'the only thing left to say is *it*.'

The effects of such stresses can do little to help make teaching easier. Some leave teaching. 'I was getting more and more involved in things and I thought it wouldn't be long before someone found out. I wanted to leave on my own terms, not be pushed out. I couldn't stand the conflicts for much longer.' Possibly for some it means that they will be reluctant to leave their school: 'the thought of going through the coming out process all over again.'

There are a number of reasons and ways that gay and lesbian teachers hide aspects of their lives from all or some of their colleagues. I do not want to fall into a trap of allowing this chapter simply to rehearse problems thereby possibly making the issue of teaching and sexual orientation more palatable to the homophobic. I am aware of the dangers of this (Johnson and Whitman, 1985). To right the balance, it is important to note that any problems had a limited effect on the teaching role and day. I do not wish to detract from these teachers' competence or humanity. Indeed, a number mentioned they felt they had an advantage, having a 'sense of natural justice', a sensitivity borne through understanding their own experiences.

Pupils and the Issues of Sexual Orientation

Given the tenacity of the corruption myths, an obvious area for this research were the classroom practices and the responses these teachers gave to their pupils' questions and behaviours. The responses I gained were at variance with the images projected by the tabloids and the recent Lords debates on clause 28. There were a number of elements which led these teachers away from any mention of homosexuality. One of these was the teacher's subject specialism. A chemist commented: 'I'm not of the opinion that pupils do confide in teachers [a fact borne out by Trenchard and Warren, 1984]. I only see them once a week and the longest I might see them would be for a two year stretch.

It would be unlikely that it would come up in chemistry.' While for an art teacher the issue might arise in class: 'They'll come and chat a lot. They work individually and some will stay late or work at lunch times. I'll talk loosely about myself. I draw the line at what I tell them. Sometimes I'll chip into their conversation.' His final comment about 'chipping in' contrasts significantly with a later statement he made about talking with colleagues: 'At the lunch table I will hold out for what I believe in. I'll show them the light.' Other teachers taking English, PSE or religious education said homosexuality might arise, but they too appeared to do little more than try to redress an iniquitous balance:

> I get frustrated and angry. It's not simply anti-gay comments. It's not their fault. The silliness that they are fed with from the press and their parents. I say that people have a right to live life. I make a statement against prejudice of any sort. It is sometimes possible to get an exchange. Kids have got more conscious of it [homosexuality]. The last 6–7 years ... there's been a lot on the television. You only have to find gay in a poem and they fall about laughing.
>
> I encourage kids to look at issues. Any prejudicial remark 'gays I hate them' or anything racist or sexist. Any comment I find offensive. It doesn't stand out. Possibly I feel a little more awkward because I'm more involved.

These comments are interesting, given the supposed indoctrination of pupils by teachers. A biologist felt impotent in the face of a pupil continually making anti-gay comments. 'If I hadn't been gay then I would have been able to say something.' An English teacher unpacked some of her fears, which give an insight into why these teachers are chary of raising the issue in class:

> The thing I find really impossible to talk about is homosexuality. I feel really bad about that — a failure. ... When it comes up in Shakespeare's sonnets or Forster I'm unable to think of anything sensible to say — it's a psychological thing — no matter how good my intentions. I feel in a false position, taking an aloof pseudo-liberal stance. ... I suppose on most subjects I hold strong opinions but I can stand it if they disagree, but if they attacked homosexuality it would strike at the roots of my character and set up a lot of conflicts for me.

The thought of being rejected and attacked as a person rather than as a teacher must be daunting. Other reasons for not courting the issue in class were offered, an important one being the fear of being found out. This led a couple of teachers to have problems with curriculum initiatives which addressed homosexuality. An English teacher spoke of a department-produced package on stereotypes:

> ... for the 4th years. It requires kids to ask questions. We didn't duck it [homosexuality]. I don't think that I could have done it without Kate. It's difficult to initiate something like that, I went in knowing that I wasn't standing on my own. ... If I had been Head of Department I rather doubt that it would have been done. The Head of Department would have to answer for it — to parents, governors....

As homosexual teachers find difficulty in raising the issue in class, it is important that their heterosexual colleagues confront their own heterosexism and work alongside on curriculum initiatives, enabling homosexual teachers to face these issues in class. Such cooperation is rarely the case, as this example from a teaching practice shows:

> Their regular tutors feared that we would provoke very hostile reactions to the subject and ourselves. Significantly they absented themselves from these two sessions. It would be nice to think that they did this because they thought that the discussion would be freer without them. Unfortunately it was clear that they did not feel that it was something that they ought to get involved with: they thought that it would damage their relationship with the pupils. (Baker, 1984)

Several homosexual teachers spoke of a sense of failure that they were not able to provide any positive roles for pupils.

> I'm very concerned at the prejudice that the kids feel — from the popular media, etc. If they were aware that you're gay, if you could be open then you could be a positive role model so they might reconsider other misconceptions, question other things. But you're inhibited from doing this.

Many felt that they had to keep some additional distance from the pupils. These fears of being found out caused anxieties about homophobia which their heterosexual counterparts might not appreciate:

> I had to cover a games lesson. It was awful having to go in the girls' changing room.

No one thinks about the problems that I have going into the boys' toilets to stop them from smoking.

While none of the interviewees had experienced a pupil 'coming out' to them, they felt that should it happen, then rather than deal with the situation themselves they would refer the pupil. Indeed the inappropriateness of revealing their own sexuality was underscored by a teacher describing a child in her class with a lesbian parent who was undergoing a custody dispute. She would not reveal herself to child or parent, saying: 'It would be the most awful thing for him because it would have to be a secret otherwise I would be worried that the other children would find out. Having a terrible secret and a mum the same wouldn't be any good for him.'

One comment that featured in the London Gay Teenagers Project (Trenchard and Warren, 1984; Warren, 1984) was the need that pupils felt for teachers to be open in the school. It is unlikely that in the current climate teachers will move from the behaviours they described.

The Importance of Gender

Faraday (1981) stresses that lesbians should not be seen simply as the counterpart of the male homosexual: 'it is essential that notions of the lesbian are reconceptualized within the context of her oppressed social position as woman and not as "female homosexual".' From the data a significant number of differences in the experiences emerged. An obvious one was that of promotion, thereby verifying Faraday's thesis that lesbians share the same situation as other women. Certainly all women would be debarred from the old-boy network, though the situation for a lesbian feminist may be worsened by the fact that she refuses to play the usual female role of bolstering male teachers or being compliant. This rejection of the male's role and power might put lesbians beyond the pale. 'How can I trust the hierarchy to support me when I share with that hierarchy no common language or experience? If men are not the center of my world, then why am I coming to them for help?' (Anon, 1984).

For lesbian feminists there may be other difficulties, in that they may fear that discovery of their sexuality may discredit their political beliefs. This may work both within the classroom and the staffroom. 'In most kids' eyes, being a lesbian is simply to do with being unattractive, desperate and unable to get a man' (Hope, 1987). Many staff 'believe that a woman who asserts herself is too aggressive and therefore must be a lesbian. The fact that a woman is a lesbian explains her views on any subject' (Hope, 1987). Thus one teacher wrote:

> In any school based meeting around anti-sexist or anti-racist issues I worry in case opening my mouth will discredit the very cause I am supporting. Of course she's bound to speak up and of course I do. (Anon, 1984)

The fear of causing problems or discrediting a cause comes out strongly in Hibbert's writing of her visits to schools:

> Would an announcement of my non-heterosexuality have done something to reinforce the feminism which I was trying to bring to their attention? ... I could easily have sent the boys off chasing lesbians. I can imagine my chair scraper in School One, consumed by heterosexual aggression, rising and shouting to the rest of the room that he was having to listen to a fucking dyke. How would the gum chewing girls have responded to that? Would their femaleness have been reinforced? Or would they have felt threatened? (Hibbert, 1987)

The equation of certain behaviours or attitudes with lesbianism in the minds of staff and pupils may give rise to problems for lesbian teachers who do not wish to make their sexuality known. This may make teaching certain material difficult, or may hamper giving the girls more attention or tackling sexual harassment, areas where heterosexual counterparts might feel less inhibited.

Gay male teachers in this survey recounted instances where they made use of female members of staff as camouflage, as confidantes and as companions. It is less likely that lesbians would use male teachers in the same way or indeed would be able to. It is possible that lesbianism makes problematic their relationships with female members of staff. The heterosexual women may fear being thought of as 'one of those'. One lesbian faced problems with a women teachers' support group which she had helped set up: 'I found it difficult to use this group for support in my specific harassment as a lesbian — in case it frightened off women who had already found it difficult to come to an "only-women" meeting.' The media also react differently to lesbian teachers, for where feminism can be levelled, it is seen as a mighty plot to neuter boys (Hemmings, 1980). This fear of political castration does not arise with male gay teachers.

BOSCHE, S. (1983) *Jenny Lives with Eric and Martin*, London, Gay Men's Press.

CONWAY, T. (1987) 'Local government', *Lesbian and Gay Socialist*, 12, pp. 12–13.

DEPARTMENT OF EDUCATION AND SCIENCE (1986a) *Education Act (2) 1986*, London, HMSO.

DEPARTMENT OF EDUCATION AND SCIENCE (1986b) *Health Education 5–16*, London, HMSO.

DEPARTMENT OF EDUCATION AND SCIENCE (1987) *Circular 11/87, Sex Education in Schools*, London, DES.

DOBSON, M. (1983) 'At school', in GALLOWAY, B. (Ed.) *Prejudice and Pride*, London, Routledge and Kegan Paul, pp. 19–34.

FARADAY, A. (1981) 'Liberating lesbian research', in PLUMMER, K. (Ed.) *The Making of the Modern Homosexual*, London, Hutchinson, pp. 112–33.

FERRIS, D. (1977) *Social Work Survey*, London, NCCL.

HEMMINGS, S. (1980) 'Horrific practices', in GAY LEFT COLLECTIVE (Eds) *Homosexuality: Power and Politics*, London, Allison and Busby, pp. 155–72.

HIBBERT, R. (1987) 'Teacher training', in HANSCOMBE, G. and HUMPHRIES, M. (Eds) *Heterosexuality*, London, Gay Men's Press, pp. 20–4.

HOOKER, E. (1962) 'The homosexual community', *Personality Research*, pp. 40–59.

HOOKER, E. (1965) 'Male homosexuals and their worlds', in MARMOR, J. (Ed.) *Sexual Inversion*, New York, Basic Books.

HOPE (1987) 'My experience as a black lesbian teacher', *GEN*, 10/11, pp. 16–17.

IRELAND, T. (1984) *Who Lies Inside*, London, Gay Men's Press.

JOHNSON, P. and WHITMAN, L. (1985) 'Heterosexism awareness', *GEN*, 5, pp. 16–17.

LEICESTER CITY NUT ASSOCIATION (1987) *Outlaws in the Classroom*, Leicester, NUT Association.

LEONARD, D. (1987) 'An interview with Di Leonard at the Institute of Education', *GEN*, 10/11, pp. 23–4.

LONDON GAY TEACHERS' GROUP (1985) *AIDS Hysteria*, London, London Gay Teachers' Group.

LONDON GAY TEACHERS' GROUP (1987) *School's Out*, 2nd ed., London, Gay Teachers' Group.

MCFADYEN, T. *et al.* (1980) *Gays at Work*, London, Gay Rights at Work Committee.

MAGEE, B. (1968) *One in Twenty*, London, Secker and Warburg.

MINSON, J. (1981) 'The assertion of homosexuality', *m/f*, 5–6, pp. 19–39.

PATRICK, P. (1984) 'Trying hard to hear you', *Teaching London Kids*, 23, pp. 7–11.

PLUMMER, K. (1981) 'Appendix 1: Research into homosexualities', in PLUMMER, K. (Ed.) *The Making of the Modern Homosexual*, London, Hutchinson.

SLAYTON, P. and VOGEL, B. (1986) 'People without faces', *English in Education*, 20, 1, pp. 5–13.

TAYLOR, N. (Ed.) (1986) *All in a Day's Work*, London, Lesbian Employment Rights.

TRENCHARD, L. and WARREN, H. (1984) *Something to Tell You*, London, Gay Teenagers Project.
WARREN, H. (1984) *Talking about School*, London, Gay Teenagers Project.
WOLPE, A. (1987) 'Sex in schools', *Feminist Review*, 27, pp. 37–46.

Part 3
Reproducing Gender Divisions

7
Schooling the Teachers: Gender and Initial Teacher Education

Christine Skelton and Joan Hanson

Recent research has shown that girls' education is different from and unequal to boys' education, and that the career opportunities and experiences of female teachers are not identical to those of male teachers (see Hough, 1985; Lees, 1986; Grant, 1987). Surprisingly one aspect of gender differentiation in education remains virtually unexplored, that of initial teacher training courses. With a very few exceptions (Spender and Sarah, 1982; Skelton, 1985; Thompson, 1986; Hanson, 1987) little research has been carried out which informs us about the role gender plays in the content and structure of initial teacher education programmes, or the attitudes of tutors and students involved in these courses. We need also to recognize that as members of the black population are severely under-represented on initial teacher education courses as students and particularly as lecturers, the research which does exist focuses on predominantly white, if not all-white, groups. Teachers have, to a greater or lesser degree, an amount of control over the official and unofficial agendas of schools; that is, over the formal curriculum content and over the host of assumptions which, although not spelled out in any curriculum statement, are implicit in all aspects of school life and effectively learned by pupils. In addition teachers' attitudes towards and assumptions about people, including their beliefs about class, race and gender, are likely to be reflected in their professional practices, whether consciously or unconsciously (Pratt, 1985; Wright, 1987). Unless teachers are born rather than at least partly 'made' (Reid, 1986), then the initial teacher education they receive has implications for their future behaviour in classrooms and for their own development and careers.

At present there are two main routes into teaching. Prospective teachers can undertake a four year BEd degree which requires them to obtain expertise in a curriculum subject (secondary) or an 'area of the curriculum' (primary) as well as developing professional skills. Alternatively those students who have obtained a first degree can opt for a thirty-six week PGCE (Post Graduate Certificate in Education) course where the emphasis is placed on acquiring skills and understanding relevant to teaching. The element of both courses which involves educational theory and practice is generally known as Professional Studies.

Initial teacher education courses offered by colleges of education and polytechnics have to be validated by the CNAA (Council for National Academic Awards). The CNAA stipulates that gender issues form a part of the course structure:

> The Council is anxious that all institutions consider the implication of the legislation (Sex Discrimination Act) when devising courses, and endeavour not only to abide by the letter of the law, but also to implement the spirit of the Act. ... These considerations should be taken into account when devising a course and admitting students, and also in the subsequent conduct of a course. (CNAA, 1980, p. 69)

On the other hand, initial teacher education programmes offered by the university sector are not subject to the same strictures, although CATE (Council for the Accreditation of Teacher Education) mentions gender in its guidelines. Whether or not gender or indeed any 'equal opportunity' issue is considered in the course structure depends on the individual institution. Because of the scarcity of information on gender issues in initial teacher education programmes we are not in a position to make generalizable statements. However, we know that some initial teacher education courses based in universities do incorporate gender into the content structure, and we know that any institution requiring CNAA validation will have had at least to consider gender. Given that there is some awareness of the question, how are these issues tackled? From the work carried out in this area it appears that gender concerns may be (a) ignored; (b) consigned to 'one-off' lecture slots; (c) consigned to optional courses; or (d) permeated throughout the programme.

Our intention in this chapter is to demonstrate the ways in which gender issues can influence the initial education of student teachers when these concerns are given an official voice and, alternatively, when they are not. We will focus specifically on our individual research studies, both of which investigated PGCE courses, one involving students on a primary course and the other a secondary programme. Our argument is that whether or not gender is given an official platform, it will nevertheless occupy a crucial position in the underlying values of the course. As Britzman (1986) states: '... teacher education, like any education, is an ideological education. It promotes particular images of power, knowledge, and values by rewarding particular forms of individual and institutional behaviour' (p. 443).

The Primary PGCE Course

In Skelton's (1985) study of a PGCE primary course she discovered that whilst gender did not feature in the written content of the course, nor were gender concerns raised in any of the lectures, discriminatory messages were transmitted via the 'hidden curriculum' of the programme. It has been found that student teachers bring with them attitudes towards teaching formed in their own school days (Shipman, 1967; Hanson and Herrington, 1976; Mardle and Walker, 1980). If student teachers already 'know' what teaching is, then they will doubtlessly 'know' what to expect of girls and boys in the classroom. As Spender and Sarah's (1982) study of PGCE students has shown, initial trainees hold deeply entrenched beliefs regarding gender. However, Skelton's (1985) research suggests that the perpetuation of gender discriminatory beliefs and practices in the classroom cannot be attributed solely to students' pre-course attitudes towards either gender or teaching. The group of students involved in the primary PGCE course frequently demonstrated an awareness of stereotyping and challenged any sexist incidents or comments which occurred *in the college setting*. When a video was shown of some girls involved in a maths project and the tutor made the comment, 'You can tell it's a group of girls by the illogical way they're going about it', he was immediately informed that he was being offensive. Yet the awareness of gender discriminatory practices and the willingness to confront sexist behaviour and attitudes which the students exhibited on campus did not extend into the school situation. Donning a 'professional' cloak seemed not only to make them oblivious to the gender discrimination they witnessed but often led them to contribute towards its perpetuation.

There were several instances on teaching practice when students accorded greater recognition to boys and boys' interests. In one school two female students carried out an environmental studies project with a group of five boys and two girls. Various pieces of equipment were distributed. Four clipboards were available to write down any findings, all of which were handed to the boys. Once out of the school the boys were given a measuring tape and asked to measure the hedge; no equipment was provided for the girls as their task was to collect plants from under the hedge. A similar situation arose on a later teaching practice when a female student gave her class of fourth year juniors the task of devising and taping a selection of programmes for a radio station. The assertive classroom strategies employed by boys (Clarricoates, 1980; Hough, 1985) rapidly emerged when the student asked the class who would like to do what. Boys secured the roles of weather*man*, news broadcaster, interviewer, quiz*master* and contestants, as well as operating the tape cassette player. The quiz itself was devised by boys who chose snooker as the subject. Domination by the boys meant that the only involvement the girls had in making the programmes was playing 'jingles' on musical instruments. The rest of the girls in the class designed posters and badges to advertize the radio station.

It became apparent in interviews that the striking division between the attitudes and behaviour regarding equal opportunities for both sexes which the students displayed as 'themselves' in the college setting and those they exhibited as potential 'teachers' in the classroom had passed unnoticed by all of them. However, by examining more closely the culture of the primary PGCE course and carrying out lengthy interviews with students concerning their individual educational biographies, it became clear that a number of factors were interacting which conspired to ensure that egalitarian students were transformed into gender biased teachers whenever they entered into their professional role.

What were these factors which brought about a marked, but unremarked, change in the student teachers' behaviour? An answer lies in the hidden curriculum of this primary PGCE programme. As already noted, gender issues were not included in the official course content nor were they raised as discussion points in any of the lectures. At the same time the underlying value system of the course communicated certain messages regarding the abilities and behaviour of girls and boys. In particular, students received messages that boys were poor readers, disruptive influences and good at mathematics. These ideas were purveyed, for the most part, in comments by lecturers and teachers in schools such as, 'It's always the girls that learn to read first' and, 'You have to keep your eye on the boys ... they tend to be boisterous.' These comments were supported further by remedial language/reading programmes and activities aimed at boys' interests and referring to the pupil as 'he'; videos and resource books which depicted boys being successful in mathematical problem-solving; children's literature with 'daring and devilish' boys and 'dreamy and docile' girls.

These messages have implications for the primary educational experiences of girls and boys. Boys' aggression in the classroom and handicap when it comes to reading are 'social' rather than 'natural' facts:

> In general intelligence, attention span, cognitive abilities and task orientation boys and girls are alike when they enter school. These are all areas relevant to school behaviour that do not differentiate the sexes. In sum, boys and girls entering school are much more similar than they are different. (Jacklin, 1983, pp. 16–17)

As 'social' facts, there is the possibility of change; that is, boys' reading ability could improve and they could become less aggressive, but such changes would presumably depend upon the teaching styles adopted and the expectations of the teachers. The problem is, of course, that if students are 'taught' stereotyped ideas about the abilities and behaviour of boys, then it is probable that these messages will be internalized and subsequently affect their future behaviour in the classroom (see Foster *et al.*'s (1975) study demonstrating that what trainee teachers are told, they tend to believe).

Another of the assumptions made on the PGCE course was that boys were better at maths. Unlike the measures taken to improve boys' reading capabilities in schools, no similar concern exists for girls' lack of visuo-spatial skills and their lesser confidence in pre-mathematical or scientific learning (Whyte, 1983). Of equal importance is the fact that the image of boys as better mathematicians at primary level is somewhat misleading. There is a welter of evidence (Fennema and Carpenter, 1981; Assessment of Performance Unit, 1982; Walden and Walkerdine, 1985) which confirms that, during the early years of education, girls do better on average in most standardized tests of mathematics attainment. But if student teachers are continually exposed to the idea that boys are better at maths, then there is a distinct possibility that this will become a self-fulfilling prophecy. So, although gender was not a concept which was openly addressed and examined on the course, traditional stereotyped assumptions formed a part of the hidden agenda and would undoubtedly affect the future expectations and behaviour of the student teachers in the classroom.

What of the students themselves? Some explanation for their contradictory behaviour towards sexism and sexist attitudes in the roles of 'student' and 'teacher' was provided in interviews. It seems that a combination of their understanding of child-centred education and their personal experience of gender discrimination at school resulted in the situation whereby gender issues were not perceived as a feature of primary classrooms. The course placed tremendous emphasis on child-centred approaches, or, as it was often termed, 'individualized learning'. Many of the handouts distributed in lectures reminded students of the importance of catering for the individual needs of children. We have sufficient evidence that a common belief of primary teachers is that they treat all children equally (Whyte, 1983; Hough, 1985). Perhaps it was not surprising to find that the students perceived teaching to the individual needs of each child as providing some kind of preventative barrier to the gender discrimination which goes on outside school. Many of the students mentioned 'society's expectations' of girls and boys, and 'parental stereotyped' attitudes towards their offspring as explanations for the continuation of gender stereotyping whilst at the same time absolving primary schools' role in the process. The students espoused the belief that 'unstructured play', an 'open-ended curriculum' and a concern for the 'individual child' unquestionably provided primary children with equal educational opportunities.

The students' 'professional socialization' partly explains the discrepancy between their attitudes towards gender as 'students' and 'teachers', but it was their personal educational biographies which allowed the subtle stereotyping of the primary school to pass unnoticed. When asked during interviews about their experiences of gender discrimination in their own schooling, they all referred to incidents which occurred during the *secondary* years of education. These incidents focused on two areas, subject choice and adolescent sexuality. Students recalled how they were discouraged from combining art and science subjects. When forced to choose, the females opted for art subjects and the male students for science subjects. Only female students referred to sexuality. They recalled the irresolvable conflicts of their adolescence; they could either concentrate on boyfriends or their schoolwork: 'I worked hard so boys weren't a problem. I didn't have a boyfriend until I was 20. The boys used to call me names like "iron knickers" or "the ice maiden".'

The evidence collected in this research suggests that when gender issues are not incorporated into the 'thinking' which underpins initial teacher education programmes, then stereotyped assumptions about girls and boys will persist. In the case of this primary PGCE course a cyclical process of gender discrimination can be identified. The students began their course already 'knowing' about teaching. As pupils themselves, the students will have absorbed the differing attitudes teachers displayed towards them and their peers by virtue of their sex. They will have 'learned' during their primary years that boys are noisier, more disruptive and better at technical subjects, and girls are quieter, less adventurous and more adept at learning to read. Their own memories of gender discrimination focused on the secondary school. The PGCE course failed to contradict any of their preconceptions and also placed emphasis upon child-centred approaches to learning which the students perceived as the essence of liberal education and a means of eradicating all forms of inequality between children. This resulted in gender stereotyping in the primary school becoming a non-issue; that is, it was not seen to exist. By ignoring gender issues on the initial teacher education course, the attitudes and expectations the students had of primary age girls and boys which had been learned during their own schooldays were compounded by their training and subsequently re-enacted in the classroom.

Not all teacher education courses ignore gender. Barry Everley (1985) and Edith Jayne (1987) have noted ways in which gender can be brought to the attention of students undertaking initial teacher education programmes. But how do these measures operate and to what effect? To provide some insight into these questions we will refer to findings of the research by Hanson (1987) into a secondary PGCE course offered by a northern university.

The Secondary PGCE Course

In order to bring equality issues to students' attention, the PGCE department Hanson studied was developing provision which included a combination of awareness-raising events, optional courses and 'permeation'. Awareness-raising events came under the umbrella of Professional Studies. Two sessions included consideration of gender, and at both students' attendance was in theory, though not in fact, compulsory. Optional courses — in which individuals could exercise a degree of choice over subject matter — provided further opportunities for students to pursue interests or to further their understanding of additional areas. Some students used these to investigate aspects of gender concerns. But the PGCE staff believed issues of equality were fundamental and too important to be consigned only to intensive events and/or to optional courses. Permeation of the whole course programme was considered the most appropriate means of ensuring that such issues were brought to the attention of all students. Equality concerns would ideally be confronted in all aspects of work.

Given that over 100 students were divided amongst twelve subject methods and ten Professional Studies groups, in addition to working in a variety of schools during teaching practice, it is hardly surprising that expectations, experiences and perceptions of the course varied considerably. Analysis of data revealed complex relationships between the various forms of provision and the attitudes students developed towards equality concerns and the various course components.

Survival in the classroom is understandably of crucial concern to all potential teachers. Responses indicated that students viewed this as largely dependent upon their practical ability to teach their specialist subjects. Aspects of the course most obviously concerned with classroom activities, with how to teach their subject, were perceived as the most valuable. Evidence from staff and students strongly supported the view that students' efforts and commitment were allocated selectively with this in mind. This selective approach was adopted within and also between course elements. It seems highly probable that from the outset subject-related method courses would have had an immediate appeal not shared by the more theoretical Professional Studies (see also Britzman, 1986).

It was an aim of the department that the three major course elements — Curriculum Work (method), Professional Studies and Teaching Practice — would interrelate. In reality a variety of factors operated to separate rather than link Professional Studies and Curriculum Work. Space does not permit detailed description of this situation but it is important to note that such factors existed and served not only to divide and invite comparisons between the two but also helped to distinguish Professional Studies as a low status course element. Subject method sessions not only occupied more of students' university-based time than any other course element, but were valued by students as the central, the most important part of the course — after teaching practice, that is! Permeation of method courses would seem to be the key way and means for equality — or indeed for any central issue — to be addressed convincingly on the PGCE as presently structured.

Although all method tutors subscribed to the principle of permeation, professional judgments differed regarding its implementation. The practice adopted by the majority involved confronting equality issues as and when they arose during course work, teaching practice or whenever. A minority considered this to be inadequate. They devised additional method sessions specifically to address such concerns. The practice of addressing equality issues as and when they arose was common to most tutors, so how did this operate and what were students' experiences? Sometimes a student would raise a point which would result in a five or fifteen minute discussion. On another occasion a tutor might observe the relative teaching time apportioned by a student to boys and girls during a lesson, and use this evidence later as a starting point for a discussion or activity during a method session. Interviews revealed a wide variety in the types of experiences encountered and in their frequency. At the same time a pattern was distinguishable in which *planning* appeared to be an influential factor. Some tutors had given considerable thought to how particular aspects of equality concerns were likely to emerge from, or might be incorporated into course work, as well as to how they might be presented and/or addressed. In other words, what came up was not left purely to chance; there were varying degrees of manipulation. On the other hand, it seemed that in certain method groups equality concerns were literally addressed only *if* and when they arose — unplanned for and incidentally rather more than intentionally.

Where planning featured more prominently, equality concerns arose more frequently and students' experiences were more varied. Individuals were able to describe readily and in detail aspects of issues encountered during the year. In those cases where little planning was evident it seemed that equality concerns were raised less frequently and had made less of an impression upon students. Even in response to careful directive questioning replies were vague. It was difficult to elicit information about what aspects had been addressed and how.

A minority of staff considered equality issues should have a place on the formal agenda of method courses as well as being considered more incidentally. A high profile was thought necessary to underline their importance, and labelled sessions to ensure they were not somehow overlooked by students. A tutor recalled an incident in support of this view:

> ... so last year I didn't do a separate session on gender issues at all whereas I did do a session where race was prominent. ... Now, although I hadn't done a special session it had cropped up on numerous occasions over the year ... but ... at the end of that year a student went for interview and was asked what she'd done on gender and [subject]. ... She said, 'Oh! We haven't done anything.' I was furious! I hadn't attached a label and shouted

> 'We're doing gender now! This is what it's about!' ... and she thought she hadn't done it. ... I'm not sure, but I think things need to be labelled at some stage, even if you are permeating it through. ...

The majority approach, adopting the practice of addressing equality issues as and when they arose, was characterized by a lower-key handling of the issues. Some tutors held strong convictions that labelling, high profiles, hype could be counter-productive; that is, were more likely to result in resentment than enlightenment. Evidence gave some support to such views. Some students indeed responded negatively and mentioned the 'high propaganda profile' as off-putting. There was talk of 'overkill' amongst some males and females. These responses are intriguing. Did students really think they had been over-exposed to the issues? Did reactions stem from the 'high propaganda' profile as suggested? If so, one might have expected all, or at any rate more, students to react similarly. Shared factors or common experiences among those complaining of 'overkill' might give some insight into this response.

In fact, these students were members of method groups where equality issues had been given a low profile and were raised relatively infrequently. Consequently they associated equality concerns with Professional Studies events rather than with method courses. Conflicting and confusing messages were being received. The department professed its commitment to equality in the course literature, provided compulsory events to address these issues, gave them a high status and called them crucial — then located them in Professional Studies. So-called important issues were placed in a lower status course element and separated from what teaching was all about — the classroom situation and method work. One student pointed out that equality issues failed to permeate throughout Professional Studies. They were doubly isolated, treated as a separate subject within a separate course:

> I think what's wrong is these issues are stuck in PSS [Professional Studies Seminars] and what's done is very separate from the classroom. If it was more *concrete* and less theoretical people might be more receptive. But, well then, its treated like a *subject* that you *do* for a few days, or half a day or whatever. It's like it's *outside* the course. ...

The combination of circumstances described here may have done little to raise awareness or increase understanding, but was it sufficient to explain hostility and complaints of 'overkill'? Evidence was not conclusive but what might have tipped the balance between apathy and antagonism was unsympathetic presentation. Limited encounters with such sensitive issues had in certain cases been accompanied by what individuals saw as an aggressive approach by a tutor, or similar reactions from fellow students.

Interesting by comparison are data from participants in two groups — one PSS and one method. There was agreement that the tutors concerned had given equality issues a consistently prominent profile whilst themselves adopting what group members regarded as a 'non-threatening' approach. Students' views were that hostility and apparent rejection of the issues had not emerged as features of their discussions. These students had arrived at the end of the year without crying 'overkill'. One male student summarized the modification of his own attitudes in this way:

> When I first came here I thought it [equality] was almost rammed down people's throats which for someone like me I think can be bad. I tend to turn off. But really, I think *now* it has made me more aware of forces that are going on. I would say that before this year I would, for instance, have been quite likely to write 'he' or 'him' all the time and not think about it. Just as a figure of speech. Now I put myself in the place of a female and, well, I think they must get really sick of it. I've stopped doing that. Some things may seem trivial if you're not on the receiving end but they mount up!

Conclusion

Clearly a great deal more research is required into the ways educational institutions approach gender issues and the subsequent implications for staff and student attitudes towards girls and boys. However, on the basis of our work we can draw some tentative conclusions. It appears that the field of primary initial teacher training is the one most likely to fail to consider the influence of gender stereotyping on the educational experiences of children. As was shown in Skelton's (1985) study, by failing to call attention to discriminatory practices evident in the primary classroom, assumptions about the abilities and behaviour of young girls and boys not only remain uncontested but are actively reinforced. We know that for some teachers, adopting practical strategies to curtail the inequalities experienced by girls in the classroom is, in itself, believed to be discriminatory towards boys (Myers, 1985). This view may be attributed to the emphasis placed by primary education on child-centredness whereby the teacher focuses teaching/learning approaches on the 'individual needs' of each child. Whilst in theory catering for the individual child might alleviate some forms of gender discrimination found within classrooms, the reality for teachers is being faced with a class of twenty-five-plus children and having neither the time nor resources to put the idea into operation. But it is not the impossibility of child-centredness which is espoused on initial teacher education programmes! Hence, student teachers embark upon teaching with *ideas* of child-centred educational aims only to be confronted with the constraints of classroom life.

Students embarking upon secondary initial teacher education courses already know something about their specialist subject areas. This, however, cannot be expected in the case of equality issues. What conclusions can be drawn from courses which do put equality issues on the agenda? The ways in which the initial teacher education course in Hanson's (1987) study tackled equality issues revealed that the approach adopted is of crucial importance. This is because Professional Studies is seen as the theoretical part of a course, bearing little relevance to what teaching is 'really about' (Denscombe, 1982). Conversely, when equality issues permeate method courses, given high status by students because they are directly linked to the reality of the classroom, then the influences of gender, race and class on children's education will be afforded a higher place among student teachers' concerns. Moreover, it was apparent that the profile of equality issues is raised when methods tutors actively structure their courses so that these concerns will be dealt with in lectures rather than leaving it to chance.

It must be appreciated that to address equality issues is not to deal with external exercises restricted to the realms of the professional or the academic; rather, it involves a challenge on a personal level. Confronting inequality involves the individual in self-examination. Personal assumptions, attitudes, expectations, behaviour are all called into question and may require change. In relation to such questions on any teacher education programme situations will probably arise which, unless managed sensitively, can easily become threatening. Tutors themselves may require help or guidance in confronting their own sexism/racism and in knowing how to raise notions of equal educational opportunities in their lectures (Jayne, 1987).

If real changes are to be brought about in the present educational experiences of girls and women, we must not only develop the knowledge and skills to implement equal opportunities in schools but also examine the institutional working and internal politics of higher educational establishments. With the current demand for an increase in the teaching population the urgency for initial teacher education institutions to review their own practices cannot be under-estimated.

References

ASSESSMENT OF PERFORMANCE UNIT (1982) *Mathematical Development, Primary Survey Report No. 3*, London, HMSO.

BRITZMAN, D. P. (1986) 'Cultural myths in the making of a teacher: Biography and social structure in teacher education', *Harvard Educational Review*, 56, 4, pp. 442–56.

CLARRICOATES, K. (1980) 'The importance of being Ernest ... Emma ... Tom ... Jane', in DEEM, R. (Ed.) *Schooling for Women's Work*, London, Routledge and Kegan Paul, pp. 26–41.

COUNCIL FOR NATIONAL ACADEMIC AWARDS (1980) *Sex Discrimination and the Equality of Opportunity*, London, CNAA/EOC.

DENSCOMBE, M. (1982) 'The "hidden pedagogy" and its implications for teacher training', *British Journal of Sociology of Education*, 3, 3, pp. 249–65.

EVERLEY, B. (1985) 'Sexism and the implications for teacher training', *School Organisation*, 5, 1, pp. 59–68.

FENNEMA, E. and CARPENTER, T. P. (1981) 'Sex related differences in mathematics: Results from national assessment', *Mathematics Teacher*, 74, pp. 554–9.

FOSTER, G. G., YSSELDYKE, J. E. and REESE, J. H. (1975) 'I wouldn't have seen it if I hadn't believed it', *Exceptional Children*, 41, 7, pp. 469–73.

GRANT, R. (1987) 'A career in teaching: A survey of middle school teachers' perceptions with particular reference to the careers of women teachers', *British Educational Research Journal*, 13, 3, pp. 227–39.

HANSON, D. and HERRINGTON, M. (1976) *From Colleges to Classroom: The Probationary Year*, London, Routledge and Kegan Paul.

HANSON, J. (1987) *Equality Issues, Permeation and a PGCE Programme*, Unpublished MEd dissertation, University of Sheffield.

HOUGH, J. (1985) 'Developing individuals rather than boys and girls', *School Organisation*, 5, 1, pp. 17–25.

JACKLIN, C. N. (1983) 'Boys and girls entering school', in MARLAND, M. (Ed.) *Sex Differentiation and Schooling*, London, Heinemann, pp. 8–17.

JAYNE, E. (1987) 'A case study of implementing equal opportunities: Sex equity', *Journal of Education for Teaching*, 13, 2, pp. 155–62.

LEES, S. (1986), *Losing Out*, Hutchinson, London.

MARDLE, G. and WALKER, M. (1980) 'Strategies and structure: Some critical notes on teacher socialisation', in WOODS, P. (Ed.) *Teacher Strategies*, London, Croom Helm, pp. 98–124.

MYERS, K. (1985) 'Beware of the backlash', *School Organisation*, 5, 1, pp. 27–40.

PRATT, J. (1985) 'The attitudes of teachers', in WHYTE J. *et al.* (Eds) *Girl Friendly Schooling*, London, Methuen, pp. 24–35.

REID, I. (1986) 'Hoops, swings and roundabouts in teacher education: A critical review of the CATE criteria', *Journal of Further and Higher Education*, 10, 2, pp. 20–6.

SHIPMAN, M. D. (1967) 'Education and college culture', *British Journal of Sociology*, 18, pp. 425–34.

SKELTON, C. (1985) *Gender Issues in a PGCE Teacher Training Programme*, Unpublished MA thesis, Education Department, University of York.

SPENDER, D. and SARAH, E. (1982) 'An investigation of the implications of courses on sex discrimination in teacher education', cited in SPENDER, D. 'Sexism in teacher education', in ACKER, S. and WARREN PIPER, D. (Eds) *Is Higher Education Fair to Women*? (1984) Guildford, SRHE and NFER-Nelson, pp. 132–42.

THOMPSON, B. (1986) *Gender Issues within a Primary B.Ed. Programme*, Unpublished MA thesis, Women's Studies Department, University of York.

WALDEN, R. and WALKERDINE, V. (1985) *Girls and Mathematics: From Primary to Secondary Schooling*, London, University of London Institute of Education.

WHYTE, J. (1983) *Beyond the Wendy House: Sex Role Stereotyping in Primary Schools*, Schools Council Programme 3, York, Longman for Schools Council.

WRIGHT, C. (1987) 'Black students — white teachers', in TROYNA, B. (Ed.) *Racial Inequality in Education*, London, Tavistock, pp. 109–26.

8
'It's Nothing to Do with Me': Teachers' Views and Gender Divisions in the Curriculum

Sheila Riddell

Introduction

All secondary schools in Britain are bound by the terms of the sex discrimination legislation of the 1970s. Despite the legislation, girls and women teachers continue to experience discrimination and disadvantage in these schools. Since teachers are 'the bearers of educational change' (Kelly *et al.*, 1985), it is vital to look at their attitudes to equal opportunities issues if we are to understand the way in which they mediate, oppose or neglect these policies. In this chapter I use interview data gathered from a group of teachers in a rural comprehensive school to examine teachers' explanations of why gender differentiation continues to be such a central feature of the curriculum, and why women and men teachers fail to secure an equal number of promoted positions. I consider the responses of subgroups of teachers and suggest reasons for the patterns found. These themes are explored at greater length in my doctoral thesis (Riddell, 1988), which looks at the reproduction of gender and class divisions in two rural comprehensive schools through the process of option choice. I used questionnaires, interviews and observation to explore the way in which teachers as well as pupils and their parents are implicated in perpetuating these divisions. Despite the fact that the majority of those I spoke to said they believed in equality of opportunity, their actions very often belied their words. Pupils' challenging of teacher authority in the classroom and teachers' reaction to this challenge often had the effect of reinforcing traditional gender codes. The way in which pupils and their parents perceived the local labour market also maintained gender boundaries. For example, working-class girls were likely to take secretarial studies not because either they or their parents were particularly keen on the idea of a job in an office, but because no other jobs seemed to be available.

The Interviews

In the summer of 1983 I carried out interviews with nineteen out of a total of fifty teachers at Millbridge Upper School. The school is a mixed comprehensive set in a small town (population 8000), and many of the pupils travel in from the surrounding countryside. Ten of the teachers whom I interviewed were men and nine were women, and they were chosen in order to provide a representative sample according to age, sex, status and subject taught. Although it is difficult to generalize from a small sample such as this, it is nonetheless valuable to examine in depth the values of a group of teachers in a particular environment. A survey could clearly not provide such detailed and specific evidence. All teachers' names are pseudonyms, as is the name of the school.

The interviews consisted of a series of questions about the third and fourth year curriculum, the option choice system, the performance and attitudes of girls and boys in particular subjects and their responses to male and female teachers. (Option choice refers to the practice adopted by most British secondary schools of allowing third year pupils to choose some of the subjects which they will study during the fourth and fifth year. Some subjects, such as mathematics and English, are compulsory. In both schools where I carried out the research almost all subjects were taken significantly more by either girls or boys, and many were also predominantly working-class or middle-class.) At the end of the interview teachers were asked about their views on whether women and men had equal chances of promotion in teaching.

I begin by looking closely at Millbridge teachers' responses to the following questions: (1) Why do you think girls and boys tend to make different option choices? (2) Do you think the school could take positive action to encourage non-traditional option choices? The purpose of these questions was to determine whether teachers attributed the production of a gender differentiated curriculum at the end of the third year to the transmission by the school of a dominant gender code, or to the extra-school environment. Ultimately I was interested in the extent to which teachers' perceptions of such issues might themselves play a reproductive role in bringing about gender differentiation. Throughout this chapter I use the term 'ideology' to refer to networks of beliefs, values and assumptions. Ways in which teachers' educational ideologies and ideologies about gender may serve as a further brake to equal opportunities in the school are discussed.

When asked why they thought girls and boys chose different subjects, teachers' responses tended to fall into one of two categories. The first category attributed different patterns of option choice to factors outside the school's control, for instance girls' and boys' differing abilities, parental pressure, peer group pressure, early childhood socialization and traditions in a rural area. The second category of responses attributed differences between girls' and boys' option choices to within-school factors, for instance, teacher attitudes, curriculum content, school ethos and organizational procedures. What follows is an analysis of the teachers' responses. It is important to note that all teachers declared themselves in favour of a policy of equality of access to all subjects for girls and boys.

The Older Group of Teachers

Four male and three female teachers over 40 were interviewed, all of whom were members of the school hierarchy. In this particular school the hierarchy or senior management team consisted of four heads of house, three deputy heads, the director of studies and the headmaster. All the teachers in this group placed a great deal of emphasis on socializing forces outside the school. Particular emphasis was placed on the traditional roles of parents in a rural area. Mr Broughton, a male Head of House who taught woodwork, had this to say:

> A lot of it is role learning from early on, attitudes of parents ... I suppose there are traditional things that men do to earn a living and women do to earn a living or cope with the home. A lot of them still don't view the woman as going out to work. They still seem to me to think of the girl being equipped for life in terms of spending time in the home, which to me is wrong.

These teachers seemed to be influenced strongly by models of social learning, according to which traditional gender identities are formed at a very early age. Mr Spiller, the Director of Sixth Form Studies who taught commerce and economics, said:

> In terms of craft skills, very few girls are given Meccano or Lego to play with at pre-school level, and it's at pre-school level

> that it matters. By the time they're at primary school it's too late. The prejudices are already formed in the child's mind.

Mr Ginger, a Deputy Head whose subject was mathematics, suggested that peer group pressure was the most important factor preventing boys from making non-traditional option choices: 'I think boys regard cooking as slightly ... Not the sort of thing you want to tell your friends you're doing at 14 or 15.'

Two of the teachers said that the first and middle schools were responsible for enforcing gender stereotypes, and a further three talked in terms of differing abilities or stages of development among male and female pupils. The inference from some teachers was that these differences were innate:

> It's also stages of development. You will find so often that a girl will work industriously and produce pages of writing that looks most impressive and when they get higher up the school you look at it and it isn't so impressive, and the boys come on and the ideas are there. (Miss Maple, Deputy Head teaching mathematics)

> When it comes to using language, girls score much higher; ... even though boys may be just as good they don't work. ... A lot of girls shy away from workshop type things because it involves physical skills, it involves three-dimensional perception at which a lot of girls seem to be rather bad. (Mr Spiller, Director of Studies)

It is interesting to note that none of these teachers was willing to accord any degree of responsibility to the school for the perpetuation of gender differences in the curriculum, and in this they differed markedly from the younger group of teachers.

When asked to consider the role of the school in the encouragement of non-traditional option choices, the older group of teachers often cited the strength of environmental socializing forces as the main reason why the school could do very little to break these long-established patterns. Mr Spiller, the Director of Studies, felt that nothing could be done because:

> ... the constraints aren't in the school's provision. ... You're fighting parental prejudice, very strong, and for the school to try and change that would simply be counter-productive. So I think in terms of school policies you have to tread in this area

> extremely softly. The other area you're treading on is employers' expectations.

All of the older teachers placed a great deal of importance on the idea of pupils freely choosing the subjects they wanted to study, and were concerned that if the school were to become over-active in discouraging sex-stereotyped option choices it would be guilty of undermining this freedom. Mr Appleyard, the Headmaster of Millbridge, who taught mathematics, said:

> I think to take over a child and tell it it ought to do something, that's just not the business of the school. ... If you try to turn the whole lot upside down then you would be pushing people to do things differently. It's not the school's job to push, it's to make opportunities available.

Miss Maple, the Deputy Head, made similar points: 'It's difficult once you start selling subjects ... I would hate to generate anything in school which is artificial and push youngsters to doing things they don't actually want.'

In terms of what the school could actually do to encourage non-traditional option choices, the most radical suggestion from this group of teachers was to appoint male and female teachers to areas of the curriculum normally associated with the opposite sex. This policy was endorsed by both the Headmaster and the female Deputy Head, who said they were very pleased to have appointed a female woodwork teacher at the end of 1983:

> It's rather nice we were able to appoint a female teacher in the engineering department. She was a very good candidate. I don't think there's any point in appointing a female candidate just for the sake of it — but it will help to confirm there's no reason why women shouldn't be appointed in that department as much as anywhere else. (Mr Appleyard, Headmaster and maths teacher)

The Headmaster made it clear that he was expecting this woman to take the entire responsibility for encouraging girls to take technology, and did not consider that any official policy statement was necessary to support her.

Only one other suggestion was made by this group of teachers as to what the school could do to break down the sex-stereotyping of the curriculum. This was to give publicity to girls and boys who had made non-traditional option choices or embarked on non-traditional careers. Mr Appleyard felt that everything that the school could do in terms of intervention was already being done: 'In careers lessons people are shown all the things that are available. Notices are up showing particular opportunities for girls in engineering. If that's intervening, yes, we do intervene.'

There are a number of ironies and inconsistencies in the positions held by the older group of teachers. For example, having placed so much emphasis on the power of extra-school pressures, they then argue that in the interests of free choice the school must remain neutral and simply inform the pupils of all the options open to them. The onus for making atypical choices is placed on the shoulders of individual pupils and teachers, with no official policy to support them. Mrs Lovell, the female Head of House who taught English, said she did not agree with the idea of an official equal opportunities policy within the school. Such a policy could only be implemented 'by an individual teacher on a personal basis — or perhaps a department might be prepared to push it.' Reporting some research on attitudes of teachers to equal opportunities policies, Pratt (1985) criticizes the notion that the school should remain neutral in this area. He argues that 'neutrality' means simply allowing the many and powerful pressures upon pupils to operate unopposed.

The stress on the determining forces outside the school led these teachers to ignore some blatant examples of the manipulation of pupils' option choices by the school. For instance, while they were still at their middle schools, pupils were asked to choose their design subjects for the following year. This group of subjects consisted of woodwork, metalwork, technical drawing, textiles and home economics. Pupils had to choose three subjects, and home economics counted as two. Not surprisingly most opted for the security of following their friends into traditional areas of the curriculum, which then restricted their choice at the end of the third year of the upper school. All of these teachers justified this practice on administrative grounds. Mr Spiller, for instance, said: 'Well, it's a question of resources. To make it possible for everybody to do all of the areas, we would need at least one more workshop, one more home economics room, and we would need extra staffing to give you the extra opportunities and times.'

On the question of curriculum content there was again a tendency to accept what was being taught in each subject area as given and unalterable. Miss Maple, for instance, could see no way in which needlework could possibly be of any interest to the boys: 'I mean the boys don't do needlework. They're scared stiff of it. It's all making soft toys and learning to use a machine at that age, and it's just not a boy's thing.'

Despite their stated commitment to equality of access, these teachers were all involved in defending the status quo in various ways. It is worth noting that the majority of teachers in this group were maths teachers, and researchers such as Pratt *et al.* (1984) and Kelly *et al.* (1985) have also found that teachers of traditionally masculine subjects such as science, maths and technology have more traditional attitudes to gender issues.

The Younger Group of Teachers

In the younger group of teachers I have included all those whom I interviewed who were under 40, and I found greater variety in their responses. There were seven women and six men. Of the women, seven were on scale 2 and three were on scale 1. Of the men, two were on scale 3, one was on scale 2 and one was on scale 1. Not only in this sample, but in the school as a whole, women were concentrated on scales 1 and 2, and men tended to occupy more senior positions. In 1983 out of twelve Head of Department positions at Millbridge, only two, home economics and French, were held by women. Subjects taught by the group of teachers I interviewed were sex-typed, the men teaching physics, chemistry, biology, maths and geography, and the women teaching English, physical education, religious education, needlework and typing.

Like the senior members of staff, the younger group of teachers believed that environmental pressures played an important part in determining the gender differentiated pattern of pupils' option choices. Four of the men and two of the women suggested that parents as role models were an important influence:

> I think some of it could go back to the home and the sort of influences girls have. You know, flower arranging is all right for a girl so you've got the sort of biological interest. But girls would not consider changing plugs and things. They would see Dad doing that and playing with the car. And so we get that sort of stereotyping fairly early on, and they see physics as related to the sort of thing they expect men to do. (Mr Jones, Head of Biology and Head of Science)

Other influences mentioned by both men and women were the media, peer groups and first and middle schools. Mr Tiller, the Head of Maths, and Mrs Marshwood, an English teacher, talked about pupils' perception of the labour market:

> I think one thing is they look at the careers these subjects lead to and you see that the careers that there are tend to be mainly staffed by men. And in biology they see that there are a great deal of women working in that area. I'm sure that some of them see biology as working with animals and think that's nice as well. But really it is this careers thing to a great extent. (Mr Tiller, Head of Maths)

Mrs Stonecroft, an art teacher who saw herself as a feminist, felt that sex-stereotyping in the curriculum was related to the construction of masculinity and femininity in Western culture:

> I think it's not very well accepted in our society that we all have masculine and feminine qualities within us — we are all masculine and feminine. ... In Western culture it's denied and I think a lot of problems arise from denying part of ourselves — I think it works like that for both boys and girls. Particularly in education that part is denied, so we have to reinforce what we happen to be, whether a boy or a girl — we almost have to prove our masculinity or femininity.

Although both women and men mentioned environmental factors in determining option choice, the men talked about these factors at far greater length than women, whereas the women placed greater emphasis on pressures within school. Only two of the men but five of the women said that they thought the school was actively involved in channelling pupils into sex-stereotyped areas of the curriculum. One of the men felt that the sex of teachers in a particular subject area was an important means by which the subject's gender appropriateness was conveyed to pupils. Mr Grant, a chemistry teacher, who said before the interview that he had never really thought about the issue, suggested that subject areas tended to reflect male and female stereotypes:

> The male of the species is supposed to be the definite survivor who's meant to be cold and analytical and therefore the emotional side comes from the female sex. You could interpret that model and say the emotional side comes in the biochemical area which is where girls tend to appear more in science and the coldly mathematical engineering, that's where the money's made in the capitalistic sense, which is usually where the boys start appearing.

The two feminist teachers were the most categorical about the overriding importance of influences within the school, particularly the importance of teacher attitudes:

> Certainly there's very much the attitude that typing and needlework will be good for the girls and it's almost unthinkable that boys should do needlework. ... I think the craft department is very male orientated and the men definitely encourage the boys rather than the girls. (Mrs Marshwood, English teacher)

This was in interesting contrast to two of the men, who specifically denied that teacher attitudes had any influence at all:

> I don't think we give physics a male image at all. That is already there in the minds of the pupils. (Mr Mottram, Head of Physics)

> I don't know why girls tend to do biology rather than physics because there's no pressure put on them from the department in any way. (Mr Jones, Head of Biology)

Mrs Stonecroft felt that curriculum content was of crucial importance in attracting pupils to particular subject areas:

> In this school I think it's got a lot to do with the way the subject's actually presented. At my last school, the people who taught home ec. had broken down that barrier where it was seen as a subject for the girls. There was the multi-ethnic side — the home ec. was to do with a dietary thing and world-wide food distribution and the idea that we are what we eat.

This teacher disagreed with the idea that peer group pressure was an important influence on the sex-stereotyping of option choices: 'We reinforce the stereotypes as adults rather than students themselves. Particularly round about 13 or younger, if they have fun doing it, they'll do it. I don't think it comes from them unless teachers foster it in the first place.' Both the younger and the older group of teachers, then, felt that environmental influences played an important part in the production of a gender differentiated curriculum, but the younger group, particularly feminist women teachers, placed much greater emphasis on the importance of within-school factors.

In answer to the question of whether the school should take an active role in encouraging non-traditional option choices, a wide range of views was expressed. In general those who emphasized the power of environmental forces were pessimistic about the school's potential for initiating reform. Mr Jones, who talked at great length about the importance of parental role models, felt that the school could do little to bring about social change:

> I was talking with Gareth Wood (teacher at a middle school) about how we teach sex education and he was saying that even at 11, 12, there is already the stereotyping that the boys are out for what they can get and it's up to the girls to say no ... and if you've got that sort of stereotyping at that age then I'm sure it applies to all spheres of activity and you're naive to think the school can change that very dramatically.

Two of the men felt that the school was already involved in counteracting sex-stereotyping in the curriculum. Mr Mottram, the Head of Physics, said they did make a conscious effort to make the subject relevant to girls, although perhaps his words suggest a rather superficial understanding of the issue:

> When we're talking about speed increasing gears instead of getting a hand drill I always get an egg whisk or what have you. In some ways you could say it was a sop to the ladies. Having said that, there's no reason why girls should say machines and mechanics aren't for me. It's just an idea that's in their minds.

Whereas all the older teachers had defended the practice of pupils choosing design options in advance while still at the middle school, all the younger teachers apart from one opposed it.

Women made a variety of suggestions about how the school could encourage non-traditional option choices. Miss Jenkins, a religious education teacher, said that girls were often placed in RE classes not because they had any particular interest in the subject but because the class needed filling, and it was felt that girls would make less of a fuss about it than boys. Mrs Marshwood said that not only formalistic equality but real enthusiasm from the teachers was necessary for changes to be made. This would probably involve changing curriculum content and subject presentation:

> I think there should be a positive sales technique for the subjects boys are choosing like craft subjects. They should be positively sold to the girls, perhaps with displays and talks, and there should be a policy of positive discrimination to make sure you get a class which is half girls. I mean nationally I'd like to see a

> policy introduced in schools to make sure that boys and girls have equal opportunities in all subjects, not just on paper.

This teacher had clearly moved beyond the liberal concern for equality of access and was arguing that equality of outcome was vitally important.

All teachers, then, placed great emphasis on the impact of socialization on subject option choice. Teachers in the older age group denied that the school had any control over this outcome because of the power of external forces, and they also tended to place some of the blame on innate differences in developmental patterns between girls and boys. Younger teachers were generally more critical of the role of the school in producing a gender differentiated curriculum, but it was only the teachers who explicitly identified themselves as feminists who were in favour of the school taking positive action to change this outcome. Among the older group of teachers women were just as reluctant as men to endorse the idea of radical change in the school. There was also an overall tendency for teachers of arts subjects to be more in favour of positive moves towards gender equality than teachers of maths and technology. However, one of the female Heads of House who taught English had extremely traditional views on issues of gender equality, and perhaps this gives some indication that once teachers occupy positions of power within a school they are less likely to criticize its practices. Another possibility is that it is women with less challenging views who tend to be promoted in the first place. I will now explore the significance of certain teacher ideologies in producing an environment unsympathetic to the implementation of equal opportunities policies.

Teachers' Ideologies and Equal Opportunities Policies

As noted earlier, equal opportunities legislation does not seem to have made much headway in eliminating sex-stereotyping from the curriculum. There is evidence that teachers react with hostility or reluctance to anti-sexist intervention strategies (Payne *et al.*, 1984) and apart from a few progressive local education authorities such as ILEA, the implementation of equal opportunities seems to be left to isolated individual teachers. The accounts offered by Millbridge teachers of why pupils opt for gender differentiated areas of the curriculum clearly show that the majority of teachers favour theories based on a view of sex-role socialization as an all-powerful and totally determining force.

A further way in which teachers' educational ideologies operated to prevent the implementation of equal opportunities policies was their belief that the job of the school was to provide a value-free environment for the pupils to exercise freedom of choice. Many teachers talked about the motivational advantages of allowing pupils this freedom, and clearly felt that there were advantages in getting pupils, rather than the school, to take responsibility for any limitations which might arise later. The value of free choice was further supported by teachers' notions of the desirability of child-centred learning (see King, 1978; Carrington and Short, 1987; and Skelton and Hanson, this volume). Normally associated with primary education, child-centred learning encapsulates the idea that teachers should respond to children as unique individuals, and should avoid seeing them in collective terms. Some teachers at Millbridge found it quite confusing when asked to consider questions concerning the differential educational experience of girls and boys, and made comments such as:

> People are individuals. I don't even consciously think of male and female. (Mrs Lovell, Head of House and teacher of English)

> I teach characters, not sexes. (Miss Maple, Deputy Head and teacher of maths)

Despite these utterances, classroom observation and other comments made by the same teachers showed that gender was a significant factor in their interaction with pupils. The ideology of child-centredness, however, discouraged them from recognizing this and acting on this awareness. The rhetoric of option choice, stressing the importance of each individual pupil picking subjects to fit his or her own needs, also served to obscure the fact that a sifting process was at work leading to very different outcomes for different groups. As Kelly (1986) puts it, 'the strongly individualistic element in teachers' philosophy, with its emphasis on helping each child to fulfil her or his own potential, blinds them to the implications of their actions for groups.' Worthy as such approaches may be, they cannot form the basis of political action.

It is important to consider why younger women teachers were more likely to emphasize structural causes of gender differentiation in the curriculum and to argue that the school could play an important part in changing these patterns. Ideologies about gender, coupled with women teachers' experiences within the school power structure and within their own families, provided some clues here. Despite the fact that the only female Heads of Department at Millbridge were in French, home economics and secretarial studies, all the senior teachers said that they thought women and men did have equal chances of promotion. The reasons given for women's under-representation in senior positions were that they were not interested, or could not cope with the responsibilities. The male Director of Studies, Mr Spiller, had this to say: 'One has to ask is schoolteaching a job for people who cannot have total domestic support certainly above a scale 1 level?' Among the responsibilities of the senior teacher's wife he listed: 'entertaining official visitors, having parties or dinner parties for junior staff, through to making sure he's got a clean shirt in the morning.' This attitude effectively placed women in a no-win situation. If they were proper women and had babies they were unfit to be promoted because of their family responsibilities. If they did not have children and were promoted they were liable to be dismissed as unwomanly, neurotic and hence incompetent. The few women who were promoted at Millbridge were the butt of much criticism. All the male teachers whom I interviewed accepted uncritically that since women made a free choice to have children, they were making a clear statement about their lack of interest in a career. Mr Mottram, the Head of Physics at Millbridge, said:

> Women do break their service. They can hardly expect to pick up where they left off. Time's gone by and other people have taken their jobs. ... I wouldn't want my wife to go back to teaching when the children are 5 or 6 because I don't think she'd be able to do justice to both, being a mother and being a teacher. ... So in a sense I'd have thought that by having children my wife had compromised her teaching career, but I mean she's quite happy to do that.

This was a view repeated many times by male teachers, and reflects their belief that because women bear children, it is perfectly natural for them to take full responsibility for their upbringing, and their position in the workforce must be regarded as of only secondary importance. Again, a belief in the importance of free choice is used to conceal the power of structural forces shaping people's lives and to justify sexual inequality. Younger women, however, even those who would not identify themselves as feminist, were very much aware of the constraints imposed on their careers by the idea that women who are mothers cannot be proper workers. Mrs Dagworthy, a scale 2 home economics teacher, said:

> There's always that awful question at interviews. Have you a family? If not when are you going to start a family? How much

> time is this family going to take up? Especially in a county like Westshire the job would go to a man because they'd expect him to be able to give it more time, which is rubbish really.

It is perhaps because younger women teachers are constantly experiencing these contradictions that they are more aware than both men and senior women teachers of the way in which the school reinforces traditional gender divisions. Even among younger women teachers, however, there were still divisions. The key factor seemed to be whether the woman perceived herself as having made a conscious choice to put home and family before work. Mrs Plummer, a teacher of secretarial studies on scale 1, had no complaints about the position of women and men in the school, and felt that most women, like herself, were not really interested in promotion. When asked why there were more men than women in positions of responsibility, she said:

> There are more men here and more capable men. A lot of the women here aren't very interested. ... I would like to go up a scale but that's about all. I don't envy women who've got to the top, but there are some who've got there which shows it can be done. I don't think women should be given an easy life. If they're not interested they're not interested.

The fact that women do not share a common perspective on male/female power relations clearly makes it difficult for them to unite in challenging their unequal position. In turn, the lack of a unified political stance makes it difficult for individual women to challenge injustice.

Conclusion

I began this chapter by exploring the explanations offered by teachers for the production of a sex-stereotyped curriculum and the power which the school might have to challenge this outcome. Differences in teachers' response based on sex, age, position in the school hierarchy and subject taught were all noted. The precise effect of each of these factors was difficult to determine because they were often interrelated. Generally, however, older teachers, who were all members of the hierarchy, believed in the overwhelming power of external socializing influences. They did not see the school as involved in a channelling process, and felt that any attempt at positive discrimination to encourage girls into science and technology would undermine their freedom of choice. The fact that senior women teachers were just as adamant as the senior men that the school was essentially a neutral institution may have serious implications for the policy of working for change through getting more women into promoted positions. Younger teachers also emphasized the power of socialization, but indicated that processes in the school were involved as well, and a small number of feminist women teachers said that they thought the school could and should embark on a programme of positive discrimination. There was some indication that teachers of maths and technology were less likely to favour active programmes to counter sex-stereotyping than teachers of arts and humanities.

Why should teachers be so reluctant to accord the school any part in the production of gender differences? Teachers' ideologies were relevant here. Teachers tended to believe in the power of early socialization to determine pupils' outlooks. They also subscribed to child-centred ideologies, which led them to emphasize *individual* needs and in the process de-emphasize *group* experiences. Moreover, teachers' ideas about work and motherhood influenced their views on pupil intentions. As beneficiaries of male supremacy in the home and the school, there was little incentive for male teachers to reappraise their own attitudes. Only some of the younger women saw their own subordinate status as structurally caused, making women's solidarity very difficult to achieve.

Teachers' reluctance to examine the part played by their school in the perpetuation of gender divisions clearly has an impact on the effectiveness of equal opportunities legislation. Apart from a few isolated women teachers, there was little enthusiasm to enforce either the letter or the spirit of the law, and the implicit and explicit sexism of senior teachers was able to continue unimpeded.

References

CARRINGTON, B. and SHORT, G. (1987) 'Breakthrough to political literacy: Political education, antiracist teaching and the primary school', *Journal of Education Policy*, 3, 1, pp. 1–13.

KELLY, A. (1986) 'Gender differences in teacher-pupil interaction time: A meta-analytic review', Paper presented at the British Educational Research Association conference, University of Bristol.

KELLY, A. *et al.* (1985) 'Traditionalists and trendies: Teachers' attitudes to educational issues', *British Educational Research Journal*, 11, 2.

KING, R. (1978) *All Things Bright and Beautiful? A Sociological Study of Infants' Classrooms*, London, Wiley.

PAYNE, G., HUSTLER; D. and CUFF, T. (1984) *GIST or PIST: Teachers' Perceptions of the Project Girls Into Science and Technology*, Manchester Polytechnic.

PRATT, J. (1985) 'The attitudes of teachers', in WHYTE, J. *et al.* (Eds) *Girl Friendly Schooling*, London, Methuen.

PRATT, J., BLOOMFIELD, J. and SEALE, C. (1984) *Option Choice: A Question of Equal Opportunities*, Windsor, NFER-Nelson.

RIDDELL, S. (1988) *Gender and Option Choice in Two Rural Comprehensive Schools*, Unpublished PhD dissertation, School of Education, University of Bristol.

9

Women's Work in a Man's World: Secretarial Training in a College of Further Education

Edith Black

During the last decade a steady flow of ethnographic studies of primary and secondary schools has greatly enhanced our capacity to understand the culture of pupils and teachers in these settings. However, large areas of educational experience remain unexplored by ethnographers. For example, there have been few incursions into the corridors and classrooms of colleges of further education, and there is little published empirical work which documents and analyzes the day-to-day experience of being a female student or a female teacher in a college of further education. Feminist researchers (Blunden, 1982, 1983; Byrne, 1978; Further Education Unit, 1985; Wickham 1986) have been critical of the ways in which vocational courses in further education reproduce the sexual division of labour. I would not want to disagree with this criticism, but would suggest that ethnographic research in this neglected area would be a useful antecedent to any attempt to introduce feminist inspired reform into vocational education.

Riverbank College: Gender Divisions

The research on which this chapter is based is an ethnographic study of full-time secretarial training in Riverbank College, a college of further education in the south-west of England. All students and all teachers are female. I shall concentrate here on data collected in informal, unstructured interviews with the teachers whose lessons I observed during a period of fieldwork which began in September 1985 and continued throughout 1986 and 1987. The starting point for my research was an investigation of Deem's suggestion that the '... sexual division of labour and curricular differentiation between the sexes may actually be much greater in further education colleges than it is in schools' (Deem, 1980). Even a cursory examination of student enrolment patterns nationally (DES, 1986a) and the location of male and female teachers in colleges of further education (DES, 1986b) would demonstrate the accuracy of that statement.

Riverbank College is no exception to the national patterns. Curricular differentiation between the sexes, particularly on full-time vocational courses, has a high level of visibility. There are three curricular areas in which all full-time students are female: the Secretarial Section of the Department of Business and Professional Studies where students are being prepared to find employment as receptionists, general office workers, typists, audio-typists, shorthand-typists or secretaries; the Nursery Nurses Section of the Department of Humanities and Social Sciences where students follow a two-year, full-time course which prepares them to find posts as nannies; Pre-Nursing courses on which students acquire the necessary academic qualifications plus work placement experience which will lead into nursing training at various levels. In contrast all full-time students in the Department of Engineering and Building are male. There were two full-time female students in the department in 1986/87, but this was a rare occurrence and was the cause of much comment. After years of co-education in primary and secondary schools most students on full-time vocational courses find themselves in single-sex classrooms or workshops.

There has been much comment on the sexual division of labour in primary and secondary schools. The general pattern is that female teachers have a strong overall numerical presence in schools but they are proportionately under-represented in posts of responsibility. The sexual division of labour in colleges of further education has received very little analysis or comment (but see Bradley and Silverleaf, 1979; Byrne, 1978; Equal Opportunities Commission, 1984). Women teachers make up 78 per cent of the overall total of teachers in primary schools, 46 per cent of the total in secondary schools, but only 25.8 per cent of the total in colleges of further education (DES, 1986b). These figures alone suggest that in any analysis of the sexual division of labour and its impact on institutional processes it is essential to differentiate between the three levels of the educational system.

In Riverbank College all but one of the eight senior management posts (Principal, Vice-Principal, Heads of Department) are filled by men. The sole woman at this level is Head of the Department of Business and Professional Studies in which the Secretarial Section is located. Below this level there are four teaching grades: Principal Lecturer, Senior Lecturer, Lecturer Grade II and Lecturer Grade I. (As part of a recent pay award Lecturer II and Lecturer I scales have been consolidated into the single grade of Lecturer. However, differentials in status, pay and conditions of service have been maintained between those who held Lecturer II posts before the award and other Lecturers.) The first three grades usually carry some extra responsibility in addition to the normal teaching load. All three grades are dominated by men. Out of a total of forty-seven such posts only nine are filled by women. Five of these women work in curricular areas which are heavily 'feminized'.

In the college as a whole women make up 34.8 per cent of all full-time appointments. Compared with the national figure of 25.8 per cent this appears to be a relatively favourable state of affairs. However, this relative abundance of female teachers in the college is concentrated in the basic grade of Lecturer I, where women make up 53.9 per cent of the total. The national figure is 36.4 per cent.

The deep gender divisions observable in full-time student enrolment patterns on vocational courses are matched by the gender divisions in staffing patterns. All teachers in the Secretarial Section and in the Nursery Nurses Section are female. For the first time in the history of the college a woman was appointed to a full-time teaching post (Lecturer I) in the Department of Engineering and Building in 1987.

As in most colleges of further education, the boundaries of women's work in Riverbank College are very clearly marked. Not only are women teachers under-represented in positions of responsibility and disproportionately over-represented in the lowest grade posts but, like female students, they are generally to be found in single-sex enclaves within the college.

The close proximity of vocational courses to the labour market gives 'common-sense' support to the gender divisions in colleges of further education. Most colleges pride themselves on their close link with local industry and commerce; the purpose of vocational courses is to provide suitably qualified entrants into the local labour market. In her study of clerical training in two community colleges in Canada, Gaskell (1986) found that 'employability' was the dominant ideology. Similarly at Riverbank College the aim of the courses taught in the Secretarial Section is to enable students to find employment in a gender-specific sector of the labour market. The college prospectus gives details of the full-time courses in the section under the headings:

duration; entry requirements; subjects studied; examinations; prospects. The employment goal of students is clearly defined and the route to employment is equally well defined as the acquisition of appropriate skills identified and measured by the possession of the relevant examination certificates.

Feminists (Cockburn, 1987; Millman, 1985; Wickham, 1986) have been sharply critical of vocational education, including the new initiatives sponsored by the Manpower Services Commission (MSC) such as the Youth Training Scheme (YTS) and the Technical and Vocational Education Initiative (TVEI). Most of this criticism repeats well rehearsed 'equal opportunities' debates about girls' general education, simply extending these debates into vocational education. It is first noted that female students make subject and course choices that limit their occupational options to traditionally female sectors of the labour market. Then the usual remedial recommendation is that they should be encouraged to make non-stereotypical choices that will qualify them for employment in traditionally male areas. When teachers in colleges of further education are mentioned in these debates, they are generally regarded as being incorrigibly conservative in their attitude towards change (Millman, 1985; Wickham, 1986).

In the many feminist-inspired reform programmes which have been based in schools, for example the Girls Into Science and Technology (GIST) project, it is recognized that teachers have a vital role to play as agents of change (Kelly, 1985; Whyte, 1986). While there have been sympathetic attempts to understand why women teachers in schools might not be enthusiastic about such programmes (Acker, 1988; Burgess, 1987; Weiner and Arnot, 1987), women teachers in colleges of further education have not received such sympathetic attention. Millman (1985) states that further education teachers '... often have no knowledge of, or commitment to, basic equal opportunities issues.' A more appreciative analysis of the occupational culture of women teachers in colleges of further education is clearly called for. I have demonstrated that women teachers in Riverbank College are a relatively powerless *minority*. In an institution so heavily dominated by men, women are in a weak position from which to initiate feminist reform, no matter how deep their commitment to it.

Interview Data

By using data collected in informal interviews with teachers in the Secretarial Section, I shall next explore their perceptions of their work as teachers and their experience of the world of office work for which they are preparing students. I will argue that what might be regarded as the conservatism of these teachers cannot be explained simply by assuming their uncritical acceptance of the status quo.

Teachers as we know them from sociological studies of schools and schooling have followed familiar paths to qualified teacher status. The majority of them progressed directly from being pupils themselves into courses in higher education which, after a probationary year, gave them qualified teacher status. There are other, largely unexamined, routes into the profession.

In colleges of further education teachers on vocational courses are expected to have experience of the work for which they are preparing their students. All the teachers in the Secretarial Section whom I have interviewed so far began their working lives as office workers. During this first phase of paid employment they worked their way up through the intricate hierarchy of office work to become secretaries. The general pattern which followed was that this first phase of paid employment ended either on marriage or just before the birth of their first child. At some later stage (there are slight individual variations) they began a second phase of paid employment by teaching on a part-time basis, usually to evening classes. They all comment on the fact that teaching in the evening made it easier for them to combine paid employment with their child-care responsibilities. The third phase began as their children grew older and they felt able to take on an increased load of teaching which included some day-time teaching to full-time classes. The fourth phase is marked by their becoming established as full-time teachers. At various stages during the second, third or fourth phases they began to feel concern about their lack of qualified teacher status and worked assiduously to acquire the required qualifications, usually by the lengthy and arduous part-time route. This path into qualified teacher status is largely unexamined, as is its effect on the people who follow it, their self-perception and their work in the classroom.

The teachers I interviewed recognized the importance of their formal teacher qualifications and often gave up their own time to gain them by attending courses in the evening. However, they draw most of their authority as teachers from their period of paid employment as office workers. During my period of classroom observation I was struck by the frequency with which teachers made reference to their experience of office work either to illustrate a general point or, more often, to legitimate an instruction they were giving to students or a demand they were making of them.

During an interview one of them said, 'I'm glad I'm not a teacher who knows it just from books.' I asked her to explain what she meant.

> I came here as a teacher, as I told you before, from an office having done all these things. Because you can draw on experience and the tips you can give them, I can't think of an example now, but they're worth far more than all the things you read in text books. Just simple things. I think it gives them confidence too if they know you can say 'When I used to deal with the mail' or 'When I did this ...' You're not just a teacher who knows it just from text books. I think they respect you for having done it and as I've told you I started from a lowly office junior and worked up to a secretarial post, so I have done all these jobs in the past.

After leaving the local grammar school at 16 she began work as an office junior with the town's biggest industrial employer. She learned typing at work after working hours and took private lessons in shorthand. She said of the department in which she worked, 'It was very good training when I look back. I mean at the time the boss was a bit severe and I wasn't too keen on him, but I think the training was excellent. I worked up through that department. First of all I was office junior, then typist, then shorthand typist and eventually I became his secretary.' The repeated reference to the way she 'worked up' through the office hierarchy reflects her obvious pride in her hard work and sense of personal achievement. She also comments on the encouragement that was given to her to 'get on'. 'There was every incentive to get on. I've got loads and loads of certificates, because each time you passed a shorthand speed you had a [pay] rise. I've got 22 certificates in all.'

These statements have been extracted from a series of informal interviews with one teacher whom I shall call Christine. Data from interviews with other teachers in the section reveal the same pattern of working from the bottom to the higher levels of the office hierarchy as it exists for women. They all express the same sort of pride in their hard work and achievement. Christine, as the other teachers do, reflects on her technical skills and qualifications, her training 'on the job' and her experience in the office world. She is proud of all these elements of her life experience which make up her expertise as a teacher and legitimate her authority in the classroom. She has technical skills which she can pass on to her students. She also has the practical experience of success in the world for which she is preparing them.

While Christine recognizes the importance of technical skills in office work, she is also aware that employers demand a complex mix of technical skills and social skills or personal attributes.

> Half of these girls that come to us now, I think their parents put them into office work because they think they can't do anything else. I don't think they realize how difficult it is to learn shorthand you know, how much all-round knowledge you need to be a secretary and it's not just that ... I mean ... there are many jobs you've got to be quite clever for, but you don't need a personality to go with it. You could use computers and be a whizz kid working out all those programs and packages, but it wouldn't matter what you looked like or how you spoke. You could still do the job and get a high salary. But being a secretary, you've got to have it all the way round. If they go for interview, I know this is sexist, but more often than not they're going to be working for a man and it's pretty obvious if they're fat and slovenly that's not going to get them the job. They may be very clever, they may be able to do all the secretarial things, but they've got to. ... It's a status symbol for a boss to have a secretary and I bet if you were to ask, but about 75 per cent of men, men being what they are, would prefer someone who's sort of ... is a good advert for him and looks quite smart as well as having common sense and being able to greet customers politely. Some of these girls have got the wrong attitude. They think the world owes them a living. When you tell them they have to make coffee and things they find it unbelievable. So I think really good secretaries with everything are hard to find.

There is a clear recognition here that looks (including body shape) and demeanour have to be pleasing to the 'boss', who is assumed to be a man in most cases. It is also recognized that while a secretary is regarded as a status symbol by her male boss she will also have to perform menial tasks such as making coffee. The key comment here seems to be '... you've got to have it all the way round.' While there is some sense of the injustice of this state of affairs, more particularly when compared with what is demanded in other forms of employment, there is also a sense of pride and achievement conveyed in '... really good secretaries with everything are hard to find.'

Later in the interview she said: 'It sounds as though you have to be a paragon of virtue. It's one of the few jobs where you need so many all-round things, where perhaps appearance counts.' I asked her to define the 'all-round things' required in a good secretary by describing their presence or absence in a particular group of students.

> Sue is the one who had most of the assets. I think she looks the part, but perhaps some of her clothes, as were Jennifer's, were a bit too revealing which could go against her. High slits up her skirt. I think a boss wants them to be glamorous but not embarrassingly so. And perhaps low necks. I mean, perhaps I'm prudish but I would say they were probably too much that way, so I'd put that against Sue. But she was a very clean and attractive girl and her hair always looked very nice. She dressed here as she might in an office. She never came in trousers and perhaps, as I say, the low necks and slits ought to be out.

These comments on the dress code for office workers illustrate the skill required in recognizing the boundary between being attractive and even glamorous and yet not embarrassingly 'sexy'. It demands very fine judgment indeed, particularly as such a boundary exists in the eye of the beholder.

Comments on dress were followed by comments on the attendance record of this particular group of students. They were mature students on a full-time Training Opportunities Scheme (TOPS) course sponsored by the Manpower Services Commission. Several of them had school-age children.

> ... if you look at the register this year, there's probably only one person who hasn't been away at all. That's bad as far as I'm concerned. You can't help the sort of health you've got, but I've worked all the time through having young children and I've been absent two days in 18 years. OK, I've been lucky with health, but to me they're absent far more than I'd expect an employee to be absent. I mean if they have young children ... they were told before they came on the course that if they had young children and they didn't have anyone to look after them they shouldn't start. I've been through this myself. You've got to make sure you've got firm arrangements and therefore I'd criticize them all along those lines.

However, Sue scored high on punctuality and attendance compared with her peers. 'She was punctual always. That was a great asset. She attended the course for I should think at least 95 per cent of the time. With young children to look after and comparing her with the others, that was good.' Only after these comments on dress, punctuality and attendance was any comment made on this student's technical skills. 'And obviously she was very good at the skills. She was a good typist and she was one of the few who passed audio-typing with distinction, so she was very good there.'

Not many employers would disagree with Christine's account of the personal qualities and skills required in a good secretary. In the assessment of their students, teachers adopt the employer's perspective. During the interview in which I was probing for Christine's definition of the perfect secretary she readily named Sue as the student who had 'most of the assets'. When I asked for her definition of these assets, she hesitated for some time and then said, 'Shall I be really personal and talk about her as though I was interviewing her?' It seemed as though she could more easily give me the definitions I was pressing her for if she projected herself into the role of the prospective employer.

The teachers I have interviewed can see the unfairness of many of the demands and expectations of employers, and spontaneously articulated them to me in interview. One teacher spoke of the responsibility she had carried as a secretary and the great pressure she had worked under, but as she spoke it was obvious that she also took pride in her ability to cope with these burdens.

> Not only did I do his personal typing but I had to supervise the typing that other typists in the department would do. You are under pressure and you carry the can. It's not just that these three letters have to go out at 5.30 but they have to be checked and they have to be correct. You sign the copy to prove you've checked it. *You* carry the can if that letter goes out wrong, not the boss who signs it. It's your job to check that letter. If he's got a good secretary he ought to be able to ... he ought not to have to read it through. He ought to be able to sign each letter and guarantee that his secretary is good enough to make sure they're all going out without any typing errors.

She did, however, express her dissatisfaction with the low level of pay for the high level of responsibility.

> And you find it's a very demanding job and very unfairly paid for what you do. As secretary I'd guarantee that I'd work harder than anybody else in his department and probably harder than the boss most of the time. He had all the trips but you did all the arranging of them. Even now you'd probably get paid at least a couple of thousand less than the people in the department you were doing all the work for.

None of these dissatisfactions emerges in the classroom. In well over 300 hours of classroom observation I have not heard any teacher express criticism of the status quo while in the presence of students.

Discussion

It would be impossible to deny that the sexual division of labour is being reproduced here. The gender divisions of the labour market meet with no challenge in Riverbank College either at the level of institutional structures or pedagogical practice. Students are not being trained to be critical of the world of office work; they are being trained in the technical and social skills that will enable them to compete successfully for a place in that world as it is. Yet the interview data demonstrate that the teachers themselves have a critical awareness of the unfair demands and unequal rewards of office work. How can we then explain their apparently willing complicity in the cycle of reproduction?

I will draw out two themes from the data that might be useful in proposing an answer to this question. The first is that the pedagogical practice of these teachers has a rational basis. They *know* the office world from their own experience of it. They know that its economic and status rewards are unequally distributed. They know that sexist attitudes and prejudices pervade its terms and conditions of employment. They also know where power resides. A rational strategy for survival in these circumstances is that of accommodation to perceived limits and constraints. The second theme is their perception of secretarial work as a highly skilled occupation. They are proud of their skills and speak with enthusiasm of the pleasure they derive from teaching what are described as the 'skill subjects': typing, audio-typing, shorthand, word-processing. In their pedagogical style they transmit their definition of these subjects as intricate skills which can only be acquired by dedication and application. These two themes indicate that we cannot regard the actions of the teachers simply as 'willing complicity' in the cycle of reproduction. The use of the reproduction metaphor is too much of a blunt instrument to explain adequately the complex processes at work here. The close relationship between the labour market and colleges of further education makes them very different institutions from schools. The sharp realities of the labour market are reflected not only in the institutional structures of colleges but also in the much deeper levels of 'common-sense' understandings of appropriate pedagogical goals and practice. Gaskell (1986) points out that '... the usual feminist response to vocational training has been to call for less gender segregation, particularly getting more women into the higher paying, more masculine programmes.' While this is true, there is also a growing awareness in the literature (Cockburn, 1987; Wickham, 1986; Yates, 1985) that extending the 'equal opportunities' philosophy into vocational education also extends the range and complexity of the problems to be solved. The realities of the labour market and employers' attitudes form one end of this problem spectrum; at the other end is the implicit devaluation of the work done by women teachers in 'feminized' curricular areas of colleges.

Conclusion

Before feminist inspired proposals for reform are extended into vocational education it is essential that more research is carried out in colleges of further education. However, this research should adopt an appreciative rather than a critical stance. It is too easy to blame teachers for their apparent lack of concern about or commitment to equal opportunities issues. A more sympathetic understanding of their occupational culture and the institutions within which they work is called for. There are many lessons yet to be learned about the limits and possibilities of educational reform, and some of them could be learned from an exploration of the experience of female teachers and their students on vocational courses in colleges of further education.

References

ACKER, S. (1988) 'Teachers, gender and resistance', *British Journal of Sociology of Education*, 9, 3, pp. 307–22.

BLUNDEN, G. (1982) *Women's Place in Non-Advanced Further Education: The Early Development of Three Colleges in the South-West of England*, Unpublished PhD thesis, University of Bristol.

BLUNDEN, G. (1983) 'Typing in the tech: Domesticity, ideology and women's place in Further Education', in Gleeson, D. (Ed.) *Youth Training and the Search for Work*, London, Routledge and Kegan Paul.

BRADLEY, J. and SILVERLEAF, J. (1979) *Making the Grade*, Slough, National Foundation for Educational Research.

BURGESS, R. G. (1987) 'Something you learn to live with? Gender and inequality in a comprehensive school', Paper prepared for the Ethnography and Inequality conference, St Hilda's College, Oxford, September 1987.

BYRNE, E. M. (1978) *Women and Education*, London, Tavistock Publications.

COCKBURN, C. (1987) *Two-Track Training: Sex Inequalities and the YTS*, London, Macmillan.

DEEM, R. (1980) 'Women, school and work', in DEEM, R. (Ed.) *Schooling for Women's Work*, London, Routledge and Kegan Paul, pp. 177–83.

DEPARTMENT OF EDUCATION AND SCIENCE (1986a) *Statistics of Education: Further Education*, London, HMSO.

DEPARTMENT OF EDUCATION AND SCIENCE (1986b) *Statistics of Education: Teachers in Service England and Wales*, London, HMSO.

EQUAL OPPORTUNITIES COMMISSION (1984) *Formal Investigation Report: Ebbw Vale College of Further Education*, Manchester, Equal Opportunities Commission.

FURTHER EDUCATION UNIT (1985) *Changing the Focus: Women and FE*, London, Further Education Unit.

GASKELL, J. (1986) 'Gender and class in clerical training', Paper prepared for the conference on Women and Education, University of British Columbia, Vancouver, June.

KELLY, A. (1985) 'Changing schools and changing society: Some reflections on the Girls Into Science and Technology project', in ARNOT, M. (Ed.) *Race and Gender*, London, Pergamon Press.

MILLMAN, V. (1985) 'The new vocationalism in schools: Its influence on girls', in WHYTE, J. *et al.* (Eds) *Girl Friendly Schooling*, London, Methuen.

WEINER, G. and ARNOT, M. (1987) 'Teachers and gender politics', in ARNOT, M. and WEINER, G. (Eds) *Gender and the Politics of Schooling*, London, Hutchinson.

WHYTE, J. (1986) *Girls Into Science and Technology: The Story of a Project*, London, Routledge and Kegan Paul.

WICKHAM, A. (1986) *Women and Training*, Milton Keynes, Open University Press.

YATES, L. (1985) 'Is "girl friendly schooling" really what girls need?' in WHYTE, J. *et al.* (Eds) *Girl Friendly Schooling*, London, Methuen.

10
Gender Joking in the Staffroom

Sheila Cunnison

Introduction

This chapter draws on data collected during three months' observation among the staff of a mixed-sex senior comprehensive school. The data are interpreted in the light of interviews with the headteachers and a sample of staff from sixteen other senior schools in the same city. Gender joking, for the most part initiated by men and aimed at women, was a fairly common sport in the staffrooms of the school. There was one large staffroom, plus minor ones attached to school 'houses' and to the maths and science departments. Some staffrooms were noted for gender joking; some people were especially prone to make gender jokes; some men and women and some groups of men and women engaged in joking often enough for a structured joking relationship to be identifiable (Radcliffe-Brown, 1952).

The aim is to analyze the role played by gender joking in maintaining the comparative success of men and failure of women in obtaining promotion within the school management hierarchies. In focusing on gender joking this chapter addresses an area which, as Delamont (1980, p. 81) and more recently Ball (1987, pp. 191–211) have pointed out, has been largely overlooked in the sociological analysis of staffroom humour (e.g., Woods, 1979, pp. 210–36).

My starting point is that the teachers in the school stand in a basically competitive relationship with one another in regard to promotion. The nature of hierarchy means that some must be more successful than others, and the limitation on resources that many have to remain for some time on the bottom scale.

My second point is that these teachers are part of a society where gender is an important principle of social differentiation, a society where men are more closely identified with the world of paid work, and women with that of home and family, although both are seen as having a role to play in each sphere. It is a society in which men are dominant, filling most positions of authority in public life, able to command higher earnings than women and thus to control the major part of family income.

Teachers believe strongly in the importance of professional training; in their view, and that of their professional associations, a qualification in the practice and theory of teaching is necessary for the job. In this sense teachers think of one another and assess one another by professional standards. Gender, race, class — all common ways people have of pigeonholing one another — should be, by these criteria, irrelevant. Race was not an issue in this school: there was only one black teacher and two or three black pupils. Class is of far greater significance in the analysis of relations between teachers and pupils than among teachers. Here I confine my analysis to the role of gender. I suggest that the practice of assessing one another by stereotypical gender roles is so deeply embedded in our society that it pervades most social situations, including those of work, regardless of whether it is formally appropriate.

An examination of hierarchies of pay and authority within the school reveals gender to be a major correlate of social positions there. There were forty-two women and sixty-eight men; 51 per cent of women but only 29 per cent of men were on the lowest scale (scale 1); only 10 per cent of women but 19 per cent of men were on scale 4 and upwards. I am interested in the social processes by which we move from the general beliefs about women's and men's roles in the family to a specific work situation: one in which men occupy most of the well-paying jobs, while women are disproportionately on the lowest salary scales. In particular I am interested in the part played by gender joking in these processes.

This chapter begins with a discussion of the processes of gender joking as a means by which women are kept in this subordinate position. This is done by analyzing specific social situations of gender joking and the more broadly structured relationships between jokers and their targets. Following this there is a discussion of responses of women to joking.

Patterns of Gender Joking

I use the term 'gender joking' to refer to jokes which have a gender content and are made across gender lines. Such jokes are usually initiated by men and take place in front of an audience, usually within staffrooms, and thus constitute a public performance.

Jokes Focusing on Femininity

Joking referred most commonly to women's appearance and thus to conventional ideas about gender and femininity. Such joking has been interpreted elsewhere as acting to control sexuality in situations where its expression is considered to be inappropriate (Radcliffe-Brown, 1952; Sykes, 1966). It does this by preventing people from taking sexual attraction seriously. Certainly sexuality is a force to be reckoned with in schools (as in work situations generally). There was, in one of the staffrooms where I was an observer, an inordinately pretty young woman teacher, already married. She attracted a great deal of attention from the men; they could not keep their eyes off her, nor stifle their comments. 'Bruised your feet have you?' said one bending over to peer at her toenails painted a shade of purple-grey. 'That does look bad!' 'Bleeding yesterday weren't they?' he chuckled, referring to yesterday's brilliant carmine, and went happily to his seat. No offence intended, and none taken. The woman was an Irish Catholic, and the same joker managed on another occasion to mix sex and religion in his staffroom jests, so directing his remarks to this woman. In a discussion which started off about a school named after a saint, he went on to ask her what extraordinary saints there were in her church and then to weave a fantasy about a 'St Gonad', the patron saint of sex. He had the staffroom doubled up with laughter. Standing up with arms stretched outwards in the form of a cross, he demanded to know whether her church indeed had such a saint.

Both incidents can be seen as defusing sexual tension. But the first had another consequence. It is representative of countless unremarkable incidents, all of which draw attention to the fact that these teachers are *women* teachers, not just teachers. Another example was when a woman raising funds for the PTA asked people to estimate the time she would take to run a mile. One man she approached responded that he would rather estimate the size of her bust. Because attention is thus continually drawn to their sex or femininity, women teachers can never escape from their gender but become associated, whether they will or not, with a stereotyped idea of woman, carrying notions of conventional femininity, and implicitly (as described below), of lesser competence and lesser commitment to the job.

Not all sexual joking was good humoured. Some jokes did not just define teachers as women, but appeared intended as put-downs. For instance, a rather stout, mature woman teacher was talking about using curtains to make costumes for amateur theatre. A man chipped in 'Should think you'd find it hard to get a pair to go round you!' It was a ludicrous exaggeration. Nevertheless, she responded to the underlying insult and left the room. He expressed surprise and ridiculed her inability to take a joke.

Jokes Focusing on Domesticity

A great many men's jokes referred to the domestic role of women, running monotonously along the line that 'woman's place is in the home'. Such jokes do not appear to be a control on sexuality. Instead they act as mechanisms for the control or subordination of women at work. They carry the message that women do not really belong at work, their proper place is in the home, that their supposed incompetence is an inevitable result of their being 'out of place'. Women in positions of responsibility found that they only had to make a small slip and it was 'back to the kitchen sink!' One of the two assistants to a house head described how her mistakes were always greeted thus, but that nothing equivalent was ever said to the other, male, assistant house head. She thought this particularly unfair as he played the traditional part of carer in his family, taking time off work to accompany his sick child to hospital appointments.

Other domestic jokes referred to reproduction. For example, an assistant house head came into the staffroom with information about mock interviews to be held as a training exercise for those seeking promotion. His opposite number, a woman, asked to see the information. He handed it over but as he did so growled at her, 'What do *you* want it for? Women are only fit for breeding.' She took it in silence. It is notable that her promotion prospects looked better than his.

A major source of the power of these jokes in subordinating women is that they referred to a cultural stereotype or ideal image of women that was largely shared by both sexes. Women did care what they looked like; they did want to be sexually attractive; most did want or had had children; most wanted to or had looked after their children in the early years; most earned less than their mates and if anyone was to stay at home it made sense for them to do so. But though women subscribed to the stereotype they did not consider it relevant to their teaching.

Making Fun of Women

There was another kind of joking. Near the end of term there was a staff party after school. It began with games and silly games: with tennis, football, a tug-of-war, a canoe race, etc. People wore whatever they wanted, mostly jeans and sweaters. Some went in for fancy dress, and two of the men dressed up as women. Both presented women as figures of fun: one, a canoeist, was a caricature of a tart with short black skirt, black fishnet tights, a wig and lurid make-up; what the other was meant to represent was unclear — he rushed around the school grounds on a little scooter, clad in a long dress with an elaborate wig and painted face. None of the women represented themselves as men.

Structures of Authority

Who initiates gender joking and why? To answer this question we must examine structures of authority in the school, the place of women and men within them, the promotion policy of the head and the teachers' perceptions of this policy.

Hierarchy and Gender

The formal management structure, as generally accepted and as revealed by the inteviews carried out within the city senior schools, is in the shape of a broadly-based pyramid. At the base are the many scale 1 teachers, at the apex a single head. This structure is best conceived of as comprising two separate hierarchies, one carrying more weight than the other: the more important is the hierarchy for 'mainstream' or subject administration, dealing with mainly internal matters such as curriculum, timetable and examinations; the lesser hierarchy is that of pastoral administration dealing with personal development, truancy, discipline, careers and relations with the community. The mainstream hierarchy moves up through department head, faculty head and deputy head and leads to the post of headteacher. At each stage the hierarchy narrows, and prospects of moving on diminish. Experience of mainstream administration is almost a prerequisite for becoming a headteacher.

The pastoral route which leads up through assistant house head and house head tends to stop at deputy. Men find it rather difficult to make the move from house head to deputy and also, with a pastoral background, difficult to move from deputy to head. For women the situation is different. The move from house head to deputy is not so difficult, but the role which the woman deputy is expected to fulfil is usually highly circumscribed, limited to girls' discipline, or, as one head rudely put it, 'tampax and tea'. Women deputies who wanted to gain experience of mainstream administration told me how they had been deliberately excluded from areas of timetabling and curriculum. For women seeking promotion the pastoral route is that most often followed. Men teachers tended to see this as more 'appropriate' for women, presumably because it did not lead along the central corridors of school power, nor to the headship. In general men seeking promotion have two main options, subject or pastoral administration, while women have only one. However, where subjects are taught almost exclusively by women (e.g., domestic science), women are almost invariably appointed within the subject administrative hierarchy at least to the level of department head.

However, there is a status ranking among subjects, and teachers who specialize in low ranking subjects are rarely appointed to the position of school head or even deputy. Technical studies, along with business administration and domestic science were ranked the lowest. Academic subjects, especially science, maths or English, ranked the highest. Thus though the head in the school observed was a geographer, two deputies were scientists, one a mathematician; of the senior teachers (a promotion awarded for outstanding contribution to the school) one was a scientist, one an English and one a classics teacher. Men from low status subjects usually tried to make their way up the pastoral hierarchy.

Promotion Policy of the Head and Teachers' Responses

The promotion policy of the head in the school observed was subject to both external and internal controls. The Burnham Committee which controlled teachers' pay at this time had set out certain rules for the allocation of scale points within schools. Scale posts ranged from 1 at the bottom to 5 at the top. Except for senior teacher level (equivalent to scale 5) points were not supposed to be awarded for outstanding merit as teachers, but for taking on particular responsibilities. Formally, therefore, teachers were only promoted to a higher scale for taking on extra responsibilities. Certain responsibilities were clearly part of the structure, for example, faculty, department and house. Others were tangential to the main structure, for example, remedial work within departments, film studies, science resources. The head was able to decide what these responsibilities should be, and thus he could, at least at the lower limits, promote as he wished. Promotion has since become subject to greater control by the local authority.

The head described his promotion policy as seeking to reward the 'good all round schoolmaster', 'the teacher who contributes more to the school than just teaching his subject'. There were in his experience very few 'all round schoolmistresses', though he was able to name one in his own school. He also preferred graduates.

His ability to reward good teachers was constrained by the Burnham rules, the number of scale points available to him (these were allocated to schools according to number and ages of their pupils), by market forces and by the need to maintain the management structure of the school. There were shortage subjects such as physics where the school was in competition with industry and in which teachers could command high salaries. The market rate had to be paid. It then made sense to appoint highly paid teachers to management posts. It may help explain why one each of the three deputy heads and the three senior teachers were physicists, and why of eighteen teachers on scale 4 and over, five were scientists, but only three were English and three maths teachers.

Maintaining the management structure of the school was important. When people in crucial positions threatened to leave, the head needed to have a few scale points in hand to try and tempt them to stay or, failing that, to employ a replacement. In the summer of 1978 a maths teacher who could also teach economics and who had already made several applications to other schools was promoted because the head felt the school could not afford to lose him. The year before a drama teacher, an expert in costume design who had been offered a job elsewhere, was even appointed to head of needlework, a previously all-female department. He was a skilled tailor and costumier and played an important role in school shows. It is perhaps worth noting that a higher salary can tempt a man to stay in his job, but a pregnant woman cannot be bribed not to have a baby.

Within the limits set by market forces and management demands, the head tried to be fair to departments and individuals. Teachers, however, saw the promotion process in a different light. They saw it as, in part, open to negotiation, using that term in its widest sense. One of the duties of the head of faculty was to keep the head informed of how teachers were developing and what they were contributing to school life. The head also generally saw teachers individually once a term, thus giving them an opportunity to broach the subject of promotion. Many did so, in most schools men more than women, although in this school the head reported an equal proportion. Teachers also approached the head on their own initiative, giving him what they considered relevant information: about getting married, taking on a mortgage, having or deciding against having a baby, etc. More men than women were reported to do so. Teachers could also attract the head's attention through successful participation in sport and drama, or unconventional presentations in school assemblies.

The major complaint of teachers about the promotion system was not about fairness, although some women thought the head favoured men. It was about the secrecy with which scale points were handed out: sometimes teachers awarded scales were asked to keep quiet for a while. Furthermore, teachers were convinced that the formal responsibilities which they were assigned when given a scale were not the contributions for which the scale was awarded. Both secrecy and the mismatch of named responsibilities with actual reasons for promotion opened up possibilities for favouritism and discrimination thus encouraging competitiveness and hostility among staff.

Structures of Joking and the Messages They Carry

Blocked Men versus Ambitious Women

Was there a connection between joking, management structure and promotion prospects? Two staffrooms were noted for gender joking, one of the lower school houses and the science department. Within the former an almost ritualized pattern of joking had become established, certain men initiating and certain women responding. The leader in this was the head of house, a scale 4 teacher, an ambitious man with considerable organizing ability. His house was tightly organized and highly competitive. He wanted eventually to have a school of his own, but he had no degree. In the contemporary climate of growing teacher unemployment this was a distinct disadvantage. To improve his chances this man was doing a part-time psychology degree. Soon, however, he might be in the category of being 'too old'. His further promotion prospects did not look very good.

His assistant, a woman, provided a contrast. She was a very successful teacher. Still in her 20s, with a BEd degree and on a scale 2, her promotion prospects were excellent. She hoped to become a headteacher or a deputy. It is well known that few women apply for senior positions in schools. Yet most schools feel they need one or two women in senior positions to undertake pastoral work, though (as mentioned earlier) they often deliberately excluded them from mainstream school management. This woman's preference was in any case for pastoral work.

Her ability and her ambition had made her known to other teachers in the school. Some, men as well as women, admired her; others resented her. One man who had watched her conducting house assemblies and other house business thought her the 'ideal *woman* teacher', firm and not easily ruffled, able to keep good discipline and yet with a sense of humour. Another who deeply resented her kept jokingly referring to her as SOB (her name was Brown) with the connotation bitch. A woman teacher criticized her temperament as being cold, that is, in conventional terms unfeminine, and suggested that her future as a woman high up in the male hierarchy would be lonely and isolated, adding, however, that her marriage and interest in sport might save her from such a fate. This observation reveals how some women teachers still see themselves as having a choice about whether to remain feminine or to go for promotion. The assistant house head herself thought that women were judged more stringently than men, and by different standards. She had heard herself unfavourably described as a 'hard woman who ought to have a baby to soften her up', whereas her comment on hearing this was that a 'hard' man was thought of favourably, as 'a man who could hold a class'.

The joking was initiated mainly by the house head and directed to his assistant. It took the form of exaggerated claims about the mental and physical inferiority of women: their smaller brains which limited their understanding of politics and the like, their smaller lung capacity which made them peculiarly suited to housework. The assistant invariably took up the challenge and responded with equally absurd counter-assertions. And so the joking insults travelled back and forth. As the jokes became ritualized so others joined in: two of the more ambitious men in support of the house head; two women who were committed to moving up the hierarchy in support of the assistant. The exaggerated nature of the jokes meant they could not be taken seriously. So any aim of putting down the women by presenting them as biologically and inevitably inferior was not achieved. But gender became a big issue and female teachers were firmly labelled as women.

The joking relationship developed here copes with the perceived threat to men of women in authority. The seriousness behind the joking was shown in the men's attitudes to staffroom darts. The darts record showed that women were as good as men, but still the men insisted that they win. If two women played one another it did not matter who won. But if one of the women played a man and beat him, and then the two women played one another, the man would want the woman who had triumphed over him to win. 'Men will accept us as equal or subordinate, but they hate to admit us as superior', was one woman's comment.

Women's Place Is Rearing Children

Another incident illustrates the same pattern of gender joking, that between a man whose advance is blocked and a woman who intends to get ahead, but the implicit message put across by the joke is more specific.

The summer term is a period of high tension as far as promotion is concerned. Points are released for new promotions as teachers hand in their notice, the men to leave for better jobs, the women to have babies or to follow their husbands. (In summer 1978 five men left from this school for better jobs, four women to have babies and two women to follow their men.)

I was an observer in a fifth form house at the time. The teachers in the staffroom were on tenterhooks waiting to see who would be 'lucky', who would be promoted. One man, a scale 2 teacher and an assistant to the house head, was particularly uptight. In his early 30s and ambitious, he worked in the technical studies department. He was quite tall and well built, and known as one of the 'heavies' — a man whose presence carried a threat of physical violence. Violence against 'kids', as they were called, was reputed to go on in technical studies. There were devices such as the 'Magic Circle', a chalk circle drawn around the feet of a standing child who was then threatened with dire consequences should he step outside. Teachers working in adjoining rooms claimed they had heard kids' heads being banged against the wall. This man had described to us how he used his own head to butt and inflict unmarked injury. However, he was a competent teacher of his subject and he could keep order.

He was also highly articulate with a gift for irony. But he was an angry man. He watched and noted as other teachers were promoted, some of whom had lesser service, were not so competent in class, had poorer attendance records or just could not keep order, and some of whom were women. His simmering anger showed in bitter attacks on those who succeeded in being promoted. But the bitterness was softened by humour. The attacks also touched a general resentment in the staffroom arising from the current squeeze on promotion. As a result the staffroom was willing to ignore the bitterness and laugh with him.

One afternoon he was in a specially angry mood. The trigger this time was that he was to join a different house. Each year a proportion of teachers was re-assigned to different houses. He was to leave our rather cosy staffroom for one with a markedly competitive atmosphere (noted for its gender joking as well as its competitiveness), and a disciplinarian and authoritarian house head. He did not want to go; he felt trapped; he paced around the room. 'It's all right for you', he moaned to two women from PE. 'But I'm in it for life. You can get out any time.' Then he leaned over one of them: 'I don't want to embarrass you', he said, 'but your husband doesn't lay on you heavily enough. You can be out by Christmas if you try!' It was taken in silence. He didn't stop his needling. As she got up to go, he pointed to her shoes, a kind of clog then fashionable, with woven leather uppers attached to wooden soles. 'Used to be lobster pots did they love?' he said. And then as she opened the door to go, 'Got your mother's dress on have you dear?' referring to a fashionable lacey creation she had on in place of the usual PE shorts and sweatshirt. The PE teacher merely smiled and went on her way.

The man in this case was clearly handicapped by being in technical studies. In his wildest dreams he could not hope for a school of his own. 'How many heads of schools do you know who used to teach tech studies?' 'None!' he answered himself. In recent years the search for 'technically literate' school leavers has made tech studies, particularly when combined with design, a much more respectable subject. In 1978 this movement was only beginning. 'Have you noticed', he said to me, 'tech studies is three feet lower than the rest of the school?' and indeed you had to go downhill to get to it. 'They've only lately let us come into the staffroom', he said. 'They used to expect us to brew up in our glue-pots!' The paradox of being in a male and macho department and yet unlikely to move up what is essentially a *male* hierarchy of school management was extremely frustrating.

The PE teacher, in contrast, was quite likely to move up from scale 1 to scale 2, thereby, in the eyes of the man, eating up one more scale point which could have come to him. Married to a lawyer, she was already financially better off than the man, whose wife was a junior school teacher. Furthermore she had no intention of starting a family for some years: she wanted to progress in her career.

The likelihood of her promotion was increased by the situation within her department. The distribution of scale points within PE was acknowledged to be unfair. The department consisted of four men and four women. Together the men held 8 points, the women only 6. Three women, all of whom had been at the school for several years, were still on scale 1. In the event the head decided that he could not afford three points for one department, and that it would be invidious to choose between the three people on scale 1. None was promoted. A year later the PE teacher left for another school and scale 2. The other two scale 1 women left to have babies.

Messages — Explicit and Implicit

The explicit message in this incident is that women are at an advantage compared with men: they have a choice not open to men; at a certain period of her life a married woman can stop work, stay at home and rear a family, becoming financially dependent on her man. The implicit messages are two. First, that men have responsibility for supporting women and children and, as such, a 'natural' right to a 'family wage', to more money than women, and within teaching more right to be promoted. Second, that women do not have the same rights in promotion nor — as a logical conclusion — the same right to a job as men: their primary role is elsewhere, in the home. When the going gets tough they can opt out.

These messages are powerful. In the first place they refer to a stereotypical ideal of family relationship widely propagated throughout the media: of a breadwinning man out at work and a dependent wife at home looking after small children. Second, even though this stereotype refers to only one phase in women's lives, it is a pattern familiar to many, especially middle-class professional or semi-professional people where husbands earn a reasonable salary. Almost all of the married women earned less than their husbands. All those with children had taken time out of work at least until their children were in primary school. With one exception all the childless women who intended to have children also intended to stay at home and look after them.

In suggesting that the PE teacher should stay at home the man raised the whole question of women's 'career break', the time lost from school while raising a family. The career break is conventionally seen as a major reason for women's failure to be promoted to higher scale posts (Hilsum and Start, 1974; NUT, 1980). The validity of this view in the case of primary teachers is questioned by Evetts in a paper in this volume.

Women who take a career break are perceived as putting domestic interests before their jobs as teachers. Hence they are defined as being less committed to the job and less worthy of promotion than men. If, on return, they seek part-time work, the lack of commitment is held to be self-evident because part-time teachers cannot be fully integrated into school life. As a result they are hardly ever promoted beyond scale 1. It could well be argued that a woman with child-care and domestic responsibilities who undertakes the further responsibility of teaching shows a very high level of commitment to the job. However, men and headteachers tend not to argue in this way. The banter in school staffrooms reinforces women's limited options. It helps structure a reality wherein promotion and femininity are seen as mutually exclusive.

Women's Responses

Gender joking is one, but only one, mechanism by which a particular stereotype or conventional image of women is attached to women teachers. In this section I consider how women respond first to the joke itself and second to the stereotype which is the burden of the message. For those who see their lives in stereotypical terms, joking poses a threat only so far as the hostility which lies behind it is perceived and resented. But for those who wish to distance themselves from the stereotype, joking is a threat, ever redefining them in terms they do not accept. Three different kinds of response can be distinguished: silence, playing along with the joke, or deliberately challenging the stereotype — through joking or in other ways.

Silence

In this school, with two men to every woman, joking took place in a male-dominated situation. More often than not it was hostile; frequently received in silence, though sometimes with facial expressions ranging from resignation through exasperation to scorn. Failure to challenge, by look or by speech, inevitably lent some degree of credence to the message. Yet it was difficult to respond. Because the hostility in any joke is veiled by humour, the joker is always able to deny any serious intention. Moreover, any serious rejoinder, as with the woman who left the room, was likely to be greeted with ridicule. Rather than be serious it was safer to be silent — with the inevitable consequence that silence would most likely be interpreted as consent.

Playing Along

Another possibility was to return the joke. Two different kinds of return joking could be distinguished, playing along and counter-joking. Both required a quick wit and an ability not to take offence. Both refused to acknowledge the serious message behind the joke, and thus refused to accept the put-down. One example of playing along occurred at the end of a busy day, when two house tutors, a woman and man, were leaving their departmental office. It had been taken over temporarily by the head of business studies who had been toiling all day over a new reprographics machine. He deeply resented having to spend time on such matters. Now, in addition, he had to work late. He looked at the woman as she put her coat on. 'Back to the kitchen sink where you belong!' he said, on the principle of 'kicking the cat'. She replied with a complaint that he had not yet reproduced some work sheets which she had handed him that morning. 'No', he said 'I've been too busy doing stuff for the Boss. I would have done it for you if you'd given me a flash', he added. 'You didn't ask me!' she said laughing. 'Didn't I?' he said 'I must have been drunk.' This woman's response did not directly challenge the gender element of the joking. But by introducing a professional dimension it defused the emphasis on gender. Furthermore it prevented the gender joke being used as a personal put-down.

The woman who responded in this way was to outward appearance quite conventional. She was also calm and humorous, and well liked by both sexes. Her general strategy for the advancement of her career was not to challenge gender conventions openly, but to make use of whatever advantages her sex gave her. Her conventional demeanour combined with competence in and out of class indicated a career in pastoral administration in the traditional area of girls' problems. Once in such a post she hoped to expand the frontiers of her job. A couple of years later she was appointed elsewhere as a deputy head, leap-frogging over the position of house head.

Challenging the Stereotype

There were several ways of challenging the stereotype. One was counter-joking, already illustrated in the ritualized pattern of joking that had emerged in one of the staffrooms (see pp. 158–9). In that staffroom the woman who figured most prominently in the joking exchanges also herself initiated joking directed against the stereotype of woman as housewife and mother.

In a comic monologue she disclaimed any liking for children: 'I can't stand babies', she said, 'When there's a baby the whole house smells of regurgitated food; it gets into the carpets and even into the walls. Children are best avoided until they are 3 and then it's best to see them for only three hours a day.' 'I don't really like them after they're 3 either, not until they're about 17, then I enjoy them. That's why I teach in senior school.' 'I would hate to teach in primary school', she said, 'It would be all yucky, tying shoe laces and taking them to the lavatory. At that stage they get their underwear outside their outerwear. I wouldn't like sorting that out. I'd just sit them on a stool and tell the class to laugh at them.' So, exhibiting a certain amount of hostility, she distanced herself from the stereotype of the maternal woman clucking over children and babies.

Another time she mocked the housewives on the new estate where she lived. 'I go out at eight in the morning and shut the door. You hear a hundred doors shutting and a hundred wives saying "Goodbye darling! Have a good day!" And I thank God I go out to work. And when I come walking home in the evening with my briefcase I can see people in windows watching, thinking "Ah she must be funny. She goes out to work." And I thank God that I do.' Both accounts caused smiles in the staffroom. At the same time they stated unequivocally that this woman teacher was different from other women, her priorities lay not in the home but with her job. She had no intention of staying home to start a family. She was a teacher.

Ridiculing the Male Chauvinist

Another possibility involved mild ridicule of men. One feminist teacher, for example, attached one or two stickers 'YBA Wife' and 'Is there a life after marriage' to the backs of selected members of her staffroom. A small pig (representing the 'male chauvinist pig') had been drawn on the office door of the head of science. It was said to have been placed there by the senior woman science teacher.

Another school made rather more of this image. A woman teacher, scale 3, had been relieved after one year of the temporary post of house head. A young man described by the head as 'a ruthless driving man of talent' had been appointed at scale 4. 'A man who would tread on many dead bodies to get where he wanted' was how one of the women described him. The women as a whole were angry. But they treated the incident as a matter for jest. Secretly they got together and at the end of term they presented the young man with an award, a stuffed pig, 'Male Chauvinist Pig of the Year'. But their plan was leaked and at the appointed time the man returned their award with a bunch of red roses. Symbolically once again the men had defined the women in a traditional role.

Of course it was possible to use non-joking means to combat the stereotype. Frequently individual teachers made serious efforts to distance themselves from it, to pronounce themselves to be exceptions. I have discussed some of these responses, which can be described as 'breaking role' (Janeway, 1972) in another article (Cunnison, 1985).

Conclusion

Gender joking is almost entirely initiated by men. It is men defining women at work in sexual, domestic or maternal terms, terms which detract from their image as professionals. As such it is a put-down, a way of controlling and subordinating women (cf. Hearn and Parkin, 1987) and one mechanism among others which militates against their promotion. The stereotype of the woman teacher is used to pass judgment on women teachers' commitment, competence and confidence. They are expected to reproduce and leave; they are expected to be less competent than men because their real concerns are elsewhere; they are expected not to need money because they are married.

I have hesitated to use the term 'sexual harassment' to apply to all cases of joking. But some clearly fall into this category as with the technical studies teacher's attack on the PE teacher. Yet some women partake, enjoy, play along with gender joking. In a society with such powerful differentiation between men's and women's roles, women teachers too can cry, 'vive la différence'. Flirtatious joking occurs periodically in schools as in any other work situation. I am not happy to apply the term 'sexual harassment' to all such behaviour. What does seem crucial is that such mundane, everyday behaviour operates to strengthen stereotypes about women teachers, thus detracting from their professional image and prospects for promotion.

Acknowledgments

My thanks to the SSRC who financed the research on which this article is based and to Kate Purcell for sharing her ideas about gender joking in industry.

References

BALL, S. (1987) *The Micro-Politics of the School*, London, Methuen.

CUNNISON, S. (1985) *Making It in a Man's World*, Occasional Paper 1, Department of Sociology and Social Anthropology, University of Hull.

DELAMONT, S. (1980) *Sex Roles in the School*, London, Methuen.

HEARN, J. and PARKIN, W. (1987) *'Sex' at 'Work': The Power and Paradox of Organisation Sexuality*, Brighton, Wheatsheaf.

HILSUM, S. and START, K. (1974) *Promotion and Careers in Teaching*, Windsor, National Foundation for Educational Research.

JANEWAY, E. (1972) *Man's World, Woman's Place*, London, M. Joseph.

NATIONAL UNION OF TEACHERS (1980) *Promotion and the Woman Teacher*, Manchester, Equal Opportunities Commission/NUT.

RADCLIFFE-BROWN, A. R. (1952) *Structure and Function in Primitive Society*, London, Cohen and West.

SYKES, A. J. M. (1966) 'Joking relationships in an industrial setting', *American Anthropologist*, 68, pp. 188–93.

WOODS, P. (1979) *The Divided School*, London, Routledge and Kegan Paul.

Part 4
Changing Directions

11
Gender and the Conditions of Teachers' Work: The Development of Understanding in America

Kathleen Casey and Michael W. Apple

During the past few years in the United States there has been a shift of major proportions in the attention being given to education. From being seen as something of marginal interest in public discussions and in the media, schools are now directly in the spotlight of public scrutiny. Elementary, secondary, technical, college and university education, coupled with the training and evaluation of teachers, are no longer topics that politicians, government officials, pressure groups, business, union members, newspaper columnists, academics, parents and others talk about when 'important' things are over. Instead of being the functional equivalent of conversations about the weather, discussions about education have again become serious and intense.

If the conservative initiative which started this debate were wholly successful in controlling perceptions and programmes, we would only hear a strident monologue on the 'failures' of American education. *A Nation at Risk* and other national reports would dictate the script that schools must follow.[1] International industrial and military competition would set the stage; the educational system would be directed by conservative elements in government and industry; and calls for 'equity' would be drowned by the demand for 'excellence'. Fortunately, while this powerful representation has gained enormous publicity, it does not represent the only interpretation of the current problems of American education, as we shall see below.

Nevertheless, we must face the force of this attempt to restructure American education. A second generation of reports, including those by the Holmes Group (1986) and Carnegie Forum (1986), taking for granted the conservative indictment of education, are now pointing a finger at those who work in schools, and their recommendations for changing the conditions of teachers' work are being implemented almost before the ink is dry.[2] Teachers are already beginning to feel the effects of increased, often hostile, surveillance, and teachers-in-training are already being subjected to new sets of regulatory and punitive decrees.

In combination with existing tendencies, and a continuing financial crisis in education, these 'reforms' have enormous potential for transforming teachers' working conditions. If present trends persist, and are reinforced, managerial techniques and ideologies will increasingly direct the work of teachers and link it with specific behavioural outcomes. Curricular goals and materials will be more closely specified and monitored to bring them into line with the industrial, military and ideological 'needs' of a relatively small but powerful segment of the American public; and 'merit-pay' and 'master-teacher' schemes will fragment and stratify the teaching force (Apple, 1987).

Schools and teachers continue to receive even more of the blame for the crisis in the economy, in cultural authority and in political legitimacy. This, of course, has a long history. As one of us has argued at greater length elsewhere (Apple, 1982, 1986), the tendency of corporate economies when they are in crisis is to export the blame from the economy to the state. Instead of examining the role of our dominant mode of economic organization in producing unemployment, instead of looking at how our economic arrangements 'naturally' generate such inequalities, our attention is diverted from the economy to the government. When millions of people are jobless or can only find part-time low-paying work, we blame the school. Don't alter the economy, it is said; 'simply' change the schools so that the ultimate arbiter of the content of the curriculum and the teaching practices within them is a set of needs defined more and more by capital and the right.

Recognizing how such a crisis is exported is helpful, yet this particular kind of reading of the relationship between our educational system and the larger society can itself have the latent effect of privileging class and economic relations to the exclusion of other major components. The crisis has also been exported onto *women* to a considerable degree. 'They are taking men's jobs.' 'They are destroying the family by not staying at home.' Their long and continuing struggle for both economic and person rights 'has gone too far' (Apple, 1986).

Judging from what we know about conservative rhetoric on women in the family, and what we know about the gendered constitution of the teaching force, the *apparent* lack of gender bias in the conservative assaults on education is remarkable. But, while the language of gender discrimination is not conspicuously present, a closer examination reveals a familiar set of masculinist assumptions. The opening flourishes of the best known and most powerful of the conservative reports, *A Nation at Risk* (National Commission on Excellence in Education, 1983), for example, are based on a militaristic metaphor which implicitly (perhaps unconsciously) criticizes a stereotypically passive (and pacifist), predominantly female, teaching force:

> If an unfriendly foreign power had attempted to impose on America the mediocre educational performance that exists today, we might well have viewed it as an act of war. As it stands, we have allowed this to happen to ourselves. ... We have, in effect, been committing an act of unthinking, unilateral educational disarmament. (p. 1)

The fact that the overwhelming majority of elementary school teachers are women, while almost all principals are men, also sheds light on the hidden gender assumptions of Secretary of Education William Bennett's calls for more administrative control in American schools: 'Hire principals who are tough. Get serious about the use of class time. Nobody's for mindless school work in elementary classes. We have to find out who is in charge of the schools' (Posner, 1986, p. 13).

It is important to realize that this is not the first time that teachers have been, directly or indirectly, blamed for national crises. During the later 1950s and 1960s the state, in concert with capital and a largely male academic body of consultants and developers, also intervened at the level of practice into the work of a largely female working force. It is not a random fact that one of the most massive attempts at rationalizing curricula and teaching had as its target a group of teachers who were largely women. The most recent attempts by state bureaucrats, industry and government to gain greater control of day-to-day classroom operation and its 'output' have simply become more sophisticated. Gender may be less visible in these strategies, but it is present in important ways once we go beneath the surface to look at changes in the labour process of teaching, how some teachers respond to current strategies and how they interpret their own work (Apple, 1986).

It is also important to recognize the tradition out of which this current conservative interpretation of the role of education, and of teachers, has been built. Like all shifts in public discourse, this construction uses elements from existing understandings to constitute a new field, and to gain political purchase. The present assault on teachers draws upon previous attempts to exert control over their work, and upon a discourse built around gender stereotypes.

Teachers' work has been the subject of continuous struggle in the United States, and competing definitions and opposing interpretations have characterized the discourse on this topic. It is the growth of, and struggle over, this discourse about teaching and gender that we want to trace in the next section of this chapter. There are four overlapping yet distinctive themes that have helped to constitute our understanding of teachers: the teacher as professional, the teacher as worker, the teacher as female worker, and the woman as teacher.

The Teacher as Professional

Many of the roots of the current dominant discourse on teachers, we would argue, can be found in the reform movement of the 1950s and 1960s, mentioned above. Dreeben's *The Nature of Teaching* (1970) and Lortie's *Schoolteacher* (1975) can be seen as summary documents for that period. Among the first works to consider American teachers from a sociological perspective, these books continue to be considered classics on the subject. Central to their analysis is the characterization of teaching as a profession, albeit a deviant one. Like current conservative reform statements, Dreeben and Lortie's recommendations for improvement of the profession through technological expertise are combined with criticism of its predominantly female (and presumably irrational and amateur) practitioners.

Assuming the 'scientific' stance of the reforms of the day, Dreeben boasts of being a 'somewhat cold-eyed sociological observer, looking in from the outside', not at teachers as people, but on teaching as an occupation; and Lortie advises teachers to abandon the 'language of caprice', and engage in 'systematic inquiry', aided by behavioural science and close empirical analysis. Both Dreeben and Lortie's proposals for change advocate 'social engineering' — manipulative 'scientific' schemes to change the minds of teachers 'who have been doing things differently for twenty years', and to select out prospective candidates who do not subscribe to the new technology of teaching.

The language of technology pervades this perspective. Technology is seen as the solution to the problem of increasing the productivity of teachers. Business and technology intersect in Lortie's focus on efficiency, in a combination familiar to readers of the current reform rhetoric. Business metaphors used in this framework not only legitimate existing institutional arrangements; they also implicitly defend the exploitation arising out of them. Both Dreeben and Lortie use market metaphors approvingly. In an example of 'cost-effectiveness' Dreeben suggests expanding the corps of student teachers, because 'most hospitals, in fact, run on the backs of their interns and residents.' Dreeben connects technology with medicine and law in a metaphor which compares videotapes of micro teaching to doctors' X-rays and lawyers' briefs. The explicit message advocates tangible records as part of a developing technology. Implicitly it associates student teachers with sick people and criminals, images of deficiency and deviance.

The notion of female teachers as deficient is deeply structured into this understanding. Professional male career patterns are imposed upon 'women's' occupations. Teachers are compared to doctors, lawyers, engineers, airline pilots, business executives and military officers, and in every case they are found wanting in terms of prestige and its 'prerequisites' — esoteric expertise, autonomy and so forth. In their explicit discussions of teaching as women's work these books consistently reinforce the most restrictive conceptions of their day. Dreeben's characterizations of teaching concur with stereotypes. 'Occupations open to women appeal more to the heart than to the mind.' He dwells upon marital status and child-rearing as central, definitive characteristics of the woman professional. Ultimately he leaves the 'dilemma' of child-care in the lap of the individual woman. 'Resolution depends on the nature of the accommodation worked out between the demands of the life cycle and those of occupational employment.'

Lortie also blames women teachers for their lack of commitment to work, again endorsing existing 'obligations associated with wifehood and motherhood.' He fails to see the significance of his own findings that, whereas women used the flexible schedule of teaching for shopping, household duties and the care of school-aged children, 'few men mentioned compatibility with family life as an attraction. More pointed out that teaching schedules allowed them to undertake further study or do other kinds of work.' Whose definitions of commitment are being employed here?

Subsequent research and analysis, as well as ensuing events, have contradicted many of the assumptions of this original construction of teaching as a women's profession. Lerner (1979) and Kaestle's (1983) historical accounts of the professionalization of teaching show how it actually worked to the detriment of women, rather than to their advantage. Strober and Tyack's (1980) reading of the history of American education also rejects what is best called the gender deficit model, pointing out the uses of gender stereotypes for social control of women teachers by male administrators.

Not only is it important to distinguish between gender deficit and gender discrimination in understanding the conditions under which American women teachers have laboured; it is also crucial to distinguish between the ideology and the actuality of day-to-day school practice. Etzioni's (1969) claim that 'women on the average are more amenable to administrative control than men' is contradicted by Strober and Tyack's (1980) interpretation of the manipulative use of such a belief. Furthermore, as we know, the 1950s and 1960s reform movement which was based on such assumptions was not entirely successful in implementing its policies. The failures of that endeavour, the supposed immobility of the educational institution, and its lack of significant change in the face of the initial onslaught of teacher-proof material were, and are, at least partly tied to the resistances of a female workforce against external incursions into the practices teachers have evolved over years of labour (Apple, 1986). Thus the gender deficit theory of teaching, one using 'professions' dominated by men as models of understanding, does not adequately deal with the way gender and its accompanying resistances and contradictions work their way out in the lives of teachers.

This does not mean that the language of professionalism has no place in talking about women teachers. In fact, the discourse of professionalism has had particular salience for teachers, especially when their working conditions and autonomy are under attack. For example, because they have been introduced under such a rhetoric, the process of control, the increasing technicization and intensification of the teaching act, and the proletarianization of teachers' work that are occurring so clearly today in the United States (Apple, 1986) can be misrecognized as symbols of increased *professionalism*, even by teachers. This is partly because, historically, professionalism has also provided a contradictory yet powerful barrier against interference by the state; and just as critically, in the struggle against male dominance, it has been part of a complex attempt by women to win equal treatment, pay and control over the day-to-day work of a largely female labour force (Apple, 1986).

The Teacher as Worker

The tensions which develop between the competing understandings of teacher as professional and teacher as worker are anticipated, and partially reconciled, in Lieberman's (1956) *Education as a Profession*, a work which chronologically coincides with the 'break-down of cooperation, trust and partnership between teachers and administrators', epitomized by the transformation and reorganization of the National Educational Association (NEA) along the lines of industrial unionism (Carlson, 1987).

The late 1950s mark the height of power for industrial unionism, with the merger of the American Federation of Labor (AFL) and the Congress of Industrial Organizations (CIO). A campaign of aggressive unionization was launched, with teachers identified as a target group of public employees whose membership could replace the declining numbers of factory workers. With the founding of the United Federation of Teachers in New York, the NEA was also drawn into the battle to represent the nation's teachers in collective bargaining (Carlson, 1987). The origins of the teacher as worker discourse are grounded in these events, as its elaboration is tied to the fact that 'in twenty years public school teachers have moved from an almost totally nonunion work force to one of the most completely unionized occupations in the United States' (Mitchell and Kerchner, 1983).

While Dreeben and Lortie see unionism as inimical to professionalism, Lieberman not only defends 'dissatisfaction with the status quo' and 'aggressive constructive efforts to change'; he recognizes the organized collectivity of teachers as an agency of change. Declaring the concept of *power* (not prestige) to be 'one of the most important and most neglected aspects' of education, Lieberman speaks explicitly political language.

Lieberman's discussion of 'the preponderance of women teachers' is consistently progressive. To say that feminization is an obstacle to professionalization is not to criticize women teachers, according to Lieberman. It is to acknowledge such factors as (1) the prejudiced attitudes against women, which are irrational, costly and ultimately devastating, and which can only be changed by an increase of men in the occupation, or, more likely, a cultural revolution concerning the role of women in American society, and (2) the absence of the objective conditions of time, place and resources for (women) teachers to mobilize in their own interests. Thus Lieberman also anticipates the effects of the women's movement on the discourse about teachers, which we will discuss below.

Neither the construction of teacher as worker, nor the connection between gender and working conditions, was unproblematically incorporated into the earliest radical conceptualizations of education in the

United States. While the upsurge of critical scholarship in the 1960s was historically concurrent with the social upheavals of that period, its early literature reflected more of the training of the white, male, left-wing academics who produced it, than it did the understandings of those it was meant to serve.

The first generation of critical writers concentrated on the relationships between economy and education (e.g., Bowles and Gintis, 1976). For them, structural regularities, not persons, explained domination and deprivation. The second generation began to ask how structures of domination were reproduced (Apple, 1979). An unintended result of both the original macro analyses and many of the micro studies which were being done at the same time (e.g., Rist, 1970; Gracey, 1975) was the presentation of teachers as shadowy puppets, or as diseased parts of a sick system. This portrayal unfortunately articulated with a trend in mainstream educational literature which blamed the teacher for school failure. It would seem as if these early works believed the rhetoric of professionalism which claimed 'middle-class' privileges for its practitioners. The working-class orientation of (male) left-wing tradition was certainly more likely to see particular students as victims, than to understand the gender dynamics of teaching conditions.

As this discourse has developed, however, the class interests of teachers have been differently conceptualized, with the rejection of 'orthodox' class divisions in favour of a theory of a 'new middle class', 'which performs an economic function not identifiable with either the function of the collective labourer nor with the global function of capital' (Harris, 1982); or a notion of 'contradictory class locations' (Wright, 1981) with teachers located simultaneously in two classes, sharing the interests of both the petty bourgeoisie and the working class (Apple, 1982, 1986). It is then possible to see how, under circumstances of fiscal crisis, worsening working conditions, layoffs and so forth, the work of teachers can be increasingly proletarianized (Apple, 1982, 1986).

Of course, teachers are different from other workers, but the similarities are still significant. Techniques used to control workers are imported from industry into teaching through such devices as 'teacher-proof' curriculum materials. Teachers are deskilled, losing the ability to make curriculum, and are reskilled as managers of classroom procedures. They thus lose even more power over their labour. Through the process of 'intensification' the quality of teaching is eroded, as teachers cannot find time to keep up with their fields, to think, to plan, to relax, or even to go to the lavatory (Apple, 1986). The understanding which sees the 'teacher as worker' reveals the sinister side of the technological solutions proposed under the 'teacher as professional' construction.

The Teacher as Female Worker

Influenced by the impact of the women's movement and feminist revisionist scholarship, American educational research has recently begun to acknowledge the role of gender in structuring the work conditions of teachers. Of course, teaching has historically been largely women's work, and at present 87 per cent of elementary classroom teachers and 67 per cent of classroom teachers overall are women. But now, rather than the subject of a few paragraphs at the periphery of a discussion of efficiency and cost-effectiveness, women teachers' gender has become the centre of an analysis of their domination and exploitation at work.

Relationships in schools are now being understood in connection to the dynamics of both patriarchy and class in a capitalist political economy. What is being recognized is that texts and other materials made available for school use look the way they do not only because of the class, but the gender (and race) characteristics of the group of people who publish the materials in the first place, as well as the class and gender characteristics of the teachers for whom curriculum materials and textbooks are produced. State bureaucrats, industry and male academics stand to gain and women teachers stand to lose from the kind of curriculum innovations which have been attempted.

The working conditions of women teachers in the United States are also being analyzed within the larger context of 'women's work'. This consideration includes a fresh recognition of the long-standing proletarianization of women workers. In fact, women were the first industrial proletariat in the United States. Though conditions have changed, the structuring of women's paid labour is still very clearly linked to the horizontal and vertical divisions of labour. The relationship between these divisions and women's paid work is laid out in more detail in *Teachers and Texts* (Apple, 1986).

All of this shows something that is striking. Not only is women's work considered somehow inferior or of less status simply because it is women who do it (Murgatroyd, 1982), but, as the labour market changes over time, the decrease in jobs with autonomy is closely related to changes in the sexual division of labour. Just as importantly, as jobs

— either autonomous or not — are filled by women, there are greater attempts to control both the content of that job and how it is done from the outside (Apple, 1986). For example, as the numbers of women in the teaching ranks increased in the United States, the job of teaching changed: women were placed at particular levels in unified, bureaucratic and public schools; curricula were graded; districts became larger and more formally organized, administrative hierarchies grew (Richardson and Hatcher, 1983); and the tasks of teachers themselves were considerably restructured.

Yet to restrict the definition of 'work' to 'paid employment outside the home' is, as feminist scholars have shown, to accept the taken-for-granted terms of a masculinist ideology. In our kind of society women have a double relation to wage labour. They are both paid and unpaid workers. Unpaid domestic labour, relations of consumption and their connections to paid work are all critically important in illuminating both how our economy functions and the shaping of women's consciousness. In addition to documenting domination and exploitation in this sphere, feminist research has begun to illuminate women's lived experiences of these relations. A pioneering study, Spencer's (1986) *Contemporary Women Teachers: Balancing School and Home*, places women teachers' non-school lives on the research agenda, incorporating housework and child-care into her analysis of the effects of women's multiple roles on their teaching and vice versa.

One cannot complete a discussion of the teacher as a female worker without reference to the issue of the control over women's sexuality and reproductive power which, many feminists argue, is the basis for gender domination and exploitation. Certainly in the past school boards have issued decrees on women teachers' marital status. In the life of a nineteenth century American woman teacher documented in *We Are Your Sisters* (Sterling, 1984), we can see the tragic connections of the control of sexuality, of racial oppression and of occupational regulation. Edmonia Highgate, 'an intense, hardworking, and self-assured' black woman, was a school principal in Binghamton, New York, and worked with freed blacks in the south. In 1870, unable to bear the consequences of her secret marriage to a white man, she died 'alone and penniless' from an illegal abortion, 'murdered', in the words of her contemporaries, 'with the world as accessory.'

As recently as 1930–31, under the economic pressures of the Depression, the National Association of Education reported that of the 1500 school systems in the United States 77 per cent refused to hire married women teachers; 63 per cent dismissed any woman teacher who married during the time of her employment (Degler, 1980). Discrimination against women on the basis of their marital status remains a possibility in times of job scarcity.

Increasingly we are recapturing the current and historical record of what it has meant for teachers to be women in the United States. However, while the growth of this discourse does illuminate many of the conditions under which teachers have worked, it still too often treats the teacher as an object of research rather than a subject creating her own history and discourse. Because of this, a new feminist approach has evolved for understanding what it means to be a woman who is a teacher.

The Woman as Teacher

What is unique about much of the feminist scholarship which has recently appeared is the way in which it has largely relinquished the act of interpretation to the subjects themselves, placing women's own understandings of their experiences at the centre of the research agenda. Using original documents, such as letters and diaries, oral and life-histories, these works give the voice of the narrator equal status with that of the academic researcher. Here we have come to the diametric opposite of Dreeben's 'somewhat cold-eyed' study of teaching as an occupation, to teachers as whole people. The teacher is placed at centre stage in a way which is totally different from the manner in which she is treated in the conservative national reports and policy initiatives.

In a group of studies which use this approach with women who have been teachers (P. Sterling, 1972; Lerner, 1973; Carew and Lightfoot, 1979; Hoffman, 1981; Lightfoot, 1983; Nelson, 1983; the Boston Women Teachers' Group, 1983; Giddings, 1984; D. Sterling, 1984; Kaufman, 1984; Spencer, 1986; Biklen, 1987; Casey, 1987), it is interesting to note that all the editors and researchers save one are women, that black teachers (almost totally invisible elsewhere) appear in many of these works, and that most have appeared following the impact of the women's movement. P. Sterling, Lerner, Hoffman, Kaufman, Giddings and D. Sterling all present teachers' own words with the briefest of background and interpretation. Carew and Lightfoot, Lightfoot, Nelson, the Boston Women Teachers' Group, Spencer and Casey use teachers' accounts as raw materials for their own extensive analyses. Through the Boston Women Teachers' Group, women teachers conduct research on themselves and other teachers.

This kind of research is based on the assumption that one will gain different, even better knowledge of prevailing conditions by respecting the 'interpretations' as much as the pieces of 'information' which are supplied by participants. Nelson (1983) credits her oral histories of teachers in Vermont with actually 'defining the issue itself.' Her interviews reveal two cohorts of teachers: an earlier one trained in teacher training courses for work in one-room country schools, and a later one trained in normal schools for work in consolidated schools. When members of the first group were transferred to graded schools, they felt like they had been turned from 'missionaries' into 'assembly line workers'; they never accepted the appeal of professionalism as their younger colleagues did. Conflicting perspectives over the role of the teacher come alive in the changes experienced by these women teachers.

Such is the power of these accounts that previous assumptions are challenged, and existing definitions of problems must be expanded, or even abandoned. The marketplace orientation found in many previous studies of teacher attrition does not appear in the teacher generated narratives which form the basis for Casey's (1987) article. For these women teaching is much more than paid employment for classroom work in a specific school; for many it is a fundamental existential identity. These women do not work for those who pay their wages; they work for the children they teach. Concerns for care and connectedness come to the fore here (Gilligan, 1982). While previous studies of teacher attrition have neglected the potential for antagonism between (female) teachers and (male) administrators, these narratives consistently condemn the repressive personnel practices of the school system, and the gender relations upon which they are based. They stand as articulate statements against the restratification of teaching that is being proposed in many of the 'teacher reform' plans.

Women teachers in both Nelson's and Casey's articles talk about their strong attachments to children. In the haste to correct earlier stereotypes of women teachers many recent interpretations have neglected or denigrated this dimension of women teachers' lived experiences. As Sara Freedman (1987) has observed in her critique of the report of the Carnegie Forum on Education (1986), 'the role of women primarily as nurturer and caretaker is seen as a relic of a best forgotten past', a view echoed in Secretary Bennett's admonition to 'get tough'. The discourse of these women stands to remind critics that, while not all women teachers are motivated by love for the children they teach, such an orientation has positive and progressive potential. Of particular importance, the desire to help particular groups of children has motivated many women teachers to engage in progressive political projects, both in and out of schools (Casey, 1987).

Reactions against job discrimination have also sometimes resulted in a simple reversal of previous constructions. For example, it is now widely assumed that women teachers will wish to pursue a career based upon upward mobility within the hierarchical structures of schools. Here again the different aspirations of particular groups of women need to be respected in any interpretation. Some women will never accept such an option, since they envision administrators as 'the enemy' (Casey, 1987).

The political understandings and activities of women teachers are now being studied from a number of angles. The personal perceptions of women teachers participating in historical moments of social change are now available in several studies.[3] Emerging evidence has begun to erode the sweeping generalizations about the conservatism of women teachers put forth by Lortie (1975) and others. But it remains for subsequent scholars to consider carefully the ways in which the political understandings and actions of women teachers correspond to, and differ from, those of their male counterparts. Here too it would be a mistake to impose male templates on the experiences of women. The ambivalence felt by female members towards the male bureaucratic domination of teachers' unions has yet to be seriously considered, and recent research has just begun to capture glimpses of the conflicts felt by the (female) elementary school teachers, who wish to engage in industrial action *and* take care of their young students (Casey, 1987).

Much of the impetus behind the various burgeonings of oral history has always come from those researchers connected to socialist and feminist projects. History itself is contested terrain, as the Popular Memory Group (1982) points out, and putting the working class, women and people of colour on its agenda has the potential to change the very terms of their struggle. With the working conditions of a predominantly female teaching force a subject of intense political debate at the present time, and with conservative policy proposals recommending more control over teachers, we must accept the challenge to publicize the past and present effects of such agendas on women teachers' lives. As this last discourse, the discourse of woman as teacher shows, finding ways for women teachers to have a voice can be part of this struggle to alter the conditions of gendered labour in America. Rather than attempting to control teachers' work from the outside, either to proletarianize them or to 'professionalize' them, rather than blaming teachers for all our social ills, we may want first to listen to them. Who knows, our society may learn how important 'women's work' is in the process.

Notes

1 Commissioned by the Reagan administration, *A Nation at Risk: The Imperative for Educational Reform; A Report to the Nation and the Secretary of Education* (National Commission on Excellence in Education, 1983) initiated the current debate with a set of sweeping condemnations of the American educational system.

2 Named after a former dean of Harvard Graduate School of Education, the Holmes Group is a consortium of education deans and chief academic officers from major research universities in the United States. The Carnegie Forum, sponsored by the Carnegie Foundation, is composed of nationally recognized business executives, political leaders, academics, high level university administrators and the heads of the two national teachers' unions.

3 Representative works include Lerner, Sterling and Hoffman's presentations of women teachers in the reconstruction south, and Kaufman's portraits of women who taught on the western frontier. Lerner's *Black Women in White America* also includes undercover slave teachers, and teachers in the Jim Crow south.

References

APPLE, M. W. (1979) *Ideology and Curriculum*, Boston, Mass., Routledge and Kegan Paul.

APPLE, M. W. (1982) *Education and Power*, Boston, Mass., Routledge and Kegan Paul.

APPLE, M. W. (1986) *Teachers and Texts: A Political Economy of Class and Gender Relations in Education*, New York, Routledge and Kegan Paul.

APPLE, M. W. (1987) 'Will the social context allow a tomorrow for *Tomorrow's Teachers*?', *Teachers College Record*, 88, 3, pp. 330–7.

BIKLEN, S. K. (1987) '"Duty in the great field of labor": Perspectives from women teachers, 1802–1890', Paper presented at the American Educational Research Association Annual Meeting, Washington, D.C.

BOSTON WOMEN TEACHERS' GROUP (1983) 'The other end of the corridor: The effect of teaching on teachers', *Radical Teacher*, 23, pp. 2–23.

BOWLES, S. and GINTIS, H. (1976) *Schooling in Capitalist America*, New York, Basic Books.

CAREW, J. and LIGHTFOOT, S. L. (1979) *Beyond Bias: Perspectives on Classrooms*, Cambridge, Mass., Harvard University Press.

CARLSON, D. (1987) 'Teachers as political actors: From reproductive theory to the crisis of schooling', *Harvard Educational Review*, 57, 3, pp. 283–307.

CARNEGIE FORUM ON EDUCATION (1986) *A Nation Prepared: Teachers for the 21st Century*, Washington, D.C., Carnegie Forum on Education.

CASEY, K. (1987) 'Why do progressive women activists leave teaching?', Paper presented at the American Educational Research Association Annual Meeting, Washington, D.C.

DEGLER, C. (1980) *At Odds: Women and the Family in America from the Revolution to the Present*, New York, Oxford University Press.

DREEBEN, R. (1970) *The Nature of Teaching: School and the Work of Teachers*, Glenview, Ill., Scott, Foresman and Company.

ETZIONI, A. (1969) *The Semi-Professions and Their Organization: Teachers, Nurses and Social Workers*, New York, Free Press.

FREEDMAN, S. (1987) 'Who will care for our children?' *Democratic Schools*, 3, 1, pp. 7–15.

GIDDINGS, P. (1984) *When and Where I Enter: The Impact of Black Women on Race and Sex in America*, New York, William Morrow and Company.

GILLIGAN, C. (1982) *In a Different Voice*, Cambridge, Mass., Harvard University Press.

GRACEY, H. (1975) 'Learning the student role: Kindergarten as academic boot-camp', in STUB, H. (Ed.) *The Sociology of Education*, Homewood, Ill., Dorsey Press.

HARRIS, K. (1982) *Teachers and Classes: A Marxist Analysis*, Boston, Mass., Routledge and Kegan Paul.

HOFFMAN, N. (1981) *Women's "True" Profession: Voices from the History of Teaching*, Old Westbury, N.Y., The Feminist Press.

HOLMES GROUP (1986) *Tomorrow's Teachers: A Report of the Holmes Group*, East Lansing, Mich., Holmes Group.

KAESTLE, C. (1983) *Pillars of the Republic: Common Schools and American Society, 1780–1860*, New York, Hill and Wang.

KAUFMAN, P. W. (1984) *Women Teachers on the Frontier*, New Haven, Conn., Yale University Press.

LERNER, G. (1973) *Black Women in White America: A Documentary History*, New York, Vintage Books.

LERNER, G. (1979) 'The lady and the mill girl: Changes in the status of women in the Age of Jackson, 1800–1840', in COTT, N. and PLECK, E. (Eds) *A Heritage of Her Own: Towards a New Social History of American Women*, New York, Simon and Schuster.

LIEBERMAN, M. (1956) *Education as a Profession*, Englewood Cliffs, N.J., Prentice-Hall.

LIGHTFOOT, S. L. (1983) 'The lives of teachers', in SCHULMAN, L. and SYKES, G. (Eds) *Handbook of Teaching and Policy*, New York, Longman.

LORTIE, D. (1975) *Schoolteacher: A Sociological Study*, Chicago, Ill., University of Chicago Press.

MITCHELL, D. and KERCHNER, C. (1983) 'Labor relations and teacher policy', in SCHULMAN, L. and SYKES, G. (Eds) *Handbook of Teaching and Policy*, New York, Longman.

MURGATROYD, L. (1982) 'Gender and occupational stratification', *Sociological Review*, 30, pp. 574–602.

NATIONAL COMMISSION ON EXCELLENCE IN EDUCATION (1983) *A Nation at Risk*, Washington, D.C., The Commission (Superintendant of Documents, US, GPO distributors).

NELSON, M. (1983) 'From the one-room schoolhouse to the graded school: Teaching in Vermont, 1910–1950', *Frontiers*, 7, 1, pp. 14–20.

POPULAR MEMORY GROUP (1982) 'Popular memory: Theory, politics, method', in JOHNSON, R., MCLENNAN, G., SCHWARZ, B. and SUTTON, D. (Eds) *Making Histories*, London, Hutchinson.

POSNER, M. (1986) 'William Bennett on new teacher salaries, education problems, and the presidency', *Newsbank*, EDU 92, B12–13.

RICHARDSON, J. and HATCHER, B. (1983) 'The feminization of public school teaching, 1870–1920', *Work and Occupations*, 10, pp. 81–99.

RIST, R. (1970) 'Student social class and teacher expectations: The self-fulfilling prophecy in ghetto education', *Harvard Educational Review*, 40, 3, pp. 411–52.

SPENCER, D.A. (1986) *Contemporary Women Teachers: Balancing School and Home*, New York, Longman.

STERLING, D. (Ed.) (1984) *We Are Your Sisters: Black Women in the Nineteenth Century*, New York, W. W. Norton and Company.

STERLING, P. (Comp. and Ed.) (1972) *The Real Teachers*, New York, Random House.

STROBER, M. and TYACK, D. (1980) 'Why do women teach and men manage?: A report on research on schools' *Signs*, 5, pp. 494–503.

WRIGHT, E.O. (1981) *Class, Crisis and the State*, London, Verso.

12
The Internal Labour Market for Primary Teachers

Julia Evetts

How can life- or career-history research, usually associated with interactionist theoretical perspectives in sociology, be reconciled with explanations on the macro level of analysis which consider the effects of expansion or contraction on an occupation? In autumn 1985 and summer 1986 I conducted a series of career-history interviews with a sample of twenty-five married women who were headteachers of primary and infant schools from two educational areas of a midlands county.[1] I was interested in the career and family strategies of women who had at some stage opted for career advancement in primary teaching in addition to having and coping with family responsibilities and who had been successful in their achievement of headteacher posts. Most of these women had achieved their headships in the 1960s and 1970s, and they were all married or had been married. The study was exploratory research designed to produce suggestive hypotheses rather than statistical generalizations.

There were clear advantages in the use of interactionist concepts and perspectives in the conduct of this research. The emphasis on meaning and its construction helped to make sense of the notions of 'work' and 'career' in the lives of these women. The interactionist concept of 'subjective career' assisted in the understanding of how these women actually experienced their careers, and the term 'strategy' helped in the analysis of how these women had coped with family goals as well as with career development.

However, if there are advantages in interactionist concepts and research perspectives, there are concomitant disadvantages that need to be recognized and confronted, such as a potential neglect of structural factors. Interactionist studies of teachers have recognized certain structural factors, namely external political and economic conditions (Sikes *et al.*, 1985; Ball and Goodson, 1985), but they have mostly ignored a second type of structural factor those peculiar to the occupation itself, that is, the nature of the labour market for teachers. External structural conditions such as economic prosperity/stringency, political optimism/pessimism and educational expansion/contraction are acknowledged and described, but then are regarded as a given set of circumstances in the context of which individuals go about constructing their teaching careers and devising their coping strategies. But we are no closer to an understanding of how these external structural influences actually bring about opportunities for certain individuals rather than others, nor how they shape the attitudes and meanings teachers attach to their careers and their work.

What has been neglected in interactionist research is any analysis of the labour market and in particular the internal labour market for teachers. We need an elaboration of the characteristics unique to the careers of teachers and of those shared with other white collar occupations and professions. If we can elaborate upon the market characteristics for teachers of different types and levels by examining the attributes that are important for promotion and progress in the teaching career, then it will be possible to explain how external structural factors are worked out in the lives and careers of individual teachers.

Certainly in my own research on the career and family strategies of the married women primary headteachers, I have made constant reference to the optimistic and expansionist economic, political and educational climate of the 1960s and 1970s. This was when the women in my study were beginning to develop their working careers and were looking for promotion. They themselves made constant references to the fact that their expertise was much in demand at that time. Those who had taken time out of teaching were sought out and their returns were encouraged and facilitated. Similarly the teaching skills of these women were recognized and they were urged to seek promotion. Such external factors as teacher shortage and educational expansion influenced how these women saw their work and constructed their careers. But I want to go beyond commenting on a particular historical era to consider what the subjective careers of the women primary headteachers in my study can tell us about the internal labour market for teachers. Only by understanding both the general and the particular characteristics of the teaching labour market can we accommodate teachers' accounts of their career histories and biographies within an explanation of wider structural influences and their effect.

Internal Labour Markets

Defining the Concept

The concept of an internal labour market developed out of attempts by labour economists in the 1950s to analyze the constraints on free competition for and free movement of labour (Loveridge, 1983). But much of its significance has come from its use by radical or Marxist economists to explain segmentation in labour markets. The labour market is seen as being made up of at least two segments: the primary sector,[2] made up of jobs with stable earnings and employment prospects, and the secondary sector of jobs offering only part-time, or intermittent employment, relatively low earnings, no job security or promotion prospects. The Piore model (1975) is the most popularly cited (Dex, 1985), and Piore introduced a further division within the primary sector of the labour market between the upper independent and lower subordinate primary jobs. The upper primary sector of the labour market was made up of professional and managerial jobs, with higher pay, mobility and turnover patterns. The lower primary sector of the labour market contained occupations with moderate levels of pay, with less variety in the content of their work and with less control and influence over the work of others (Dex, 1985, p. 132).

According to Doeringer and Piore (1971) primary sector occupations develop *internal labour markets* where competition for promotion to the upper primary sector is restricted to those already in the primary sector occupation. This internal labour market thereby constitutes a career structure whereby some members can progress and achieve promotion in the career whereas others are left behind to occupy lower primary sector jobs.

Teaching as a Primary Sector Occupation

Using such a model teaching is a primary sector labour market occupation. It offers relatively high wages, good working conditions, responsibility and control over the work in the classroom and employment stability. Teaching also has its own internal labour market with a nationally recognized career structure. Through the internal labour market some teachers are promoted into upper primary sector occupations (educational management) whereas others remain in lower primary sector jobs (classroom teaching). In the internal labour market of teaching, competition for promotion is confined to those already qualified and employed as teachers. The headteacher position is located in the upper primary sector of the labour market since these posts involve management and administration, higher pay, more responsibility, variety and control over the content of their work, opportunities for individual initiative and decision-making and control over the organization of the work of other teachers and over their promotion prospects. Secondary schools have further forms of 'middle management'. But in infant and junior schools there is a more stark divide between headteacher posts and others. Compared to heads, classroom teachers have less variety in their work, no control over other teachers and less opportunity for individual initiative beyond the classroom. Their positions are best located in the lower primary sector of the labour market.

Internal Labour Markets in Primary Teaching

There are certain gender-specific characteristics of the junior and infant (in contrast to secondary) teaching labour force that have consequences for the internal labour market and promotion prospects. First, women teachers outnumber men. According to national statistics (DES, 1987b) 78 per cent of teachers in maintained primary, junior and infant schools in England and Wales are women. A second characteristic of the primary, junior and infant teaching labour force is the ready availability of part-time and supply work. There are local variations in the opportunities for part-time teaching posts but there has been a more or less constant pool of supply work, in general taken up by married women rather than men teachers.

Also there are certain gender-specific characteristics of the upper sector of this labour market. Overall men have a higher proportion of the headteacher positions (55 per cent) and thus predominate in the upper sector of the labour market for primary teachers. But there are further significant gender differences *within* the upper sector. Women predominate as heads of infant and nursery schools, while men predominate as heads of primary and junior schools. Women have a virtual monopoly of the infant headteacher position. There are more separate infant schools than junior and primary schools. But because infant schools are smaller and their pupils necessarily younger, and because of the operation of the unit total system,[3] these (female) infant heads are less well paid than most heads of junior and primary schools.

The Characteristics of the Internal Labour Market for Primary Teachers

What are the important characteristics of the internal labour market for teachers in the primary school sector? What ideologies underpin the market? What attributes are necessary for promotion from the lower to the upper sectors of the internal labour market, and do such attributes affect men and women teachers equally? Finally, how are the mechanisms of the internal labour market modified under different external conditions of expansion or contraction? In order to approach such questions, the remainder of this chapter discusses the characteristics and processes that operate in the internal labour market of primary teaching.

Beliefs about Promotion in Primary Teaching

Individual Striving. The first characteristic to consider is the various beliefs surrounding promotion in teaching and how such beliefs bring about acceptance of unequal opportunities. Crompton and Jones (1984) examined three organizations (banking, insurance, local government) to investigate differences in the characteristics of their internal labour markets. But there were common features as well. All three internal labour markets achieved control through compliance because employees were engaged in individualistic striving within the organization. Similarly for primary teachers, both men and women, the ideology is individualistic with an emphasis on equal opportunity and promotion for special merit and for taking on additional responsibilities. The belief system that supports the internal labour market of primary teaching involves the idea that men and women primary teachers begin their teaching careers with similar sorts of qualifications, attitudes and ambitions. Among young primary teachers both men and women are thought to want interesting work, enjoy classroom contact with children, and have ambitions for more responsibility and for a career.

As careers progress, an ideology of equal opportunity is sustained, despite the fact that men generally do better in promotional terms.

Gender differences in career achievement are accommodated by invocations of the effect that family responsibilities have on women's attitudes. Both men and women primary teachers explain the gender inequalities in promotion by claiming that older married women teachers are resigned to their dual family and work responsibilities and are unwilling to take on extra teaching duties because of family commitments.

The belief that individualistic striving for promotion positions explains differential career achievements is widely held in primary teaching as well as in other white collar occupations. The biographies of the headteachers in my study to an extent confirm the presence of such an ideology. For most of these women (although not all) their careers were not developed until their family responsibilities began to ease. However, a teaching career was important to them, and although they might attribute their own career success to chance or luck, nevertheless the stereotype of the belief system does not adequately explain the variation and variety these headteachers showed in their career attitudes.

The Compatibility between Women Teachers and Young Children. The primary teaching labour market shares such sustaining ideological components as individualistic striving with other white collar occupations, but there are additional components in primary teaching that need to be elucidated. Perhaps of most significance is the idea that women are better than men at teaching very young children. The teaching of the very young, nursery and infant children, is almost exclusively female. There are promotion opportunities for women in infant education, and most heads of separate infant schools are female. Some of the women in my study had moved to infant education from others sectors specifically to achieve a headship post. This aspect of the ideology that sustains the internal teaching labour market reflects the general belief that women as mothers are the most appropriate carers and educators of young children. Women heads of infant schools can continue to see themselves as primarily mother-figures, as unambitious, as not competing against men in such roles. Some of the heads in my study espoused such a view of themselves. They were ambivalent about their career successes; their family accomplishments were as important to them.

However, this was not the case with all the women heads I interviewed. Several heads gave examples of discrimination, particularly in the 1960s, when women were encouraged to apply and were selected for the headships of infant schools but were discouraged from competing for the more prestigious and higher paid junior and primary school headships. Apparently it was felt by appointing committees that women would find it more difficult to handle the 'older' (up to age 11) boys! The women heads reported changes in the 1970s, but clearly some selectors (and some women themselves) remain unconvinced, given the continued gender differentiation in this respect.

One consequence of the beliefs about women's suitability for teaching young children is that the typical career route to a primary headship is different for women and men. The women primary heads in my study had moved to primary headships following successful infant headships or after holding posts as heads of small village primary schools. This was the case whatever age group the women had been trained to teach and had, in fact, been teaching. The route via an infant headship is not a career route that men can follow. Successful men will proceed directly to junior or primary headships from deputy headships or classroom teaching.

The general belief in individualistic striving and the more specific belief in the gender appropriateness of certain teaching roles constitute the ideology that shapes the promotional opportunities within primary teaching. It is necessary also to specify the qualities and characteristics the internal labour market requires as qualifications for promotion into the upper sector, the headteacher position.

Qualifications for Promotion

Geographical Mobility. Occupations vary in the extent to which promotion is indeed internal in geographical and/or job terms (Crompton and Jones, 1984). Primary teaching does constitute a stratified internal labour market at the local education authority level. None of the women heads that I interviewed had achieved any of their promotions out of the county in which they were currently employed; indeed many of the heads had taught in only one administrative area of the county (Evetts, 1987). This finding suggests that the internal labour market of primary teaching for women is defined and specified according to local educational authority boundaries and may even be constricted further to operate within administrative areas or districts within those boundaries. How the market is defined for men primary teachers cannot be ascertained from my research. It is possible only to hypothesize that it will be similarly local, for the most part, although men primary teachers will be more likely to have the option of moving to a different LEA in order to advance their career prospects should this prove necessary.

In certain internal labour markets employees are required to be geographically mobile, usually to gain experience in various branches/establishments, in order to work their way up the promotion hierarchy. Crompton and Jones (1984) indicated that there will be important differences between the operation of internal labour markets according to whether employees have to operate with an 'occupational' career strategy (moving from employer to employer) or with an 'organizational' career strategy (where advancement can be sought within an employing organization). (This distinction was developed in Brown, 1982.) Clearly primary, junior and infant teaching is complex in this respect. Primary teachers need to develop an organizational career strategy in that promotion is sought within an employing educational authority. But educational administrators claim the desirability of experience in a range of schools. This aim is not necessarily achieved in practice, however.

In general, married women primary teachers are not as mobile as men primary teachers. Few married women will be willing or able to move their families to develop their own careers. Nevertheless, for the women heads that I studied, lack of geographical mobility did not seem to have been a handicap, especially in achieving an infant headship. Indeed, stability seems to have been a characteristic that helped these women advance their careers. Of those teachers who had been geographically mobile early on (in pursuit of their husbands' careers), promotions did not begin until they were able to become established and to get themselves known in an area. For men primary teachers, family constraints are probably less prominent. Geographical mobility may be a significant gender difference, therefore, in the career strategies of men and women primary teachers.

Continuous Service. Another usually important characteristic for promotion into the upper sector of internal labour markets is continuous, unbroken service. The ability to work continuously differentiates the working careers of men from those of most married women in many occupations, including primary teaching. The National Union of Teachers has estimated that approximately 65–70 per cent of the female teaching population (both primary and secondary) eventually break their service (NUT, 1980). Some women (and some men) break their teaching service for reasons other than child-care, but it is this break that is by far the most significant for women. Of my twenty-five primary and infant headteachers, fifteen had broken their teaching service. Of the other ten, one had been a late entrant to teaching, eight had had no children and one had continued to teach without a break.

The women heads in my study who had broken their teaching service were not out of teaching for long periods, nor did most experience these periods at home as real interruptions in their careers (Evetts, 1988a). The 'breaks' for this group ranged from eighteen months to eight years. But if part-time and supply teaching are calculated as the equivalent of half a year's service, then the large majority of this group was out of teaching for under three years. Most of these women had kept in touch with teaching either through intermittent supply work or through more regular part-time teaching, or at the very least through experience of setting up and assisting with play groups. One important consequence of this kind of incomplete break was that these women were not anxious about their abilities to do the teaching job upon return.

The internal labour market for primary teachers might be unusual, therefore, in that continuous service is not a prerequisite for promotion into the upper sector for women teachers. Clearly a break in service *might* explain some of the gender differences in achievement of headteacher posts. But a break, particularly if it is short and incomplete, does not always stop women achieving promotion posts in primary and infant teaching. Certain features of the teaching labour market, such as the availability of part-time and of supply work, allow women to maintain contact with their teaching work while they are at home working as housewives/mothers. The availability of part-time and supply work for married women primary and infant teachers might distinguish the primary teaching labour market from other professional and semi-professional occupations. Moreover, in the primary teaching labour market a break in service and the manner of the subsequent return (for example, when women are sought out and their returns encouraged) might have positive career implications. Certainly for the women in my study the break in service *increased* their self-confidence. Their experiences at home had added to their understanding of the needs and capabilities of young children and had increased their confidence in their interactions with parents and with teaching colleagues. However, such positive implications of a break in service might be a unique feature of the primary teaching labour market.

Post-Entry Qualifications. Crompton and Jones (1984) identified considerable variations among their three organizations in the extent to which post-entry qualifications were essential for promotion. In primary teaching the precise significance of post-entry qualifications is difficult to specify categorically. For current headteacher post holders, both men and women, there seems to have been no necessity to acquire additional qualifications (Evetts, 1986). Similarly in the interview research, of the twenty-five women primary and infant heads, seven had gained an additional post-entry qualification (three had achieved an in-service BEd, one had an Open University BA degree and three had acquired advanced diplomas in education). But most of these post-entry qualifications were not undertaken with promotion in mind, and most were achieved *after* the women had gained their headteacher positions. The heads claimed they were undertaken in order to update knowledge. However, there was a feeling amongst some of the headteachers that since the teaching certificate had been downgraded by its replacement with the BEd degree for all new entrants, qualifications would become increasingly important in future in the promotions race.

For the heads I interviewed, length of experience and satisfactory teaching service (particularly if this had been noted by significant authority figures) had been sufficient for seeking promotion in the internal labour market. But there are signs that in the future post-entry qualifications might become an increasingly important way of getting oneself known as wanting promotion, and an increasingly necessary requirement for headteacher posts for both men and women.

Promotion Processes

So far I have discussed some ideologies that support the internal teacher labour market and certain qualities which are thought to influence promotion prospects. Primary teaching shares certain of these characteristics with other white collar and professional occupations, while other features are peculiar to the internal labour market for primary teachers. Next I want to consider two processes — sponsorship and the operation of an occupational community — which regulate access to promotion opportunities in the internal labour market of primary teaching. Other occupations might share certain features of these processes. In respect of primary teaching these processes became apparent from my research into the headteachers' career histories.

Sponsorship. The belief in individualistic striving and meritocracy within the teaching profession, namely that promotion does not come automatically with age and length of service but rather that promotion has to be applied for and is the reward for merit, for ability and for taking on additional responsibilities, has already been discussed. What remains to be examined is how in primary teaching such promotional qualities are identified and how individuals are sponsored by 'gatekeepers' (Lyons, 1981). In internal labour markets some individuals are recognized and encouraged to go for promotion whereas others are not so identified, have to motivate themselves and even then may find it difficult to achieve a promotion post. The internal labour market model itself gives no indication of how promotable characteristics come to be identified and how the individuals who possess such characteristics are encouraged and backed in their attempts to secure promotion.

Headteachers are one such source of sponsorship. Giving encouragement to apply for promotion is clearly different from having the power actually to allocate promotion posts. But heads can and do apply for scale promotions (now incentive allowances) for individual teachers, although the advertizing, application and selection procedures for deputy head and headteacher positions are rather more formalized. Inspectors and advisers also practise sponsorship. Winkley (1985) has suggested that inspector/advisers have more influence over career prospects in primary than in secondary schools. He claims that inspector/ advisers 'define as tightly as possible the rules under which teachers may be short-listed for jobs. The inspectorate may, for example, insist on forming the short-list. There are L.E.A.'s where it is the inspector and not the head of the school who makes the final decision as to who should be appointed' (Winkley, 1985, p. 113). Clearly there are also cases where heads and inspectors work closely together to determine appointments and promotions. Generally speaking, in the teacher labour market within local education authorities there are important links between heads, inspectors and teachers, and these links seem particularly important for promotion prospects in primary education.

It is necessary also to consider whether there are differences between men and women primary headteachers in the process by which they become career ambitious. Elsewhere (Evetts, 1987) I have described the part played by 'gatekeepers' in motivating the women heads that I studied to seek promotion. The women heads frequently mentioned the influence of inspectors and of their own headteachers in giving the initial push and guiding the teachers into appropriate courses of action. Although not all of the women heads attributed their career success to the initial encouragement of such 'gatekeepers' — some were clearly self-motivated — nevertheless such sponsorship was important to the women I studied.

It is possible, therefore, that teachers who wait to be sponsored for internal promotions such as incentive allowances (women more than men?) are likely to take longer to achieve initial career promotions than those who motivate and push themselves. This, together with any differential support given to women and men by 'gatekeepers', means that gender differences in the origins of career ambition could have important consequences for the numbers of men and women in headteacher posts.

Occupational Communities. A related factor that seemed to be important for promotion for the women heads and which became apparent in their career-history accounts was membership of an occupational community or teacher network. There was a very real sense of community amongst these women that had existed when as teacher-mothers they had shared difficulties, experiences and solutions with other women teachers and with their own headteachers. This sense of community continued when, as headteachers themselves, they tried to assist their own women staff to work out compromises in their teaching and in their family responsibilities (Evetts, 1988b). The concept of 'occupational community' has been used to refer to instances where various characteristics of the man's work have resulted in the formation of a community of families who live together in a relatively isolated residential location and who share a common lifestyle, common values and so on. The necessity of a common residential location as a characteristic of an occupational community has been challenged by Salaman (1974). It is highly likely that communities which develop in connection with female occupations will have rather different sorts of characteristics. These women did not live in the same geographical area; their husbands had different kinds of occupation and to that extent their lifestyles varied. However, there was a strong sense of shared identity and there was considerable fellow-feeling amongst these women facing conflicting demands on their time and energy. They had similar sets of (family and teaching) obligations; there was broad agreement concerning the expectations they set themselves; they had experienced common problems and difficulties; and they pulled together to fulfil the tasks and to share solutions that had worked. Out of necessity, women teachers in primary education had worked, cooperated and supported each other in diverse ways.

The implications of this female teaching community for promotional opportunities in the internal labour market are many. Where married women, as heads, have achieved a measure of control over the scale promotions (incentive allowances) of their staff and their resources in schools, then manoeuvrability, cooperation, assistance and mutual support could be maximized. In such a situation there are more opportunities for heads to take decisions and make arrangements with women teachers' career and family obligations and career strategies in mind. The consequences for men primary teachers are perhaps rather different. But men teachers have for a long time benefited from the operation of gender-specific promotional networks.

Following the identification of these two processes in the internal labour market of primary teaching, it is possible to indicate further promotion-related characteristics which become apparent from career-history research data and are additional to those Crompton and Jones have described for other white collar workers. These additional characteristics arise out of and are related to the presence of an occupational community in primary teaching. They are also explained by the existence of close ties between management and classroom practitioners in primary teaching whereby it is possible for heads and inspectors to sponsor and encourage certain teachers in the competition for promotion. These additional characteristics seemed to work in a number of different ways. But in order to trigger the sponsorship and community networks, it was necessary for individuals to display the following sorts of attributes: an ability to get oneself known in the local educational area through special teaching achievements and/or through attendance and prominence at in-service courses; a willingness to take on extra responsibilities in school and to show leadership qualities particularly in times of crisis; an educational philosophy and pedagogical practices that accord with the headteacher's and are currently in favour at the local authority inspector/adviser level; a familiarity with innovative schemes. In addition it is important to emphasize tenacity and a willingness to put oneself forward for promotion and to continue to apply for promotion posts even following rejections.

In the past both the general characteristics and the features specific to the primary teaching labour market have seemed to favour men teachers for promotion posts, although women have always succeeded in achieving the headships of infant schools. Thus gender has been a significant factor in the internal labour market of primary teaching. However, if more women achieve the headships of junior and primary schools, in addition to the headships of infant schools, then there will be more opportunity for the teacher-community and sponsorship features of primary education to work in women's favour.

Conclusion

I have been concerned to demonstrate the characteristics and processes that operate in the internal labour market of primary teaching to manage and control promotional opportunities into the upper sector of the labour market. In conclusion, it is necessary to consider how the characteristics of the internal labour market are modified under different external conditions of expansion or contraction. This will help to demonstrate how the gap that exists between interactionist concepts and macro contexts can be filled by the notion of an internal labour market. It is important to note that the characteristics identified as significant for promotion success will be applied differently in times of teacher shortage and in times of plentiful teacher supply. In the former case preferences for geographical stability, continuous service and post-entry qualifications can be relaxed (as in the 1950s and 1960s), and teachers who do not meet such criteria might nevertheless be promoted. But when there is educational contraction and a ready supply of teachers (as in the 1980s), these characteristics can form the basis for selection.

The teaching community and sponsorship mechanisms of primary education will also serve different purposes in times of teacher shortage and teacher abundance. When there is a shortage of teachers, the occupational community can work to bring women teachers back into teaching and to assist them in devising and negotiating family and teaching strategies; the sponsorship mechanisms can operate to encourage both men and women teachers to apply for promotion and to succeed. On the other hand, when there is a plentiful supply of teachers and of applicants for promotion posts, there will be fewer opportunities for the community of women teachers to support individual members in their attempts to resolve pressing family and teaching dilemmas. But the sponsorship mechanisms continue to operate. In the tighter economic and educational climate of the 1980s and 1990s, when there are fewer promotion posts and less movement generally within the teaching profession, it is probable that only those with continuous (or almost continuous) teaching service, with post-entry qualifications and with strong local links and connections will be sponsored for promotion.

The concept of an internal labour market can assist our understanding, therefore, of how external structural conditions are mediated in occupations and come to influence the lives and careers of individual teachers. By examining the detailed processes whereby certain individuals or categories of individuals are identified, encouraged or even sponsored for promotion, we can appreciate how professional occupations vary in the operation of their internal labour markets. Perhaps even more important, we will learn how different external conditions of expansion or contraction are worked out in particular occupational groups. Conditions for promotion depend on a range of factors (both internal and external to the occupation), and these factors are outside the control of any particular individual, whatever their attitude to career.

Nevertheless, the strengths of life- and career-history research are many. Through such research we can understand the detail of how external structural factors and internal labour market processes are worked out in a variety of individual careers. Such detailed accounts help to develop, expand and refine more general explanations at the structural level of analysis. Thus career-history research needs to be accommodated within wider explanations of structural factors and their effects. Analysis of internal labour markets is a way of profitably integrating the two levels of analysis.

Notes

1 The sample consisted of one in two of the women primary and infant heads in the city area of the county who had been 'once married' and two in three of the 'once married' women heads from another, generally more rural, county area. The headteachers' names and school addresses were obtained from the local education authority, and they were contacted initially by a letter asking if they would be willing to take part in the research. All but two headteachers agreed. The transcribing of some of the interview material was done with the help of a small grant from the Nottingham University Research Fund.

2 An attempt will be made to avoid the potential confusion here between 'the primary sector of the labour market' and 'the primary sector of education' by using the terms in full where necessary.

3 The criteria for determining the responsibilities and the salaries of headteachers of schools of varying sizes, and for deciding the number and types of promotion posts available in a school, are the number and age of pupils on roll. These are compounded into one basic operating principle called the 'unit total' (see Hilsum and Start, 1974, p. 307, and for the latest update see DES, 1987a, p. 28).

References

BALL, S. J. and GOODSON, I. F. (Eds) (1985) *Teachers' Lives and Careers*, Lewes, Falmer Press.

BROWN, R. (1982) 'Work histories, career strategies and the class structure', in GIDDENS, A. and MACKENZIE, G. (Eds) *Social Class and the Division of Labour*, Cambridge, Cambridge University Press.

CROMPTON, R. and JONES, G. (1984) *White Collar Proletariat*, London, Macmillan.

DEPARTMENT OF EDUCATION AND SCIENCE (1987a) *School Teachers' Pay and Conditions Document*, London, DES.

DEPARTMENT OF EDUCATION AND SCIENCE (1987b) *Statistics of Education: Teachers in Service in England and Wales, 1985*, London, DES.

DEX, S. (1985) *The Sexual Division of Work*, Brighton, Wheatsheaf.

DOERINGER, P. B. and PIORE, M. J. (1971) *Internal Labor Markets and Manpower Analysis*, Lexington, Mass., D. C. Heath.

EVETTS, J. (1986) 'Teachers' careers: The objective dimension', *Educational Studies*, 12, 3, pp. 225–44.

EVETTS, J. (1987) 'Becoming career ambitious', *Educational Review*, 39, 1, pp. 15–29.

EVETTS, J. (1988a) 'Returning to teaching', *British Journal of Sociology of Education*, 9, 1, pp. 81–96.

EVETTS, J. (1988b) 'Managing childcare and work responsibilities', *Sociological Review*, 36, 3, pp. 503–31.

HILSUM, S. and START, K. B. (1974) *Promotion and Careers in Teaching*, Slough, National Foundation for Educational Research.

LOVERIDGE, R. (1983) 'Sources of diversity in internal labour markets', *Sociology*, 17, pp. 44–62.

LYONS. G. (1981) *Teacher Careers and Career Perceptions*, Slough, National Foundation for Educational Research.

NATIONAL UNION OF TEACHERS (1980) *Promotion and the Woman Teacher*, Manchester, Equal Opportunities Commission.

PIORE, M. J. (1975) 'Notes for a theory of labour market stratification', in EDWARDS, R. L., REICH, M. and GORDON, D. M. (Eds) *Labor Market Segmentation*, Lexington, Mass., D. C. Heath.

SALAMAN, G. (1974) *Community and Occupation*, Cambridge, Cambridge University Press.

SIKES, P. J., MEASOR, L. and WOODS, P. (1985) *Teacher Careers: Crises and Continuities*, Lewes, Falmer Press.

WINKLEY, D. (1985) *Diplomats and Detectives: LEA Advisers at Work*, London, Robert Royce.

13
Prima Donna inter Pares? Women in Academic Management

Miriam E. David

This essay aims to explore women teachers' careers in higher education, focusing on academic social scientists. Because of the dearth of literature, except for Acker (1980) and Sutherland (1985), I have unashamedly decided to reflect upon my own experiences as an academic social scientist to try to tease out some of the issues and factors which construct such female academic careers. In this journey I have come to the realization that my own career experiences — both the pleasant and the painful — are not unique but mirror those of other women academics. Inevitably, of course, the particular complex combination of personal and professional experiences is unique, but there are parallels and similarities with other women's experiences. Feminist academics in North America, especially Keller and Moglen (1987), have begun to explore the effects on academic women's lives of interpersonal questions. I do not think that male academics have the same experiences in the academy as do female academics. I want to argue that gender is indeed a significant variable in the construction and experience of academic careers, as it is now recognized to be in other educational careers, such as schoolteaching and educational administration and management.

This argument about the significance of gender is, however, quite difficult to sustain at the statistical level. In Britain we have such a paucity of statistics about women's place in the academy, especially as social scientists. What we do know, from studies such as Williams *et al.* (1974) and Rendel (1984), is that the expansion of the higher education labour market entailed an expansion of the social science disciplines including sociology, social administration, social policy and social work, and an increase in the numbers of women employed as social scientists. In the early years of this expansion, however, women's careers were typically different from men's. Women were more likely than men to be found in temporary research, rather than tenured teaching posts. In recent years we have witnessed a return to this pattern of academic social science careers. For a brief period in the 1970s women were appointed to tenured teaching posts in proportionately greater numbers than hitherto. From the early 1980s, with the general contraction and tightening of the higher education labour market, there has been a disproportionate reduction in social scientists and a consequent reduction in the representation of women. Nevertheless, because of the consolidation of women academics' careers in the 1970s, this reduction has not had uniform effects. Rather a curious phenomenon has emerged of the diversity of women's career patterns. In this situation some women have been afforded opportunities for career advancement such as promotion through the academic hierarchy to senior academic positions, including professorial and/or head of department posts and deanships. The spread of women's academic positions, from temporary researchers to tenured posts to deanships and beyond, is now typically greater in the social sciences than it was in the past, especially a decade or two ago.

For some, academic posts are a 'position for life' — as with the classroom teacher so with the tenured academic — a career grade. On the other hand, career progression may entail the acceptance of some minor or more substantial administrative or managerial responsibility. Typically in Britain, although not in other higher education systems such as those in the USA or Canada, managerial and administrative responsibility is of a permanent rather than temporary and rotating kind, and it is usually so substantial that it takes one away from the 'chalk-face' or classroom. Increasingly educational management within the academy has begun to take on a distinctive flavour different from that of the 'career-grade' academic. This change in job definition has occurred more by incremental changes in the majority of institutions than by deliberate design. It has at least something to do with the redirection, nationally, of higher education policy and the characteristics and nature of the constituent institutions. The effect, however, is to make career prospects and promotion realities rather at variance with one another. The old assumption, which held true for at least two generations of academics, that promotion through to professor or head of department was as much to do with seniority as anything else is no longer tenable. Being 'primus inter pares' is not an adage that fully rings true. Instead, the job now entails some management responsibility covering not only academic guidance and/or leadership but also the deployment of resources, both physical and staffing. In the current harsh economic climate this means making difficult, and often tough, choices between people and the necessary materials to carry out academic tasks.

The generation of academics currently empowered to make these decisions was not brought up to expect to be engaged in this kind of exercise. Rather the assumptions made at the beginnings of academic careers were about the pursuit and implementation of intellectual ideas through course design and development, as well as research. A different gloss is now put on academic life from that of the post-war construction of academic careers. The expansion of social science departments, especially sociology and social administration, in the two to three decades after the end of World War II brought with it hope and optimism in designing new courses, new curricula and new research endeavours, and contributed to rising expectations for career creation and construction. These hopes and expectations are no longer easy to sustain.

The initial development of the social sciences accepted the form of the wider social context in terms of the relations between the sexes: it was completely gender-blind. No specific consideration was given in the social sciences either to questioning the relations between the sexes in the subject matter nor in the gender composition of the students who chose to enter higher education. The academic careers that initially developed for the social sciences flowed from this and were very much in the general academic mould — new specialized careers, essentially for men, although the exclusion of women was not by design. This pattern remains generally unbroken.

Margrit Eichler (1986) has provided an extremely useful critique of the way in which the social sciences as a discipline have developed. She tries to apply the Kuhnian notion of paradigmatic shifts to the ways in which the discipline might have responded to the various recent feminist appraisals of it. She suggested that the discipline could have been radically altered by the feminist contributions either by accepting a totally feminist reorientation or by developing an explicit, non-sexist approach. More modestly the discipline could have been slightly modified by the addition of a liberal feminist approach. However, on close investigation she discovers that the enterprise of social science has been relatively untouched by the various feminist critiques and has remained within the traditional 'business-as-usual' gender-blind paradigm.

I am particularly attracted to trying to use Eichler's approach for a reconsideration of the development of academic careers in the social sciences, which in a sense are the other side of the (subject) coin. Elsewhere I have applied Eichler's approach to my own career progression through doing contract research to becoming a tenured teacher (David, 1987). I would like to use it again to look at my becoming an academic leader and/or manager, committed to the notion of being a feminist of some variant. This commitment has implications for the ways in which one might teach and work with others. The commitment, as I had previously understood it, came largely out of a somewhat negative reaction to the ways in which I had experienced my academic relationships, especially within largely male hierarchies. On reflection, however, there are two other more positive reasons for this commitment: one is the developing network of feminist colleagues and friends, which I acknowledged in part before; but the other is the growing realization of the nature of the student clientele. The vast majority of my students — at all levels within the academy — have been women, themselves searching for some new and exciting understanding of their own life situations. Their quests have greatly influenced my own and continue to do so.

Eichler's critique can be used first, and briefly, to re-assess whether or not the pattern of academic social scientists' careers was any different from that of the discipline developments. Although I noted above that in the 1970s in Britain the proportion of female social scientists in tenured teaching posts increased, it increased only at the margins and only relatively temporarily. Despite these accretions to the profession, the effect was not to alter its essence. It did not even go so far as the relatively minor change of 'adding on' a feminist touch. The general structure and pattern of the profession essentially remains that of 'business-as-usual'. Of course what is 'business-as-usual' is only that in its widest gender sense. The enterprise of social science, especially for the managers and academic leaders of social scientists, has changed to a more business-like style. In other words women have entered the profession in greater numbers and proportionately more have risen in the academic hierarchy, but that, in itself, has not altered the characteristics of the profession. Insofar as a small number of those women promoted have had feminist inclinations or leanings, this has not, sadly, had a distinctive effect on the general characteristics of the profession or its academic offerings. It has not entailed any paradigmatic shift. I do not wish to suggest any indictment of the women themselves nor of the growth of feminist scholarship. It is merely to point to the tremendous difficulties entailed in such a task of trying to alter a now well established academic profession. Also I would not want to dissuade others from the pursuit of this objective of attempting, in some ways, to feminize and/or humanize the endeavour of social science, and to try to do so through those involved in teaching and research.

Eichler's approach can also be applied to my own situation. Indeed, in my own case, and presumably that of other feminist social scientists, I believed — and still believe — that I have something qualitatively different to present as a woman academic leader. I would want to go further than trying to 'add-on' a feminist approach to the conventional one, but would want to develop an alternative feminist perspective or an explicitly non-sexist strategy for the social sciences, which takes seriously the variety of feminist critiques.

My own belief that I have a distinctive approach came from several different sources. With growing maturity based not only on chronological age but also on research knowledge and experience of educational management, I began to realize what the various styles of academic leadership in the social sciences might entail. Inevitably as a social scientist I was familiar with different theories of organizations and their management but, more than that, I had even tried to investigate them in my doctoral research. Distinguishing chief education officers, or directors of education, into 'conciliators' or 'educators' (David, 1977) made me keenly aware of the inter-personal skills necessarily involved in that kind of job. Through the growing network of feminist scholars I realized that inter-personal skills could not be used without a recognition of gender relationships, too, and the purpose for which they would be applied. It was this network which began to develop a sound basis for the assumption that we, as a group of feminist social scientists, had more than a set of critiques of the discipline to offer. We also had the personal qualities we thought necessary to try to transform the discipline through our own activities, such as in the professional associations and in the departments as academic leaders. This growing assurance, however, was not born of arrogance, it also derived from the exciting developments in teaching both on conventional social science courses and in the specialisms of women's studies. The inter-personal relationships between women staff and students were both exhilarating and encouraging, building up both bonds and knowledge and pointing the way to highly creative new ways of working. However, the translation of some of these non-hierarchical, cooperative ways of teaching and learning from their origins in informal settings into the academy was not easy. Given academic hierarchies, such cooperative ways of working could only be achieved fully on the edges. It was important at this stage, however, to identify alternative strategies, possibilities and their potential for implementation.

These exciting new possibilities were often on the brink of being eclipsed by the difficult milieu in which we were increasingly required to operate. Just as we were beginning to realize quite how innovative they might be, through our various experiments and investigations, the wider context began to throw shadows over our achievements. With the benefit of both distance and hindsight it may now be important to record that for me personally, along with the Bristol Women's Studies Group, the realization of our goals coincided with Mrs Thatcher's election to power. *Half the Sky: An Introduction to Women's Studies* was published in the summer of 1979, within months of the Conservative victory.

However, that victory could not gainsay our own achievements and recognition of new ways of working in the social sciences. What it did was to modify and limit the possibilities for implementation. Relatively quickly the Thatcher government began to require new, more 'cost-effective' ways of working from institutions of higher education. The impact on universities and polytechnics differed, as did its impact on the disciplines within and between different institutions. At Bristol University, where I then worked, the impact was resounding and dramatic. It rapidly forced us all to reconsider our roles and prospects although our immediate day-to-day teaching and research were relatively untouched. In retrospect the senior managers of Bristol University responded to government requests with amazing alacrity and apparently in a very traditional, sexist mould. The long-term effect appears now to confirm the university in its élitist, patriarchal form, obscuring the contribution built up by an active, cohesive group of feminist scholars in the social sciences. Although we were all by now self-assured in our knowledge that our new ways of working in teaching and research were of value to other such scholars and students, we could not avoid the regular bruises to our confidence as the institution assiduously seemed to ignore us. The opportunities for career advancement within the institution began to recede into the dim distance. Gradually I, amongst others, recognized the reality of this — its effects on our daily lives, on our ambitions, on our teaching and research. I began to look elsewhere to realize my ambitions to transform the nature of the social sciences, still confident in the belief that I could be an academic leader and that I had something distinctive and creative to present that students and scholars alike seemed to appreciate.

Having convinced myself of my capability, I was soon offered the opportunity to test my abilities as head of a department of social sciences at South Bank Polytechnic. The interview for the post confirmed me in the belief that my qualities were appropriate. I had mentioned on my application form my feminist commitments and activities, and I was given the chance to discuss them in the interview. I was asked about my strengths and weaknesses, and I offered as one of these weaknesses 'my sex'. The rejoinder was that the institution was committed to equal opportunities. I remarked that the commitment was not self-evident from the interview panel, there being only one woman out of a panel of twelve, and she was an external advisor (a professor from a university). I quickly realized that this repartee was very risky and might have cost me the post, but fortunately (or unfortunately) it did not.

Nevertheless, I had reckoned without a range of other factors, which all became critical in preventing me realizing any of my ambitions. On reflection this problem could have been an indication of my lack of self-awareness and maturity, but I think not. I think the problem arose from an extraordinary conjuncture of at least four other factors. First was the gulf in daily working procedures and practices between universities and polytechnics. Although part of my early educational research had been focused on the setting up of polytechnics and the creation of one polytechnic, I was only aware of the working relationships at a theoretical level. I only knew how it felt at one remove — through colleagues and friends who worked or studied in polytechnics. The crucial difference to me, it now becomes clear, is nothing to do with committee structures or forms of decision-making, but rather with how power and authority are exercised and experienced. I remain astonished at how it is with ease that the power in Bristol University is exercised as compared with South Bank Polytechnic. At the latter the senior managers or directorate have constant struggles to impose their will and have in the end to exercise heavily coercive forms of control. By contrast the unquestioning acceptance of the authority of the university's senior management, or rather the fact that it is a tacit assumption that they would brook no opposition to their rules, leads to a less overtly combative situation. Negotiations appear, on the surface at least, to be carried out with consummate gentlemanly ease, as compared with the pitched battle at South Bank. I do not think the differences are to do with the resource base, as many have tried to argue, but rather, to use Weberian terminology, the traditional authority of a university institution as compared with the rational-legal or bureaucratic authority of a polytechnic. In other words the maturity or age of the institution contributes to the ways in which it is able to run itself.

The second, and indeed third, factors have to do with unique facets of South Bank Polytechnic. They have to do with aspects of the history of the institution as a whole and the department's place within the institution. The polytechnic had experienced a series of rapid changes in its management and the incumbent personnel over a short period prior to my appointment. Immediately following my interview and in the six months prior to my taking up the post on a full-time and permanent basis, three successive Directors (the equivalent of the university Vice-Chancellor) left. Several more members of the directorate team left in the first six months that I was in the post. I began to feel that I might have something to do with this exodus. The interregnum lasted a full year, but had been preceded by lacunae in authoritative personnel. Again there had been a similar interregnum at Bristol University which was managed by a senior pro-Vice-Chancellor and certainly did not provoke so many anxieties or uncertainties.

Similarly at the departmental level there had been an interregnum lasting for over two years, and during that time the department had been managed by a succession of acting heads. Taken together, these various changes in management provoked tremendous anxieties and uncertainties for the department. Finally, the fourth factor was that the threat of reductions in resources, both staff and equipment, had hung over the institution and been implemented on a piecemeal basis, rather than savaging one department, discipline or course. Equal misery, as opposed to selective butchery, had also taken its toll on morale, creating almost permanent uncertainty.

It was into this context that I stepped and tried to find a way to lead the department: a department which in a university context would approximate a faculty of social science, having almost fifty members of staff. The four different strategies that Eichler's analysis suggested were all ones with which I toyed. Obviously I was not at all sympathetic to the idea of maintaining the 'business-as-usual' approach, both because of its sexist implications and the fact that I had some particular ideas that I wished to pursue. I certainly believed then, perhaps somewhat naively, that I could develop exciting new courses both for undergraduates and postgraduates, and that I could develop the potential of my staff to explore new ideas in both teaching and research. I was particularly keen to try to implement some of my feminist notions, through courses in women's studies and new ways of working with the staff.

However, it was in the exploration of how to implement these ideas that I quickly began to experience difficulties. I did not merely want to 'add-on' a liberal feminist or woman's approach to the usual social science frame. I was inevitably different in style from the previous permanent incumbent not just because I was a woman but also because I was an active feminist. In any case being a woman in this context implied being rather motherly as opposed to being patriarchal or fatherly. Yet in all sorts of ways that style of leadership itself posed rather a lot of problems for the department — and perhaps for myself in terms of self-image and personality. This left me to consider either the separatist feminist or non-sexist approach. Both of them also posed difficulties, and I pursued both somewhat unevenly. For example, I suggested, almost on taking up office, new non-sexist ways of working to try to allow for more democratic, cooperative methods. But this initiative was quickly misunderstood and interpreted to mean that I was a 'soft touch', incapable of providing a firm, directive framework of leadership. I also suggested new course developments to take account of these predilections, but again my speed — and timing — were too hasty for such a nervous and somewhat demoralized group to accept.

I also tried some separate forms of feminist organizing, as well as proposing women's studies teaching. For example, I invited all the women on the full-time academic staff to lunchtime meetings to discuss our ways of working together. This group made up half the total full-time teaching complement of thirty staff. What immediately became clear was that their various interpretations of the term 'feminist' were very different from mine and did not have the same implications for their teaching, research or organizing activities. There was very little enthusiasm for developing such group understanding. For the most part they were chiefly committed to some notion of implementing equal opportunities: that is, improving the workplace opportunities for women and blacks or minority ethnic groups. They were not particularly keen to develop a collective notion of feminist scholarship. Indeed many of them poured scorn on such an endeavour, seeing it as élitist, since it initially at least excluded part-time teachers and the research staff. These distinctions have been nicely raised by Weiner (1986).

Thus I quickly drew a blank in every direction I pursued, and I rapidly became extremely disheartened. I felt like a stranger in a foreign land, not understanding the language, habits or culture of the people of whom I had become a part. It seemed even more foreign to me than my various sojourns in North America had — it was more the fact that we spoke the same words but they had different meanings. The Mad Hatter would have found life easy! The culture and its framework were different at every level. Although they taught BSc and MSc courses in social policy, sociology, sociology of education, all of which I had taught and written about, I found them hard to grasp. The staff of the department appeared not to understand me, and I clearly could not understand them.

More than that, I found very little support or help in interpretation from the rest of the faculty, from the directorate or the Personnel Officer, all of whom I turned to in turn and in increasing desperation. There were, of course, different and special reasons for each one failing to interpret for me. The over-reaching reason, however, was that they too were deeply absorbed in this culture and could not see its special characteristics. The rapid turnover of personnel in the directorate meant that they were all far too busy with crisis management to lend a supportive ear or to suggest styles of leadership.

I was left to 'sink or swim' for at least a year, and by the end I felt I had almost drowned and was incapable of ever being able to get a grip on the management, never mind academic leadership, of the department. Increasingly I became shrill and almost hysterical — and the more that happened the more stubborn and resistant to my authority the staff became.

The only ray of light for me at this juncture was the appointment and imminent arrival of the new Director — the first woman to direct a polytechnic. I was excited and pinned all my hopes on her transforming the polytechnic and therefore my life. In fact, things in my department initially became much worse immediately after her appointment. I think I was frequently confused with her; together we escalated rather than soothed their fears and uncertainties. The only readily available model of a woman leader is and was Mrs Thatcher. In retrospect now I think that we three became indistinguishable in the eyes of the staff of my department (and I suspect others too).

The crisis escalated in my department to such a pitch that I began to hate my job and planned to leave. At the next departmental meeting, when the majority of the thirty academic staff had left early, as they tended to do, I decided to brave it and ask the remaining half dozen how they wanted me to manage the department. One or two supportive women academics, experienced in issues of social service management, proposed some form of external consultancy to review the department's processes and procedures. This idea was agreed with alacrity by other members of staff still present.

It was an idea which had already begun to germinate in my own mind and which I had discussed with other colleagues outside the college, particularly to find a consultant sympathetic to these feminist issues. It seemed to be the only way forward — and it might at the same time return me to my former state as an academic rather than crisis manager. I took further soundings on the matter both within the polytechnic and with outside consultants. Various possibilities were considered, within the over-riding constraint of limited resources *and* the fact that the new Director was herself considering a plan for senior management training.

My own feminist inclinations led me in the direction of *consultancy* rather than training, where the skills of psychodynamics or psychotherapy might also come into play. At both a personal and an intellectual level I find the feminist revisions of psychoanalysis extremely appealing and had used such work for both teaching and research. In particular I had found Chodorow's (1978) work extremely illuminating in attempting a synthesis between psychoanalysis and social structure in order here to understand mothering.

This led me to choose a woman consultant, suggested to us through a member of the department. She had a range of relevant experience from a degree in social policy to social work to psychotherapy to management consultancy to local authorities and their women's committees. She seemed too good to be true! That proved not to be the case — she was simply excellent!

She helped us to develop a two-stage process for *recreating* the department, first to deal with the management structure, and second to develop a new culture and set of identities for the staff. At the time of writing this second stage has only just started. It is a stage of development that is necessary and relevant not only to South Bank, but also to all social scientists in the last decade of the twentieth century. It is also central to the issue of what academic and social science careers are to be in the twenty-first century — in other words who will we ourselves be, and who will we be teaching and preparing for what kind of lives and careers?

The fact that these questions were once again open to debate and discussion gave me renewed enthusiasm for the job, and helped me to get over the painful two-year initiation rites that I had undergone.

In any case the process that the consultant facilitated exorcised, by externalizing, the spirit of that pain. A two-day staff development event was held to discuss the problems that we had all experienced and the ways in which these might be overcome. Once the feelings were aired and shared, it became much easier to put them to one side and start again. We quickly devised a new management structure in which power could be more evenly spread throughout the department. Built into that was a system of regular review, by an advisory team of the department, composed chiefly of sympathetic and supportive staff. The task for the last six months has been to get that new system into smooth working order, to free us to think afresh about our futures as academics, as teachers, as social scientists.

The constraint of our internal working procedures was but one of several preventing our clear thinking. Another is the rapidly changing context of our work, due to changes emanating from the Conservative government and built into the Education Reform bill, destined to receive royal assent in July 1988. The changes alter the financial status of polytechnics and have led already to major administrative redesigns, internal to the polytechnic, to fit us for our new corporate, accredited status. The speed at which all the changes are occurring is too rapid for most of us to assimilate easily. The implications of the changes are massive: they imply resource changes, administrative and management development and, most importantly, course developments which require new visions of our subject or discipline base. The uncertainty that the now classic notions of social science will have any place in the academy in the twenty-first century is ever-present. The changes clearly require and have already set in train a cultural transformation. Our values and visions with which we all entered academic careers in the social sciences are no longer tenable. Rethinking our identities as teachers and researchers and what we wish to convey to our students is the major task facing us. It is, however, a task that we can now face together, having opened up and shared the ways in which the uncertainties deformed us each individually and forced us into combative working relationships. My particular visions as a feminist, teaching a largely captive female student audience of aspiring social scientists, also need revision. We are now required to go into the marketplace to seek students, and although we know that there are still plenty of potential mature students, it is difficult as yet to know how we or they will find the resources for such study.

The context in which we are all now operating is completely new: there have been paradigmatic shifts in both academic life in general and in the social sciences in particular. They are probably in part due to the impact of social movements, including feminism, on the nature of the discipline and the wider social context. The effect, however, has been to transform what is 'business-as-usual' into a search for 'business-enterprise', which may include feminist reappraisals insofar as they are in tune with potential student demand. The tragedy is that these transformations have been imposed from the outside rather than being the result of creative search for new ideas and new clientele; to that extent there has been resistance. Yet the effect may be to create an exciting new discipline and scholarship to fit future generations of men and women for the twenty-first century.

References

ACKER, S. (1980) 'Women, the other academics', *British Journal of Sociology of Education*, 1, 1, pp. 81–91.

BRISTOL WOMEN'S STUDIES GROUP (1979) *Half The Sky: An Introduction to Women's Studies*, London, Virago.

CHODOROW, N. (1978) *The Reproduction of Mothering*, Berkeley, Calif., University of California Press.

DAVID, M. E. (1977) *Reform, Reaction and Resources: The 3Rs of Educational Planning*, Windsor, National Foundation for Educational Research.

DAVID, M. E. (1987) 'On becoming a feminist in the sociology of education', in WALFORD, G. (Ed.) *Doing Sociology of Education*, Lewes, Falmer.

EICHLER, M. (1986) 'The relationship between sexist, non-sexist, woman-centred and feminist research', in MCCORMACK, T. (Ed.) *Studies in Communication*, Vol. 3, Toronto, JAI Press.

KELLER, E. F. and MOGLEN, H. (1987) 'Competition between women', *Signs*, 12, 3, pp. 493–511.

RENDEL, M. (1984) 'Women academics in the seventies', in ACKER, S. and WARREN PIPER, D. (Eds) *Is Higher Education Fair to Women*? Guildford, SRHE and Slough, NFER-Nelson.

SUTHERLAND, M. (1985) *Women Who Teach in Universities*, Stoke-on-Trent, Trentham Books.

WEINER, G. (1986) 'Feminist education and equal opportunities: Unity or discord?' *British Journal of Sociology of Education*, 7, 3, pp. 265–74.

WILLIAMS, G., BLACKSTONE, T. and METCALFE, D. (1974) *The Academic Labour Market*, Utrecht, Elsevier.

Notes on Contributors

Sandra Acker is Lecturer in the School of Education, University of Bristol. She has published on the subject of women and education in journals including the *British Journal of Sociology of Education* and *Sociological Review* and has contributed chapters to a number of collections. She has co-edited the *World Yearbook of Education 1984: Women and Education* (Kogan Page, 1984) and *Is Higher Education Fair to Women?* (SRHE, 1984). She is currently conducting research into teachers' work and culture in primary schools.

Michael W. Apple is Professor of Curriculum and Instruction and Educational Policy Studies at the University of Wisconsin, Madison. His most recent book is *Teachers and Texts: A Political Economy of Class and Gender Relations in Education* (Routledge and Kegan Paul, 1986).

Edith Black has taught English in secondary schools and colleges of further education since 1964. She is now a part-time PhD student in the School of Education, University of Bristol.

Kathleen Casey is a Lecturer in the School of Education at the University of Wisconsin, Madison. She has taught in Africa, Britain and the United States. She is currently completing an extensive study of the life-histories of politically active women teachers.

Sheila Cunnison is an Honorary Fellow at Humberside College. Following a first degree in economics and a year's study of sociology in America, she joined the Department of Social Anthropology of the University of Manchester in 1955 as a Research Assistant. Since then she has been engaged in a variety of participant and observational research projects in factories, school and care jobs. Her particular interests are in gender and work and in gender and trade unions, including teacher unions.

Miriam E. David has been Head of Department of Social Sciences at South Bank Polytechnic since January 1986. Previously she taught social policy at the University of Bristol. Her main research interests are women, family and education, and she has published widely on these topics in scholarly journals and in book form. Her most recent book, co-authored with Caroline New, is *For the Children's Sake* (Penguin, 1985). She is involved in research on parents and education and in an evaluation of the implications of the 1988 Education Reform Act for the changing role of parents.

Julia Evetts is a Lecturer in the Department of Sociology at the University of Nottingham. Her research interests include a study of women primary headteachers' careers. Recent articles, published in education and sociology journals, have included analyses of career ambition, of career breaks or interruptions and of women's management of family obligations alongside career development.

Rosemary Grant, after a period as a radiographer, trained and worked as a primary school teacher in Sheffield. Her interest in research arose from her experience of the promotional system and has since extended to include enquiry into primary practices, evaluation and teacher-based research. She is currently seconded to Sheffield City Polytechnic where she is working with teachers in-service who are engaged in curriculum change initiatives in their schools.

Joan Hanson was educated in fine art at Liverpool University. She has had thirteen years' teaching experience, working with all ages and abilities of children in the junior sector. In 1986/87 she undertook an MEd at Sheffield University.

Barbara McKellar holds a BEd, an MSc in Sociology and Social Policy and a Diploma in Access Studies. From 1973 to 1985 she taught in primary schools in East London. She is now Senior Lecturer in Multicultural Education, South Bank Polytechnic. Her interests are in race and language in education.

Sue Middleton is a New Zealander who has taught in primary and secondary schools. Her teaching includes schools in multicultural communities and a class for 'slow learners'. Since 1980 she has lectured in the Education Department at the University of Waikato, Hamilton, New Zealand, where she is now a Senior Lecturer. Her doctoral thesis was a life-history study of New Zealand feminist teachers of the post-World War II generation. Current research interests include the youth cultures of pubescent girls, curriculum theory and the politics of women's studies. She recently edited a book, *Women and Education in Aotearoa* (Allen and Unwin, 1988).

Alison Oram works half-time as a Tutor-Organizer for the WEA (Workers Educational Association), London District, and also teaches women's history for London University Extra-Mural Department. She is writing a book on women teachers and twentieth century feminism, and has published several articles on women teachers and government policy between the wars.

Sheila Riddell taught English in a rural comprehensive school for over six years before beginning her doctoral thesis on gender and option choice at the School of Education, University of Bristol. For the last five years she has lectured in communications and sociology at Weymouth College on a part-time basis. She has also tutored on adult education women's studies courses and has done some teaching in higher education.

Christine Skelton is a Lecturer in Education at the University of Newcastle upon Tyne. She was a primary school teacher for nine years during which time she developed an interest in the implications of gender stereotyping for the experiences of girls and women teachers working in primary schools. As a result of this interest she undertook an MA at the University of York, focusing her research on gender issues in the initial training of primary school teachers.

Gillian Squirrell is currently a Research Fellow in the Division of Education, University of Sheffield. Formerly a secondary school teacher, her main research interests now are in the initial training of teachers and in the coping and resistance strategies deployed by new entrants into the profession.

Index